MENDOCINO

& THE MOVIES

Hollywood and Television Motion Pictures
Filmed on the Mendocino Coast

Compiled & Edited by Bruce Levene

Gallery Bookshop
Mendocino, California

Gallery Bookshop P.O. Box 270 Mendocino, California 95460
(707) 937-2665   info@gallerybookshop.com

Fourth Edition

ISBN: 0-933391-14-5
Library of Congress Catalog Number: 98-65343
Printed in the United States of America

Mendocino & The Movies is dedicated to Toni Lemos, in recognition of her 50 years of work to bring motion pictures to the Mendocino Coast.

Thanks and acknowledgements to the following individuals, organizations and resources who provided help, inspiration, remembrances, books and photographs for this compilation. My apologies to anyone inadvertently omitted.

First, and foremost, I wish to thank *The Mendocino Beacon,* and the *Fort Bragg Advocate-News,* whose files made this book possible-Toni Lemos, for use of her movie albums and her memories-Bill Wagner and Mendocino Historical Research (MHR), for photographs and photographic help.

In memory of Laing Chambers, Hal Ogle, and Addie Reis, for their albums, photographs and

films. Joe Ribiero and Wally Smith, for the use of their photographs and scrapbooks.

Stephen McLaughlin, David Torres, and Lisa Walters, of the *Independent Coast Observer,*

Gualala. Virgina Sorensen, for the use of her *Treasure* materials.

Delores Anderson-Bob Avery-Ed Barff-Dave Belew-Tom Cahill-Eleanor Campbell-Neva Cannon-Megan Coddington-Cammie Conlon-Betty Cox-Judy Curry-Lee Edmundson-Margot Farrar-Jill Fosse-Marilyn Helela Gomez-Marlene Hall-Verna Hayter-Grace Helela-Shirley Hess-Francis Jackson-Jone Lemos Jackson-Ken Jackson-Gloria Jacobs-Pete Kalvass-Kentucky John-Audrey (Ball) Kirkman-Sylvia Kozak-Budd-Scott Kuhn-Bill Larkin-Kate Lee-Dee Lemos-Jack Lemos-Lila Longo-Mary McBurney-Christianne McLees-Alvin Mendosa-Lotte Moise-Mark Morton-Jewell (Coverston) O'Connor-Hazel Paoli-Lena Paolinelli-Barbara Reid-Grace Sandefur-Oliver Seeler-Ron Silva-John Skinner-Denise Stenberg-Richard & Barbara Tanis-Pat Turner-Jeff Walsh-Lillian Welsh-Eleanor White-Ted Wurm-David Youssoupoff.

Margaret Herrick Library, Academy of Motion Picture Arts & Sciences, Beverly Hills-California State Library, Sacramento-Nancy Goldman, Pacific Film Archive, Berkeley-San Francisco Performing Arts Library & Museum, San Francisco-San Francisco Public Library, San Francisco.

Bay View Cafe-Black Bear Press-Mendocino Graphics-Mendo Video-Visual Feast.

The map on the inside front cover was adapted from *The Magnificent Mendocino Coast Visitor Information Guide,* published by Fort Bragg-Mendocino Coast Chamber of Commerce. Used by permission.

The excerpt on Page 28 is from an interview with Clarence Brown by Kevin Brownlow, in *The Parade's Gone By,* Ballentine Books, N.Y., 1969.

The quotation by Ole Hervilla is from *The Finn, The Twin and The Inn* by Mel McKinney, The Abalone Press, 1994.

Photographs with the citation *Blum* are from *A Pictorial History of the Silent Screen* by Daniel Blum, Grosset & Dunlap, N.Y., 1953

To my wife, Gail Lauinger, and my daughters, Mara Levene and Sarah Levene, for their love and patience.

Contents

Introduction · · · · · 5

Preface · · · · · 6

1904—Caspar Lumber Company—*Silent* · · · · · 7

1916—The Promise—*Silent* · · · · · 9

1919—King Spruce—*Silent* · · · · · 12

1920—The Man Who Dared—*Silent* · · · · · 15

1921—Kindred of the Dust—*Silent* · · · · · 16

1922—Strange Idols—*Silent* · · · · · 19

1922—Soul of the Beast—*Silent* · · · · · 21

1922—Timberland Tales Two Reelers · · · · · 24

> Giants of the Open—*Silent*
>
> Blue Blood and Red—*Silent*
>
> The Doomed Sentinels—*Silent*
>
> Hearts of Oak—*Silent*
>
> Kings of the Forest—*Silent*
>
> Knights of the Timber—*Silent*
>
> Rustlers of the Redwoods—*Silent*
>
> Timberland Treachery—*Silent*

1923—The Signal Tower—*Silent* · · · · · 27

1925—In Search of a Hero—*Silent* · · · · · 30

1943—The Uninvited · · · · · 31

1943—Frenchman's Creek · · · · · 32

1947—Johnny Belinda · · · · · 38

1954—East of Eden · · · · · 45

1954—The Strange Case of Dr. Mesmer · · · · · 50

1963—Island of the Blue Dolphins · · · · · 51

1965—"The Russians Are Coming" · · · · · 57

1966—The Spirit is Willing · · · · · 63

1969—The Dunwich Horror · · · · · 64

1970—Summer of '42 · · · · · 67

1970—Is there a Doctor in the House?—*Television* · · · · · 71

1971—Glen & Randa · · · · · 72

1971—Young Goodman Brown—*Educational* · · · · · 74

1971—The FBI-Bitter Harbor—*Television* · · · · · 75

1972—The New Healers—*Television* · · · · · 76

1972—Slither · · · · · 77

1973—Haunts · · · · · 79

1973—"…And God Bless Grandma & Grandpa"—*aka* Evil Town · · 80

1973—The Runaway on the Rogue River—*Educational* · · · · · 81

1976—Jeremiah of Jacob's Neck—*Television* · · · · · 82

1977—The Boy Who Talks To Whales—*Television* · · · · · 84

1978—"Same Time, Next Year" · · · · · 86

1978—Strangers: The Story of a Mother and Daughter—*Television* · · · · · 89

1979—Humanoids from the Deep · · · · · 91

1980—Dead & Buried · · · · · 94

1982—Cujo · · · · · 97

1982—Treasure—*Videodisc* · · · · · 100

1983—Racing with the Moon · · · · · 102

1983—Sutter's Bay—*Television* · · · · · 109

1984-89—Murder She Wrote—*Television* · · · · · 110

1985—Dark Mansions—*Television* · · · · · 118

1986—Destination America—*Television* · · · · · 120

1986—The Killing Time—*Television* · · · · · 121

1987—Overboard · · · · · 123

1988—Wired · · · · · 127

1989—The Karate Kid-Part III · · · · · 129

1990—Dying Young · · · · · 130

1992—Forever Young · · · · · 133

1993—Pontiac Moon · · · · · 137

1994—The Haunting of Sea Cliff Inn—*Television* · · · · · 142

2001—The Fugitive—*Television* · · · · · 143

2001—The Majestic · · · · · 144

2007—Shark Swarm · · · · · · *145*

2013—Need For Speed · · · · · · *146*

2015—Crabs! · · · · · · *147*

2015—The Impact of the *Frolic* · · · · *148*

Introduction

The first public showing of a motion picture in America occurred in New York in 1896. Only eight years later, in April, 1904, Miles Brothers Photographers of San Francisco came to the Mendocino Coast, not for a Hollywood production (there would be no Hollywood until 1912), but to make what is now called an industrial film.

Abbie Krebs, owner of the Caspar Lumber Company, commissioned the photographers to make a silent film showing how lumber was produced.

Twelve years later Hollywood did come to the Mendocino Coast, for the first of 63 films—17 silent and 46 sound—made here between 1916 and 2015. That film, *The Promise*, was a major production, produced by a well-known early film-maker, Fred J. Bulshofer.

But a sad fact of our cultural history is that perhaps 80% of all silent films no longer exist in any form, except stills, if that. After 'talkies' began in 1928, the silents languished, were allowed to deteriorate, then ground up by the thousands for their cellulose during World War II.

We cannot watch *The Promise*, which showed lumber camps, log drives, the dynamiting of a log-jam, and scenes following a train wreck at night. Or Harold Lockwood and May Allison, major movie stars of their time. Or the numerous 'oldtimers' who were extras.

We cannot view *King Spruce*, *The Man Who Dared*, *Strange Idols*, or the eight two-reel *Timberland Tales*. The only silent films made on the Coast currently available on DVD are *The Soul of the Beast*, which shows an escaped circus elephant swimming in the Noyo River, and interesting railroad scenes in *The Signal Tower*.

Because there was so little historical awareness that silent films were even made on the Mendocino Coast, these movies have been notated extensively. And it should be understood that the silent stars of their day were just as popular (perhaps even more so, considering how new mass entertainment was then, and how little there was of it) in their films as are present-day heroes and heroines.

It is also possible that more silent films were made than are listed in this book and that no articles about them were printed in newspapers. Or if they were, the complete files of the newspapers themselves—like the *Fort Bragg News* and the *Point Arena Record*—may not exist.

It was relatively easy to make a silent movie. A small film crew could have arrived at Point Arena on a 'Dog-hole Schooner,' shot a film, then left the following week, with few people the wiser. If the locale was to represent, say Maine, who would remember the film company had even been there?

It is also quite likely that films were made in or near Willits or Ukiah (east of the Coast), as it was so easy to take the Northwestern Pacific passenger train north from Sausalito. The latest film made there was *Heartwood* in 1996. But that is beyond the range of this study, as are the more than 60 commercials (beginning in 1969) filmed on the Coast.

Supposedly a film was made east of Caspar in 1935, however no information about it has been found. But in the 1940s the Mendocino Coast was "re-discovered" by film makers. In 1943 *Frenchman's Creek* with Joan Fontaine was filmed on and near the Albion River and Big River. In 1948 *Johnny Belinda*, for which Jane Wyman won an Academy Award for Best Actress, was filmed at Noyo, south of Fort Bragg and in Mendocino.

Two movies were made here in 1954: *East of Eden*, with James Dean and Julie Harris—for this writer one of the greatest American films—and *The Strange Case of Dr. Mesmer*, definitely filmed around Fort Bragg, but apparently never released.

In the 60s came *Island of Blue Dolphins*, made at Anchor Bay, and *"The Russians Are Coming!"*—a favorite of the many locals hired as extras—filmed at numerous locales.

Avant-garde film titan Bruce Baillie lived in Caspar in the late 1960s and made some experimental films there, including *Tung*, *All My Life* and portions of *Quick Billy*. His films can be viewed on YouTube.

Three 'student' films of note were also made during the 1970s. The first, *Thunder Under The Sea* (1972), used Pomo Indian students and was filmed by professional film-makers. The other movies—*When The Bough Breaks* (1972) and *Scarlet Ibis* (1977)—were made by UCLA film graduate students.

Praise should also be given to the 'art' films —particularly *After the Caspar Mill*, *Today I Saw*, and *Woman of the Butterfly Man*—produced by local artist Ray Rice.

Some films have also been made on the Coast without even a ripple of notoriety. For example, a few scenes in the 1995 television movie *Fudge-A-Mania* were filmed in Mendocino (perhaps the footage was purchased from a stock film company) with no local awareness.

Then there was Fred Astaire, who told an interviewer that *Finian's Rainbow* (1968) had been filmed in Mendocino. The movie would have been welcomed, but was made elsewhere.

Beginning with *The Dunwich Horror* in 1970, to the present, movie-making on the Coast has become almost commonplace

Other than films, the Coast has had other associations with Hollywood. The two most famous heroines of silent serials were Pearl White *(The Perils of Pauline)* and Ruth Roland—the latter went to school in Fort Bragg for a few years in the early 1900s.

Ruth Roland advertising
Ipana tooth-paste in 1910.

Two articles about Mendocino-born actress Daisy Henderson appear in *The Mendocino Beacon* in 1922. She toured for six months on the Orpheum vaudeville circuit in the Marks Bros act, then had small roles in three little known silents: *Melting Pot, Spanish Gold and Alias Jimmy Valentine.* Strangely, the only other information discovered is of her death in 1926 from 'consumption,' at Comptche, east of Mendocino.

A year after she gained the title, in 1926, the Coast's own Miss America, Fay Lanphier, appeared in Paramount Picture's *The American Venus,* a film reviewed favorably by the critics.

A well-known actress of the 1940s, Ilona Massey, owned property at Little River for awhile, which could be one reason Hollywood paid so much attention to that area when filming for *Frenchman's Creek* began in 1943.

The Coast even has a relationship with America's most famous movie, *Gone with the Wind.* Cammie King Conlon, who at age four played the role of Bonnie Blue Butler, has lived here for many years and was marketing coordinator for the Mendocino Coast Chamber of Commerce.

During the late 1970s and early 80s, current Hollywood star Winona Ryder (Nonie Horowitz) attended the early grades at the Elk grammar school.

Rumors exist of other film personalities, both silent and sound, who have lived here anonymously. Most certainly, like other tourists, numerous film stars have visited the Coast to experience its tranquil beauty.

Mention should also be made of the occasional problems of the movie companies. Warner Bros. was to begin filming *Practical Magic* in Mendocino in early 1998, but a small group of disident residents made threats to disrupt the production. Because of this controversy Warner Bros. cancelled the project here and made the film in Washington state.

This might have meant that no Hollywood film company would ever make another movie in Mendocino, but by 2001 matters seem to have quieted down and the film companies returned to the coast.

Whatever happens in the future, the making of motion pictures here has had a wonderful long run. The Mendocino Coast's permanent place is assured in America's continual love with its greatest contribution to the dramatic arts—the movies.

Cammie King Conlon and Clark Gable in *Gone With The Wind.*

Nonie Horowitz at Hendy Woods State Park, June, 1981. *(Morton)*

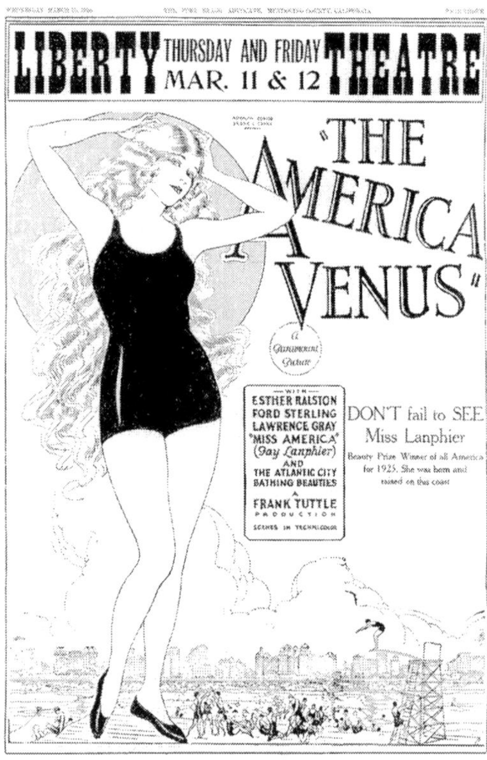

Preface

The history of the Mendocino Coast must certainly include the natural beauty of this entire area which has been recorded for posterity on film by the motion picture industry. Many Oscar winning films depict the ever-changing Pacific Ocean, its rugged cliffs, pristine beaches, winding rivers and giant redwood trees

During the past fifty years I have been fortunate to have been involved in the filming of numerous motion pictures and television commercials. Some of them have become classics, such as *The Russians Are Coming!, East of Eden,* and *Summer of '42.*

So many interesting stories can be told about the behind the scenes happenings on the sets, such as when Ronald Reagan visited his then wife, Jane Wyman, on location for *Johnny Belinda;* when Bette Davis danced in a thin print dress for scenes in *Strangers*—portraying a hot Fourth of July celebration on a freezing day in December in Mendocino.

Bruce Levene has compiled a wealth of information on filmmaking in this book. He has devoted countless hours to interviews and to obtain the priceless photos shown here. I know you will enjoy his presentation.

—*Toni Lemos*

Caspar Lumber Company — 1904

THE SEQUOIA SEMPERVIRENS — TO BE ADVERTISED IN A SCIENTIFIC MANNER.

The Caspar Lumber Company Through its Able President, Mrs. Abby E. Krebs, is to Advertise Redwood, as Finishing and Building Lumber.

Mr. Miles, a professional photographer of San Francisco, has been spending the past week with Mr. C. J. Wood. He is here in the interests of the redwood exhibit at the St. Louis Exposition, and has been taking views of the redwoods and the manufacture of lumber from the tree to the vessel.

Mr. Miles is a "moving picture" expert and has taken moving views of a redwood tree being felled, of steam donkeys hauling logs, of a moving train of logs, of the logs going down the chute into the pond, of the logs going up into the mill, of the sawing of a log in the mill and of the wire chute bringing up freight and sending down lumber.

He has also taken a great many stationary views. They will be gathered into a lecture which will be given in the Forestry building at St. Louis, and as the lecture is delivered the views will be thrown on a screen 16 feet by 20 feet.

The admission to this lecture will be free to all, the primary object being to educate the visitors regarding the growth, methods of manufacture, etc., of redwood and to incidentally impress upon their minds that they should buy redwood to finish their houses with. These views are to keep the crowd interested while this fact is being impressed.

Mrs. Krebs, the President of the Caspar Lumber Company, has charge of the exhibit at St. Louis, and is leaving nothing undone to show the advantages of redwood. Under her direction Mr. Miles has been afforded every facility at Caspar. The roof of the mill has been removed for a considerable distance, the side of the mill torn down, stands erected to the pond from which to take the views, as well as in the woods. In one place a stand 40 feet high was put up. Mrs. Krebs has contributed all this expense herself, besides her time, and she is entitled to a great deal of credit.

She has forwarded to St. Louis a piece of a redwood bridge stringer and two redwood ties that have been in continuous service on the Caspar company's railroad since 1876, during which time they have been exposed to the weather without any protection. They are still sound and show in a striking way the durability and lasting qualities of redwood.

—*Mendocino Beacon*, April 16, 1904

The Caspar Mill and pond. A portion of the mill roof was removed to enable interior filming. Miles Brothers cameraman is at left.

Two stills taken by Miles Brothers of San Francisco during the filming of the Caspar Lumber Company's motion picture to promote the redwood lumber industry that was shown at the 1904 World's Fair in St. Louis ("Meet Me in St. Louis").

At right, the movie photographer is holding a hand-cranked camera atop a swaying train of logs in Hare Creek Canyon.

Below, the Miles' Brothers cameraman is standing in the foreground on a tree stump filming "Hercules" pulling a logging train on the Caspar, South Fork & Eastern Railroad.

After the Fair, the film was placed in a closet in Caspar Lumber Company's San Francisco office and forgotten. The logging company, which began in 1862, disbanded operations in Caspar in 1955. Discovered in the1970s, the film was stupidly destroyed because of the fear of ignitable nitrate film, a tragic loss to the histories of Mendocino County and American technology. Although a copy of the entire film might exist, at present only about 10 minutes are available on videotape—luckily the rarest scenes—taken inside the mill. This was probably the first industrial film—perhaps the first motion picture—made in California north of San Francisco.

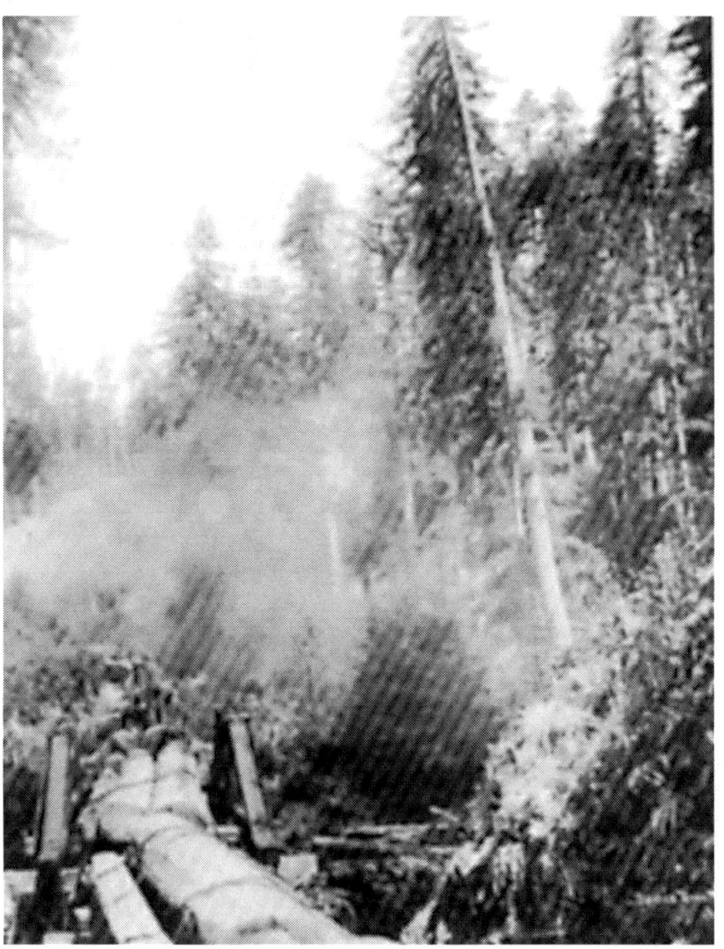

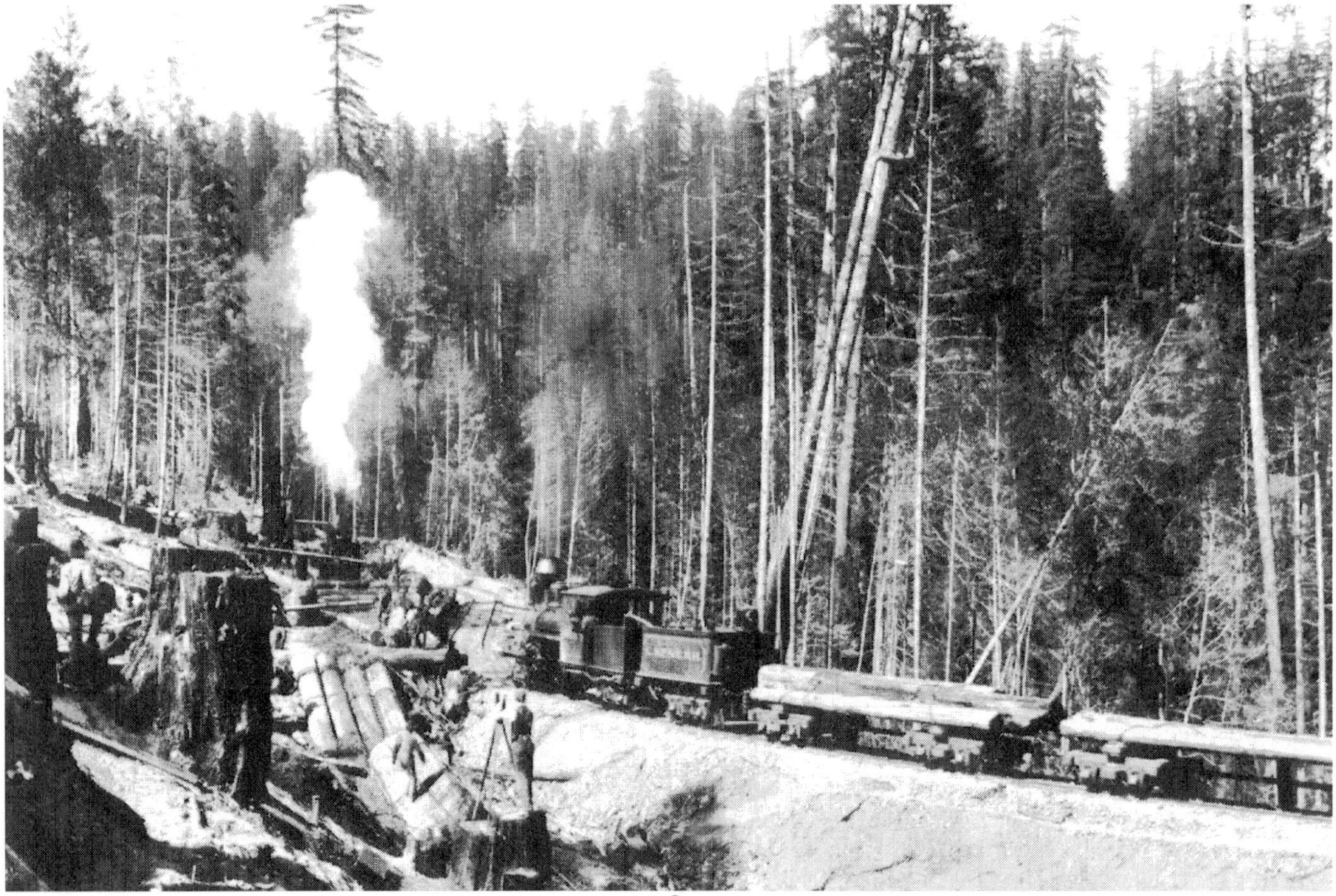

COAST SCENERY IS SOUGHT BY MOVIES

Coast logging scenes are to play an important part in the production of "The Promise," a feature film which a troupe from the Metro Company of Los Angeles are now making in this vicinity. They arrived here last Wednesday evening for a three weeks stay and are in charge of Fred J. Bulshofer, general manager, and producer for the company. They are making their headquarters at the Windsor Hotel.

The troupe has already made several visits to the "booms" on Big River, and various parts of the Caspar woods. It is understood that they also intend to take several pond pictures on Pudding Creek.

Harold Lockwood is the star, and Miss May Allison is the 'heroine' of the picture. Some of the others are Lester Cuneo, Lillian Hayward, Charle Hallings, Dorothy Barrett, Tony Gaudio and others adapted to this line work.

—*Fort Bragg Advocate,* December 27, 1916

The Mendocino Lumber Company 'Boom' up Big River. The photograph was posed for the filming of *The Promise. (MHR)*

May Allison and Harold Lockwood were two of the most famous film stars of Hollywood's early days, and they teamed together in 22 successive romantic dramas, making them the most popular pair of screen lovers of their time. May Allison began her film career in 1915 and appeared in more than 30 films through 1926—one of Metro Pictures greatest box-office attractions in the early 1920s. Harold Lockwood was popular from the first moment he appeared before a camera in 1911 and that popularity increased through another 120 films. He died at the height of his fame, at age 31, during the influenza plague in 1918. Tony Gaudio's career as a cameraman began with *The Mirror* in 1911 and ended in 1949 with *The Red Pony.* According to a local tale, Lawrence Stallings, later co–author of *What Price Glory,* was location manager for *The Promise,* but no evidence of this has been discovered.

MOVIE STARS PERFORM ON BIG RIVER

SECURE LOG-DRIVING SCENE AT "BOOM"

At last Big River and the "Boom", which never fail to attract the passing stranger with their picturesque scenery, are to come into fame. The habitat of the celebrated "singing fish" was invaded this week by a Los Angeles motion picture troupe and in the near future the beauties of this celebrated coast stream will be shown on screens throughout the land.

The play in which these scenes will be introduced is "The Promise." It deals with the great woods and Indians and includes a dramatic river scene in which the leading man is precipitated into the stream from a log jam through the discharge of a shot of dynamite under the jam by the villain. A thrilling escape follows.

Not only do the members of the company, numbering fifteen, appear in the scene taken, but also the men at the boom and a crew of men under Woods Supt. Ed Boyle who are employed with some work there at present. Practically all of Thursday and Friday were given over by the movie company to picture-taking at the boom. They also filmed the mill, and the fore part of the week took pictures at the Caspar pond. It is said that films will be taken of logging scenes adjacent to Fort Bragg. The troupe is making its headquarters at the Windsor hotel at that place and will probably remain some days on the coast.

The troupe includes three women, May Allison, Lillian Haywood and Dorothy Darret, the first named of which plays a leading part. Harold Lockwood is the bright and shining light among the men, and his salary is said to run into the neighborhood of seven or eight hundred dollars a week. The York Motion Picture Company is the concern for which the films are being taken. It is said that the play will be ready for the screen within a few weeks and that it will be shown at Fort Bragg and possibly here soon after that.

—*Mendocino Beacon*, December 30, 1916

Lester Cuneo and Harold Lockwood in log-driving scene.

Harold Lockwood, Ed Boyle and Lester Cuneo in fight scene. *(Yorke Film*

Cameraman Tony Gaudio.

Woods Boss Ed Boyle. *(MHR)*

"The Promise," Five-reel Drama Featuring Harold Lockwood and May Allison.

THE GENUS "fan" ought to be well-pleased with "The Promise," a five-reel drama of the outdoors, in which Harold Lockwood and May Allison are the featured players and which was produced by the Yorke Film Corporation for release by Metro. While the production comes under the general classification of drama, it may perhaps be better described as a visualized novel of the same general description as those stories that are commonly considered light reading. In that same sense "The Promise" is light entertainment—there are no deep problems to solve, and the viewer is held interested without having to use his mind overmuch. The story unfolds itself smoothly on the screen despite a tendency toward over-titling. While there is no great originality to the story by James B. Hendryx, the screen treatment given it has lent an added interest. The story appeared in the *All-Story Weekly*, and was scenarioized by Richard V. Spencer.

The exteriors in the production are worthy of special note. All of them are good and many are excellent. Especially commendable are those scenes showing the lumber camps, log drives, the dynamiting of a log-jam, and the scenes following a train wreck at night. All through the production the backgrounds are consistently true to the story.

Mr. Lockwood and Miss Allison are pleasing in their portrayals of the leading parts—the former as a wealthy youth who makes good in a lumber camp in the West, and the latter as the society girl he leaves behind him. Lester Cuneo is a capable villain. Others in the cast are Paul Willis, Lillian Hayward, George Fisher, W. H. Bainbridge, Leota Lorraine, John Steppling and T. H. Gibson-Gowland.

Fred J. Balshofer directed the production. Photography, which is uniformly excellent, was done by Tony Gaudio.

—*Motion Picture World*, March 10, 1917

UNION THEATRE
For Sunday, July 22nd

See Harold Lockwood and May Allison in a Metro Wonder Play of a wild life that was tamed by a life in the wilds—"The Promise." Everyone should see Mr. Lock-wood in "The Promise." As you saw them making the picture, why not see how it looks on the screen? Look for Mr. Ed Boyle and other prominent men of the Mendocino woods. Would you risk your life for a promise? See what Mr. Lockwood did. The climax of the play answers this question with tremendous power. Special matinee beginning at 2 P. M. for the accomodation of the public. Those who possibly can attend in the afternoon will be greatly appreciated by the management.

—*Fort Bragg Advocate,* July 18, 1917

Harold Lockwood and May Allison (*Yorke Film Corp.*)

"THE PR0MISE" TONIGHT AT SKATING RINK HALL

Tonight at Skating Rink hall "The Promise" will be shown on the screen. This is the play about which so much interest centers among coast residents because of the fact that many of its principal scenes are laid at coast points, a number of which were taken on Big River. In the river and logging scenes the familiar faces of a number of local people will appear.

The play itself is said to be remarkably interesting and a large number will no doubt avail themselves of the opportunity to see it.

Mr. Nichols has gone to considerable trouble and expense to secure it for this early date.

On next Wednesday evening Marguerite Clark will appear in "Little Lady Eileen."—*Mendocino Beacon*, July 21, 1917

King Spruce — 1919

LOG JAM AND DAM TO BE BLOWN UP FOR "MOVIES"

"King Spruce" Production Will Show Ten Mile Camp Life, Falling of Big Trees, Spectacular Glen Blair Runaway, and Big River Blow-Ups. Hi School Girls to be "Shot"

The wonders of Mendocino redwoods and scenery are to be portrayed abroad in "King Spruce," a six reel motion picture now being taken here by the Mitchell Lewis Co.

The novel has as its original setting an eastern logging village in the winter where the villagers are all run out by the Sheriff, and on retreating start an immense forest fire.

To this end scenes of camp life and the falling of big timber are being taken on Ten Mile, a spectacular runaway scene was staged at Glen Blair, and a dam and immense log jam on Big River are to be blown up.

The company has as its stars Mitchell Lewis and Mignon Anderson, and directed by Roy Clements.

At Ten Mile the falling of nine giant Sequoias has been taken and Sunday numbers of camp scenes were "shot" which included locomotive No. 11 and its crew as follows: Jack Cummings, Chas. Plummer, Ben Scott, T. Golden and M. King.

Next Sunday scenes are to be taken to represent a camp going in for the winter, in which all the employees of Ten Mile Woods will take part.

The latter part of this week, pictures will be taken at Ten Mile of village life in which Esther Rivers, Julia Lessa, Gertrude Rushing, Thelma Sawdey and Mildred Bishop, all local High School students, are to appear. Twenty-five small children will also take part.

Yesterday one of the spectacular features of the production was taken at Glen Blair when a runaway logging scene was pulled off. It consisted of a buggy, followed by four large work horses, running down the hillside at high speed in advance of on-rushing logs. The scene comes about, in the story, when the line attached to the logs which the horses are pulling breaks, causing a general runaway. The stunt was pulled off in the hills to the east of the Burwash home in Little Valley.

It is understood that pictures of the immense redwoods on Pudding Creek, which are now being logged by the Glen Blair Company, will also be taken.

On Big River the large log jam of over 15,000,000 feet which formed on the North Fork last winter is to be blown up in part. A hundred pounds of Hudson powder will be used to create this scene, and all damages to the timber will be paid for by the picture company.

An old dam on the North Fork, which was previously used in starting the winter log drive, is to be reconstructed, and will be blown up, after the water has been raised to a height of seven or ten feet.

Pictures will also be taken of the "Boom," five miles up Big River, where piers which were constructed of redwood logs fifty years ago to form a bumper to stop the millions of feet of logs which come down the river each year in the freshet, are being repaired for the first time. The fact that the wood below the waterline is as firm as the day it was put in, is additional proof that the redwood has remarkable decay resisting qualities.

It is not altogether certain whether this particular scene will be needed in the "King Spruce" production, but it should make a splendid feature for the Pathe Weekly or like films.

The "King Spruce" photo play is estimated as a $50,000 production and will practically be taken in this locality, with the exception of the snow and forest fire scenes. Three weeks is the time alloted for the local work, but if weather conditions are favorable it may be done in less time. On account of the moisture in the air, camera work cannot be don eafter 3 P.M., and it is sometimes quite late in the forenoon before the light is strong enough to start work.

The daily expense of this company of twenty members, including salaries, is $1680.

Messrs. Clements and Lewis state that our local scenery surpasses almost all other parts of the State for motion picture work.

Mr. Clements states that he is highly pleased with the courteous treatment received by the people of this section.

—*Fort Bragg Advocate*, November 26, 1919

Mitchell Lewis had one of the longest acting careers in Hollywood, beginning with *The Million Dollar Mystery* in 1914 and ending with *Trial* shortly before his death in 1956. During those 42 years he appeared in 100 films, achieving perhaps his greatest fame in the 1926 epic *Ben Hur*. Considered one of Hollywood's most distinguished actors, Lewis was a founder of the Motion Picture Relief Fund. Mignon Anderson had a short film career, beginning with *The Merchant of Venice* in 1912 and ending 14 films later with *Kisses* in 1922. Melbourne MacDowell (born 1857) was a dramatic actor on the American stage from about 1880 until he sppeared in his first film in 1917. He made 23 more until retirement in 1928. Director Roy Clements wrote or directed 14 films between 1918 and 1926.

The crew of Union Lumber Company's Camp 1 on Ten Mile River as extras and some actors in crowd scene in *King* Spruce. Actor Mitchell Lewis is fighting left of center, facing right. To his right, facing left, is woods boss Walter Ball. *(Mitchell Lewis Co.)*

MOVIE COMPANY
TO TAKE SCENES ON BIG RIVER

The Mitchell Lewis Movie Company, members of which have been at Fort Bragg getting timber scenes in the woods of the Union Lumber Company for a production to be known as "Spruce King", will shortly transfer their activities to this locality where Big River is to be utilized as a setting for additional scenes for this play.

Permission has been granted the movie management to build a dam across Big river near the foot of the big Hill for one of the scenes. Water is low at this period and a dam suitable for the occasion can be constructed without much difficulty. Some six miles further out near the Company ranch is a considerable log jam where a large body of logs hung up in last year's drive. A blast will be put in near this so that the proper effect may be gained for a scene which is supposed to depict the breaking up of a jam. Only in reality the logs will not move from their present resting place as the water is still very low and the most of them are hard aground.

The Company will assemble here next week when the camera will "shoot" the Big river scenes.

—*Mendocino Beacon*, December 6, 1919

"King Spruce"

Hodkinson Presents Mitchell Lewis in a Picturesque Melodrama of the Lumber Camp. Story of a Big Hearted Man of the Woods Who Straightens out the Difficulties of a Spruce Magnate and Wins His Daughter. See the Impressive Forest Scenes in This Swiftly Moving Melodrama of the North Woods.
Reviewed by Louis Reeves Harrison

Cast: Dwight Wade: Mitchell Lewis~John Barrett: Melbourne MacDowell~Elva Barrett & Kate Arden: Mignon Anderson~Colin McLeod:Arthur Milleter~Rodburne Ide:James O'Neil~Nina Ide: Betty Wales~Tommy Eye-: Joe Ray~Ladder Lane: Gus Soville~Prophet Eli: Frederick Herzog. Directed by Roy Clements. Camera: Fred G. Hartman. Length, Seven Reels. Based on the novel **King Spruce** by Holman Day (N.Y. 1908)

"King Spruce," a Hodkinson release, is strinkingly graphic in scenes of the North woods. It is against an interesting background of wild woodland and rude lumber camps that most of the action takes place. This necessitates skilled photography, fine in detail and effective in contrasts of light and shadow. The camera work is of such high order that, whether it be of mountain torrent or falling monarchs of the forest, it abounds with the vivid imagery of the truly picturesque.

The story is straightout melodrama. Accidents and incidents dominate the characters. They are controlled by circumstances, woven into a pattern designed to present them in heroic or villainous roles. Attention is focused upon a central figure of kindly motives and great physical strength. He is an optimist who stands up for the right and brings those guilty of wrong-doing to either punishment or to repentance. This is largely done by his superior physical strength. He wins out whenever it is called into play, and brings about a happy ending for those who deserve it and for some who do not.

Mitchell Lewis plays the lead with good-natured confidence, and his support is strong, notably Melbourne MacDowell as John Barrett and Mignon Anderson in the dual roles of Elva Barrett and Kate Arden. The other types are well-chosen without exception. Care shown in preserving the atmosphere and mood of "King Spruce" and the capable performance of all its actors rank it as good melodramatic entertainment.

The Story

"King Spruce" is personified in John Barrett, lumber magnate of the North woods. His domineering character is shown when his daughter Elva falls in love with a school teacher, Dwight Wade. Barrett conspires with his foreman, McLeod, to entice Wade away to the lumber camps and finally decides to accompany the gang of men himself. He starts in to eject and burn out all "skeeters" who have settled on the land without domiciliary rights. Wade has shown his fighting blood by thrashing McLeod for an act of cruelty and he now vainly opposes Barrett from motives of humanity.

From the first shack burned emerges a wild girl, Kate Arden, who sets the forest afire in revenge. There is another vengeance awaiting Barrett. Kate is his own daughter by the wife of a woodsman who has waited years to get even. It is she who ties Barrett to a tree, where he must be burned in the fire now raging, but he is rescued by Wade.

Barrett now acknowledges Kate to be his daughter. When his daughter Elva comes to take care of him the resemblance between the two girls confirms his confession.

Barrett attempts a half-hearted redemption by bribing his foreman to marry the wild girl, but he is brought to his senses by Wade and Elva. Wade has become a power through his feats of strength and kindly humanity and he finally wins the high regard of the spruce magnate himself. He is given a partnership in a newly organized business by Barrett, and Elva, to use her own terms, is thrown in for good measure.

—*Motion Picture World*, March 27, 1920

Cast of *King Spruce* on porch of Ten Mile Camp I office. Known actors, sitting: Betty Wales, Mignon Anderson, Mitchell Lewis, Arthur Milleter, Melbourne MacDowell.

—*(Mitchell Lewis Co.)*

Mignon Anderson, Joe Ray, Mitchell Lewis, Jewell Coverston, Audrey Ball, Betty Wales.

Audrey Ball Kirkman's father, Walter Ball, was the Woods Boss of Camp 1, Ten Mile. She provided the still photographs from *King Spruce,* probably the only existing visual record of the movie. Audrey remembered being paid $50 as an extra but this was likely the amount paid to her father.

Jewell Coverston Carlson's father was David Coverston, the Head Bucker (who sawed downed trees into log lengths) in the Camp 1 woods. Jewell's remembrance: "We lived in Camp 1 and we had to go over on the other side of that big hill, where they were making the picture. I was five yeards old and my sister was seven. She didn't want to go back for a second day but the movie people said she had to. My sister was watching me constantly and said, "Don't get burned on that stove!" Because they had built a fire under it and I stood there with a spoon stiring what was supposed to be melting snow. What amazed me more than anything else, when we got all through, they set the darn hillside on fire and they couldn't control it until it burned out. I got a doll and my sister got a doll. No money."

MOVIE TROUPE
AFTER WESTPORT SCENES

Fort Bragg, March 12—The Fox Movie troupe, some 27 in number, arrived here by train Wednesday evening with a carload of paraphenalia to produce another Coast film.

The scenes for this particular film are to be laid in and about Westport and the old Bonton saloon, relic of former days, is to be woven into the story which will depict a coast milling town of thirty years ago. Lumbering scenes of the present day will be woven into the picture and already the troupe have spent a couple of days at the Noyo camp. A mob scene will be taken in Fort Bragg Sunday morning in front of the Grand hotel and local citizens are invited to come out and participate and it is anticipated that there will be a big crowd.—*Mendocino Beacon*, March 13, 1920

In front of the Bonton Saloon in Westport, circa 1918. *(MHR)*

Eileen Percy *(Blum)*

William Russell *(Blum)*

The Man Who Dared

When Mamie Lee's father, Sam Corwin, is sentenced to jail for forgery, the sheriff, Ed Cass, offers to cover the debt in return for Mamie Lee's hand in marriage. The distraught daughter agrees, and Cass robs the saloon to obtain the money, framing Jim Kane, his rival for Mamie's affections, for the crime. Jim is sent to jail an embittered man. In the adjacent cell he watches an Italian stonecutter, a condemned murderer, spend the night before his execution chiseling a figure of Christ. After the sculptor collapses from exhaustion, Jim is astounded to see the spirit of Christ appear and minister to the condemned man. His religious experience converts Jim to Christianity. Meanwhile, Mamie Lee discovers a confession to the robbery written by Cass and brings it to the judge. Realizing tht he is doomed, the sheriff kills himself, thus freeing Jim to begin life anew with Mamie Lee.

—*American Film Institute*

> The above description, plus a review that appeared in the October 29, 1920 issue of *Variety*, seems to make *The Man Who Dared* a candidate for the worst motion picture ever made on the Mendocino Coast.
>
> William Russell was a well-known leading man of the silent screen, acting in 86 films between 1912 and his death in 1929. Eileen Percy appeared in 48 films between 1917 and 1931.

The Grand Hotel in Fort Bragg (northeast corner of Main & Alder Streets), 1920.
(Haggard Photograph/MHR)

Kindred of the Dust — 1921

SETTING HERE FOR A FAMOUS MOVIE PLAY

John B. O'Brien, a moving picture director of broad experience and recognized ability, is here making arrangements for the R.A. Walsh Co. who are coming next week to "shoot" Peter Kyne's famous novel, "Kindred of the Dust," in this locality.

It is planned to take scenes in connection with the lumber industry at Caspar, Fort Bragg, Glen Blair and Ten Mile.

Mr. O'Brien is highly elated with our wonderful scenery, and spoke very highly of the courteous manner in which he has been treated by all he has come in contact with.—*Fort Bragg Adovcate,* September 14, 1921

SHOOTING LOG WILL WRECK GAS LAUNCH

Eighteen or more members of the Walsh Co. are expected here the latter part of this week to film the big parts of "Kindred of the Dust."

One of the thrillers of the picture will be the destruction of a gasoline launch on the Caspar mill pond, which was purchased from a Noyo fisherman for $600.

It will be placed in such a position that a big log which is shot down the chute will crash into it.

Mr. O'Brien and camera man Lyman Broening and Byron Haskin have already taken scenes of the saw mill at this place, logging operations at Ten Mile and the falling of big trees in the Albion woods.

—*Fort Bragg Advocate,* September 28, 1921

The Caspar Mill pond, where a big log shot down the chute and crashed into a launch. *(MHR)*

Peter B. Kyne was a well-known writer from about 1913 until the 1930s. He wrote hundreds of magazine articles and 25 novels, a dozen of which, including *Kindred of the Dust,* each sold over 100,000 copies. *The Valley of the Giants,* a tale of the California redwoods, was filmed four times, in two silent and two sound versions, in Humboldt County, California. Kyne's most famous character, "Cappy Ricks," first appeared in a collection of short stories in 1916.

Falling a big tree in the Albion woods. *(MHR)*

When the logs came

crashing down

A SURGE of waters—the boom of crashing logs—a weak call from the Old Laird battling in the rapids—the crazy dash of a lumberjack—and a leap!
Remember that in the story? Aye; but now feel the thrill of what you really see.

The story of "Kindred of the Dust" is laid in the heroic northwest—the home of drama and romance. Miss Cooper plays the role of "Nan of the Sawdust Pile," a refined girl with a voice of operative calibre, who is forced by poverty to live in one of the squalid sections along the Puget Sound, in the State of Washington.

She meets Donald McKaye, son of the millionaire lumberman, who owns the land on which she and her grandfather are living without legal right, and both fall in love. Parental interference interrupts their love affair and it is many years before they are reunited and find peace and happiness.

"Kindred of the Dust" is the type of picture which the patrons of this theatre prefer, and we are sure that you will enjoy every foot of it. The mere fact that it was written by Mr. Kyne, and produced by Director Walsh, and that the leads are in the capable hands of Miss Cooper and Mr. Graves, are sufficient guarantee that it is worthwhile entertainment.

R.A. Walsh or Raul Walsh directed 114 films between 1912 and 1964, including *What Price Glory, St. Louis Blues, Battle Cry* and *The Naked and the Dead.* He also wrote, produced and acted in numerous movies and portrayed John Wilkes Booth in *Birth of a Nation* in 1915. Miriam Cooper appeared in 64 films between 1910 and 1924, including *Birth of a Nation* and *Intolerance.* Ralph Graves acted in 48 mostly forgetable motion pictures between 1918 and 1949 and was briefly a director during the 1920s.

Kindred of the Dust has been restored but is not available on home video.

"I miss him so!"

Miriam Cooper, from the title card for *Kindred of the Dust.*

Ralph Graves, the leading man. (*Blum*)

Big Picture Taken at Caspar — Here Thursday and Friday

Manager Triguerio of the Liberty Theatre makes the following statement concerning "Kindred of the Dust," which will be shown at the Liberty Theatre tomorrow and Friday evenings:

"Just a year ago, Mr. Walsh decided that Fort Bragg was the ideal background for his wonderful production of "Kindred of the Dust." Mr. O'Brien and myself personally visited all the mills on the coast and after a careful study, decided that the Caspar plant was the most ideally situated.

"The very first shot of the picture shows the Caspar mill as the lumber mill of The Laird of Tyee, at Port Agnew. The success of the production is largely due to the splendid co-operation given by the Caspar Lumber Co. and Mr. Fred Stickney in the use of their plant and adjoining property.

"Owing to the big rush of work at the Los Angeles Studio, it was impossible to send Mr. Ralph Graves and Mr. Lionel Belmore to Fort Bragg so the big task of finding a double for these two men fell upon Mr. O'Brien. Happy Berkovits and Max Ware were picked as perfect substitutes and for a few days became movie stars.

"The Fort Bragg station figured several times in the production and Arthur Hanson and Johnny Pimentel are central figures.

"I have just returned from San Francisco, where I saw the picture and can honestly say that it is a wonderful production.

"What could be finer than a thrilling Peter B. Kyne story, enacted amid the redwoods and mills of our own vicinity?

"The Liberty Theatre is surely proud to be the first theatre in California to offer this mammoth production during its first run at the Tivoli Theatre in San Francisco.

—*Fort Bragg Advocate*, October 11, 1922

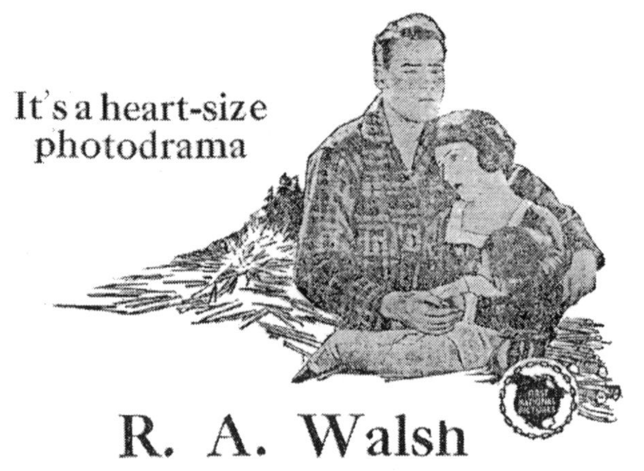

MOVIE TROUPE HERE
FOR LOGGING SCENES

FORT BRAGG, March 24—A company of moving-picture actors numbering some 25 arrived here Monday evening in a special car. They are to take pictures of local logging camps for the production of "Strange Gods." Dustin Farnum and Doris Pawn are the leading stars and most of the camera work will be done around Glen Blair. The picture will be under the direction of Bernard Durning. Before coming here, the company produced a picture with scenes taken on San Francisco Bay.—*Mendocino Beacon*, March 25, 1922

Glenblair Ready For Film Company

Glenblair is all decorated awaiting a good bright sunny day so the Fox Film Company can "shoot" their scenes. Inclement weather has delayed shooting.

The management reports that C. A. Curtis, Superintendent, and E. A. Sinclair, head of the Glenblair plant, are extending their numerous courtesies for which they are thankful.—*Fort Bragg Advocate,* March 29, 1922.

Richard Tucker and Doris Pawn in scene from *Strange Idols. (Fox Film)*

BAD WEATHER CAUSES MOVIE TROUPE TO DEPART

FORT BRAGG, March 31—The movie troupe headed by Dustin Farnum departed for San Francisco Thursday evening, a portion going down the coast by machine while a large contingent went by the night freight to Willits to connect at that place with the night train from Eureka. Owing to rainy and cloudy weather of the past week it has been impossible for these people to shot satisfactory outdoor scenes so they concluded not to further prolong their stay at this time but will return here at a later date when they can be sure of better weather.—*Mendocino Beacon*, April 1, 1922

Very Poor Story
Fails to Make Entertaining Picture

The old, old situation of the countryman marrying the actress is retold in this story of Jules Furthman's, a plot that is so hackneyed and worn out that nothing could make a satisfying entertainment of it. It runs so true to the recognized formula for this type that the specator anticipates every step in the development, gradually but definitely lessening the interest because there is no suspense and not a single new twist to put you off the track.

Everything happens along just as you expect it until finally you figure it's a waste of time waiting around for an ending that is so certain. The story material in this is all so familiar viewers might easily enough believe you were showing them something they had seen before. They will have to be mighty easily satisfied to be pleased with this one.

—*The Film Daily,* June 4, 1922

Dustin Farnum and Philo McCullough *(Fox Film)*

Strange Idols star Dustin Farnum *(Blum)*

Perhaps the bad weather made *Strange Idols* another candidate for the worst film made on the Mendocino Coast, but as no prints likely exist we can't know.

Dustin Farnum was a member of a famous American theatrical family that had its roots in 19th Century theatre. He acted in 35 films between 1914 and 1926, including two famous movies of the 'Teens: *The Squaw Man* and *The Virginian*.

Doris Pawn acted in 18 films between 1914 and 1923. Richard Tucker acted in 152 films between 1913 and 1940. Philo McCullough acted in 113 films between 1914 and 1954 and even had one television role, in *Tarzan the Fearless* (1964).

(Fort Bragg Advocate, October 11, 1922)

MOTION PICTURE STARS
COMING WITH CIRCUS

A real three-ring circus is to furnish the background for a motion picture production with the all-star cast living the life of the "big-top" for several weeks during the making of the picture, according to producion plans announced for "Someone to Love."

John Griffith Wray, the Ince director, will take over the circus "Howe's Great London Circus," for three weeks to permit the Ince players to film the scenes of "the elephant girl" story from the pen of C. Gardner Sullivan, the author of "Hail the Woman."

The "Someone to Love" Company includes Cullen Landis, Madge Bellamy and Noah Beery. They will be with the circus at Fort Bragg, afternoon and evening, on Sunday, May 14.—*Fort Bragg Advocate,* May 3, 1922

BIG CROWD AT CIRCUS

People from all parts of the coast were here Sunday to attend Howe's London Circus, which gave creditable performances here in the afternoon and evening

There were fourteen cars in all, one of the cars which housed the elephant and camels being eighty feet long.

This was the first circus to visit Fort Bragg, and one of the remarkable features to the coast people was that they arrived at 5 A.M., unpacked and had their tents up and ready to show at 2 P.M., and after showing in the evening had everything loaded back on the cars and left at 12:30 that night. All the animal cages were on wagons and were run right in the cars that way. Horses from the circus were used in moving the apparatus.

There were about one hundred people in the circus.

It is understood that the management spent $200 for feed and $300 for provisions here. It is also said that the total cost of coming here from Willits and return amounted to $2,000.

No figures were given out as to the exact amount taken in but it is understood that the management was well satisfied and expects to return here next year.

—*Fort Bragg Advocate,* May 17, 1922

Thomas Ince was a major Hollywood producer during the 1920s.

Beautiful Madge Bellamy acted in 58 films between 1920 and 1936. She portrayed an innocent screen image, but in 1943, after her acting career was over, she made headlines by shooting her millionaire lover.

Cullen Landis appeared in 60 silent films between 1916 and 1930, but his voice prevented the transition to talkies.

Noah Beery's long dramatic career began in 1916 and he acted in 187 films before his death in 1946. He was always a character actor and usually portrayed villians.

John Griffith Wray directed 20 films during the 1920s, then acted in 60 movies during the 1930s.

Oscar, whose circus name was Rubber, would not be the last elephant to perform along the Noyo River.

Soul of the Beast is one of three silent films made on the Mendocino Coast known to exist and is available on DVD or YouTube.

The movie set of the Canadian village of "Medicine Bow," located near the Noyo River east of Fort Bragg. *(Metro Pictures)*

The Screen
The Girl and the Elephant

THE SOUL OF THE BEAST, with Madge Bellamy, "Oscar," an elephant; Cullen Landis, Noah Berry, Vola Vale, Burt Sprotte and others, by C. Gardner Sullivan, directed by John Griffith Wray.

Wlthout "Oscar," an amenable elephant fortunately not trained to the point of reading subtitles or studying the vehicle in which he supports Madge Bellamy, "The Soul of the Beast," now running at the Rivoli, would indeed be a dreary production. As it is, the goodnatured pachyderm—given a bale of hay one minute and a tiny piece of suger the next, with the assistance of Miss Bellamy, manages to drag the picture along.

This Thomas H. Ince film opens with a series of circus scenes, in the Canadian village of Medicine Bow that are quite well done, spoiled a little by the comedy introduced by the Director, John Griffith Wray. Noah Berry has the part of a whole-hearted tyrant—Caesar—who even stoops to killing and cooking a pet rabbit and trying to make his master eat it.

In the beginning Ruth Lorrimore, played by Miss Bellamy, was a luckless girl. Silas Hamm (Bert Sprotte), the circus manager, received notice to leave from his pet wild woman, and forthwith put Miss Bellamy in the costume and cage to take her place, letting the attendants feed her on raw meat for the delectation of the crowd—just to prove that she was really wild and found on the left bank of the Amazon.

Ruth is locked in the cage when a storm flings down the tents. But there is nothing to fear, as "Oscar" comes along, pulls out the iron bars and ambles off with Ruth on his great head.

"Oscar's" best efforts are in the scenes in which he punishes Caesar. He did not have any affection for Hamm, as the circus manager has a nonchalant way of striking matches on his trunk. He liked Caesar less, because that individual fired a shotgun at him. "Oscar" loped after the tyrant, who fled to the river. There is a wicked look in "Oscar's" eye, as he observes that Caesar has reached the other bank and is grasping a slithering rock. The elephant trudges into the stream, fills his trunk with a good load of water and lets fly at Caesar, until the latter slips from his uncomfortable position into the river, where the big beast awaits him. By the time the elephant has finished with the villain the latter is limp and humble.

"Oscar" shows his jealousy of the hero, his hate of Caesar and the circus manager, and his joy at finding his young mistress. Cullen Landis plays the part of the pathetic lame Paul Nadeau, who recovers the use of his knee through an operation. In the last scene "Oscar" rocks the baby, and Paul and Ruth are happy in their little Canadian home with both villians out of sight.

—New York Times, May 22, 1923

At far left, Madge Bellamy; on ground, Cullen Landis; with hand raised, Noah Beery, Sr; center, Vola Vale.

Oscar the elephant chasing Noah Beery, Sr., into the Noyo River.

MOVIE COMPANY TAKING PICTURES HERE

Twenty-two members of the Universal Film Company are here to shoot eight two-reel pictures concerning lumbering and logging stories.

Robert Hill is director of the company. Roy Stewart and Miss Andree Tourneaur play the leading roles. Albert Smith and Buck Connors also take important parts.

The company will take pictures of the local logging woods, mill, and street scenes. This work will probably take five weeks.

The Robinson Crusoe picture which is now being at the Liberty was made by this company.

—*Fort Bragg Advocate*, August 9, 1922

MOVIE COMPANY TAKING PICTURES ON BIG RIVER

The movie troup of the Universal Film Company which took up headquarters at Fort Bragg recently to take pictures embracing coast logging and milling scenes, have spent most of the past week in this neighborhood. They spent most of their time at Boyle's camp where logging operations are near at hand to the Willits road and where Big River can be easily reached. The latter part of the week they have been at The Boom where river driving and the towing of log rafts can be pictured. The troupe comes down each morning from Fort Bragg in machines and returns to that place in the evening. Roy Stewart is the star actor of the company.

—*Mendocino Beacon*, August 19, 1922

MOVIE TROUPE GIVE ED BOYLE LOVING CUP

The members of the film company which has been taking pictures in the coast section, and which filmed many logging scenes at Ed Boyle's camp on Big River, tendered Mr. Boyle and Leland Milliken, the stock man, a banquet at a local restaurant Monday evening out of consideration for the many courtesies shown them by these two gentlemen. Mr. Boyle was presented with a loving cup by the members of the company.—*Mendocino Beacon*, September 30, 1922

Giants of the Open

Dorothy Lewis sees the unconcious form of a man, later known as "The Drifter," prone on a log floating down Sawdust River. She rescues him and takes him to her father's logging camp, where he incurs the wrath of Peavey, a timber smuggler employed as Lewis's foreman. In a fight with "The Drifter," Peavey is beaten. Lewis receives word of a shortage found in the timber sent from his camp and determines to locate the leak.

"The Drifter," suspicious of Peavey's actions, takes the log raft down the river himself, while Peavey races to head off his substitute. The pirates unsuspectingly board the raft to collect their tribute and in a knockdown and dragout fight on the shifting logs they are overpowered and put timber arrest by the Company's logmen and "The Drifter," who reveals himself as a U. S. Forestry Agent.—*Universal Weekly, October 14, 1922*

LIBERTY THEATRE
——FORT BRAGG——
Big Attractions!

Thurs. and Fri., Oct. 5--6

WILLIAM S. HART, in

"Travelin' On"

One of the Earth's strays forever prospecting the face of it. Searching for nothing in particular but eternally "travelin on." Such is the character of J. B. played by Wm. Hart. His only name was a cattle brand. His only reputation—bad. So it didn't seem so hard to shoulder the guilt of another's crime. But the soul stirring sacrifice he made—only a woman knew.

=== Special Added Attraction! ===

The First Run in California, of

"Giants of the Open"

Featuring Ray Stewart

For the past seven weeks Mr. Stewart and a company of Universal Players have been with us making a series of eight Lumber Jack stories. The first one, "Giants of the Open," was made at Montgomery Grove, Comptche and along the Albion and Big Rivers. These pictures are the only ones that have been entirely made in this vicinity. Don't miss the first one. Owing to the extreme length of the program—Travellin On Giants of the Open and Harold Loyd—shows begin promptly at 7:15 and 9:30.

Admission .... 30c and 50c.

(*Fort Bragg Advocate*, October 4, 1922)

Blue Blood and Red

Jim Allen, foreman of the Frazier's Forest Preserve, saves the owner's daughter, Betty, from a nasty fall into the river. He later rescues her father from being crushed to death by a felled tree. His bravery in saving Frazier makes an ally of Swede Knudson and antagonizes the superintendent, Philip Archer, who plots to gain control of the preserve.

Later, Knudson's suspicions of Archer are aroused and he accuses him of trying to double cross the hands. Archer makes his getaway, jumps on a passing train and flees pursued by Allen. Jim overtakes him at the end of the run, and in a thrilling fight on a swaying scaffold, gets the better of him. Archer breaks away and dives a hundred feet to the water below. Jim jumps after him and brings him back to camp, where his guilt is proved by many incriminating letters found there.

—Universal Weekly, October 21, 1922

Timberland Treachery

Bob "calls" Caswell for running rough-shod over the young shoots in his automobile. They argue and Bob knocks Caswell down, then makes him replant one of the trees. Caswell drives away, then goes to Rose's cabin and tries to kiss her. Bob sees him and knocks Caswell down again, telling Rose that he will protect her in the future. "Slim" and Caswell talk and Caswell offers Slim $1,000 to get control of the Bedford homestead. The following day Slim and Caswell blast a tree trunk on the homestead. Bob saves Rose's life by lifting her to her horse from the trunk just as it blows up. Next morning, after Slim promises to file the necessary claim on Rose's homestead, Slim and Caswell lock her in a powderhouse, and boarding a lumber train, start for the line office to cheat her. The engine of the train sets fire to the forrest and the flames surround the powderhouse. Bob sees the smoke and rides like fury. He gets Rose safely away, just before the house is blown to bits. Having learned of Caswell's plot, Bob tells Rose of it. They canoe toward the land office, arriving there just as Slim and Caswell arrive. They fight and Bob licks them both. Rose then files her claim.

—Universal Weekly, November 24, 1922

Kings of the Forrest

Bob is shown through the Occidental Lumber Mill. He meets Lewis and Redwood Joe, bitter enemies. Joe later goes through the lumber office for some money. A man hands Rose a contract, drawn between Bentley and an independent company for some outside logging and cutting. Rose is disappointed, for her father, Lewis, has wanted the contract. Joe becomes abusive and Bob comes in and throws him out. Bentley comes along. Joe tells him that Bob and Rose are sore. Bentley says he wishes he himself did not have the contract after all, for he has made an error in bidding. Joe offers to steal it for him, and does. But he is seen by Rose. He gets away, though, and hides the contract in a nearby log.

Joe then goes to the office and tells them that Lewis stole the contract. Lewis is summoned, accused, and locked up to await trail for theft. Bob, worried, wanders about, while Joe demands money from Bentley. Bentley demands the contract first. Joe goes after it but sees that the log is being drawn into the mill. He follows and get the contract but is seen by Bob. They fight. The contract falls into the conveying chains. Bob overpowers Joe and knocks him unconscious. Bentley sees him and knocks him unconscious with a rock.

Rose has seen everything and she goes into the mill after Bob, evading Bentley's attempt to stop her. She stops the machinery in time to save Bob and recovers the contract. On the latter is a smudged fingerprint—Joe's! Joe and Bentley are convicted of the crime, while Lewis is set free and given the contract.

—Universal Weekly, December 2, 1922

Hearts of Oak

Callahan tries to kiss Mary as she rides through the forest. Bob arrives in time to beat up Callahan. Later Bob, suspicious of Callahan, manages to get a job with the latter's lumber crew. Next day Mary discovers that Callahan is cutting trees down on her homestead. She confronts him but he denies it, then knocks her down. Again Bob interferes and after beating Callahan, makes him apologize to Mary. He tells Mary that the night previous he saw Callahan deliberately move his claim-stake more than 600 feet into Mary's homestead. Bob tells Mary he is a timber inspector for the Government.

Some days later, from his lookout, Bob sights a fire starting near Mary's tract. He rides madly. Mary and several men fight

the flames and finally extinguish the fire. Then Mary accuses Callahan of deliberately setting the fire; she shows him a peculiarly shaped pencil, ostensibly Callahan's, found near the source of the fire. Callahan tries to attack her, but she runs away, leaps over a bank and onto a passing runaway lumber train flat car. Down grade, the car hits a terrific pace. Bob arrives and immediately obtains a motor-driven handcar and sets out after the flat car. He saves Mary just in the nick of time.

Back to the scene of the fire, Callahan has been caught and is being held for Bob's return. Bob tells him that the pencil is incriminating evidence and that Callahan better leave the country, at once and forever. The crowd leave Bob and Mary alone.

—Univesal Weekly, December 16, 1922

25

them of the danger of leaving fires in the woods. Walton resents the warning and words follow, ending in blows. Larry is the victor and as such incurs the displeasure of Madge.

Grant tells Walton to try to persuade Larry to allow the work to go on, and by persuading the men to continue working, he can show whatever ability he might have. The men have gone to Larry's cabin to talk things over.

Larry, however, is chasing a wild animal. Madge, out with her dog, is hunting the same animal. She loses her way and and as she comes upon Larry's cabin she sees the men approaching. Not recognizing them, she runs into the cabin and locks the door. Larry returns just as the men are about to force the door. He fights them off and as one of them goes away he drops a lighted match, starting a fire. Larry enters the cabin and is very surprised to find Madge there. When he comes out with her he finds Walton there, who starts trouble and runs into the woods with Larry after him. Madge follows. Larry is again the victor. He carries Madge, suffocated by smoke, to her canoe at the edge of the river. Returning to the canoe with Walton, he finds it ablaze, floating down the river. —*Universal Weekly,* January 1, 1923

Knights of the Timber

While riding to her home from the railroad station, Jean Lowring is told by Jake that she should dispose of her father's timber lands before they become absolutely worthless. Jean has been away at a school in the East for several years. She is returning to see her father, who has been seriously injured in an accident in the woods. Jake is secretly in the employ of one Nelson Trent, agent of the unscrupulous lumber trust.

Ned Gregory of the Forestry Bureau, tells Jean that the timber is worth more than she had thought. When Trent comes to make an offer to buy it, she refuses and with the aid of Ned, starts to work developing the property.

Having been ordered to secure the land at any price, Trent orders Jake to blow up the dam. Jake refuses, so Trent decides to do it himself. Jean discovers him at the last moment and her father hears the altercation that follows. In a supreme effort he gets outside the cabin. He falls, however, and lands on the plunger which is set to blow the dam.

Ned learned of the plot and was captured by Trent and imprisoned in a cabin right in the path of the swollen river. Jake, in a dying condition, reaches the cabin, releases Ned and signs a dying confession, implicating Trent in the plot. Ned is carried over the falls by the rushing water, but is rescued in the nick of time by Jean, who had made a wild ride to save him. With Jake's confession she is able to collect from Trent's company for the damage. Her father recovers the use of his limbs through the effort made to save his daughter.

—*Universal Weekly,* February 13, 1923

Doomed Sentinels

Larry Newton, field agent for the Bureau of Forestry, comes upon the camp of Grant, a wealthy timber man. Grant is having trouble with his men because they object to the conditions of the camp. They have refused to continue work unless the conditions are bettered. Larry orders all existing hazards removed before work goes any further.

In the woods he finds Madge, Grant's daughter, with Walton, a young society man, suitor for Madge and for her father's timber land. They are toasting marshmallows over a fire. Larry warns

Film Stars Arrive at Noyo

Virginia Valli, Wallace Beery and Rockcliff Fellows, famous Universal stars arrived at Noyo River Tavern last week to begin work in the production of "The Signal Tower" which is being filmed by the Universal Film Company in the redwoods between Fort Bragg and Willits.

Rockcliff Fellowes plays the part of the signal towerman and comes in for a lot of heroic work in wrecking the runaway freight train to avoid running head-on into the limited approaching on the same track.

Special trains, both freight and passenger have been working for the past two weeks in the making of this super-production on the line of the CWR.

—*Fort Bragg Advocate,* October 31, 1923

Dining Room, Noyo River Tavern *(MHR)*

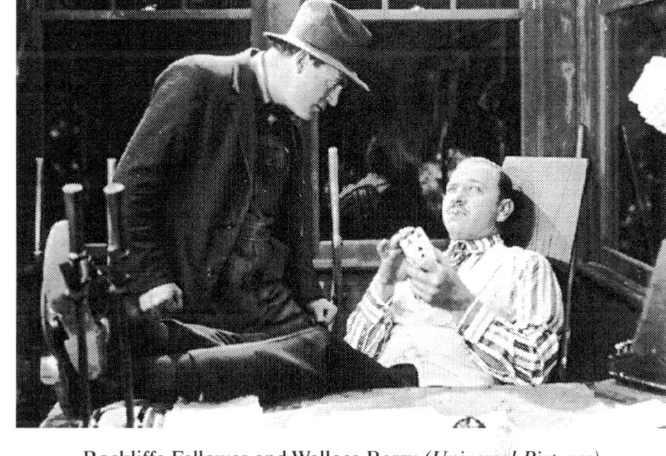

Rockliffe Fellowes and Wallace Berry *(Universal Pictures)*

Virginia Valli and Rockliffe Fellowes *(Universal Pictures)*

Rockliffe Fellowes and Wallace Beery in fight scene. *(Universal Pictures)*

Frankie Darro and Rockliffe Fellowes *(Universal Pictures)*

Noyo River Tavern was a resort on the California Western Railroad (the 'Skunk') located 21 miles east of Fort Bragg near Northspur on the banks of the Noyo River, that offered "walking trails, horseback riding, fishing, hunting, swimming, dancing and other amusements, making it an ideal place for outdoor life." The main building, containing a dining room, was surrounded by fully furnished bungalows, tents on platforms, and "a dancing pavilion with an excellent floor."

Inside the signal tower. J. Farrell MacDonald and Rockliffe Fellowes. *(Universal Pictures)*

Villain Wallace Beery and heroine Virginia Valli *(Universal Pictures)*

Rockliffe Fellowes and Virginia Valli *(Universal Pictures)*

Wallace Beery and Virginia Valli *(Universal Pictures)*

Film Company Finishes Taking Picture

The Universal Pictures Corp. have finished taking their big railroad feature picture, "The Signal Tower" and have shipped their equipment from Burbeck on the CWR&N back to Universal City. It took three large freight cars to handle it, and a special Pullman car was sidetracked at Northspur to accomodate the company. This car was picked up last night by the regular Pullman train.

Over forty persons have been working night and day for over a month on this picture, and with the exception of a few interior scenes, the entire story was filmed along the lines of the CWR. This picture should be released sometime during next March and will be shown at the local theater.

—*Fort Bragg Advocate,* November 21, 1923

"I signed a contract with Universal and made five hits in a row: *The Acquittal, The Signal Tower, Butterfly, Smouldering Fires,* and *The Goose Woman.*

For *The Signal Tower,* we took over a railroad in northern California and worked among the big trees for six weeks. Ben Reynolds was my cameraman. We used to get up at five a.m. and shoot the locomotive climbing the gradient, with the sun coming up and the steam mingling with the trees . . . it was just beautiful. We made everything on location, even the interiors of the signal tower, which I had built at a switch track. When it got too bright outside we fitted amber glass in the windows to balance the exposure.

The whole railroad was ours. They had one train a day. Once we let that through, it was our set. I had a terrific wreck in the picture, when the train broke loose at the top of the mountain and came down wide open."

—Director Clarence Brown, interviewed by Kevin Brownlow in *The Parade's Gone By,* 1967.

THE SCREEN
The Switchman's Dilemma.

THE SIGNAL TOWER, with Virgina Valli, Rockliffe Fellowes, Wallace Berry, Frankie Darro, James O. Barrows, J. Farrell Macdonald, Dot Farley and others, adapted by James O. Spearing from a story by Wadsworth Camp. Directed by Clarence L. Brown. At the Mark Strand.

After viewing "The Signal Tower," the celluloid melodrama at the Strand this week, one is impressed with the confining duties of a railroad signal man in a tower on a lonely forest division. Such a job might be a boon to omniverous readers and students who have good hearing and a familiarity with the Morse code. During the time these signal experts are on duty they are never safe in wandering out of call of the dots and dashes of the busy little telegraphic instrument. Should anything happen in their own home—say half a mile distant—about the time the limited is due to pass, they are obliged to stick to their guns.

Although the subject of this film is not new and there are a number of sequences in which the director has been forced to utilize minatures, the narrative is told in such a way as to make it emphatically gripping.

In his scenerio James O. Spearing dwells carefully on certain details. He gives a lucid idea of the atmosphere and works up to an effective climax. Obviously, he could have done even better with a more original theme in which there was a little more relief than there is in this narrative. The story was written by Wadsworth Camp, and there are certain situations which it is apparent Mr. Spearing has been bound to accept.

The villain, an arch-fiend of a strange, nonchalant type, falls precipitously in love with Sally Taylor, his colleague's wife, the instant he sets eyes on her. He is known as Joe Standish, his nickname being "the railroad sheik." Gertie, Sally's giddy cousin, fawns upon Joe when he arrives, but her absurd attentions are rebuffed even by Standish. For the sake of the story the signal men work on twelve-hour shifts. Hence there are only two of them in the isolated spot, and to add to complications, Sally, angered with her cousin, sends her off to her home, and thus she is left at Joe's mercy, he having rented the room in the Taylor house vacated by his predecessor.

Joe loses little time in snatching his first kiss, with the result that Dave, white with anger, turns the scoundrel out of his home, giving his wife an unloaded revolver with which to intimidate Standish should he ever return. The uncanny Joe bides his time for revenge. One stormy night Dave receives a message to the effect that a freight train has become uncoupled and that several of the cars are rushing down hill, endangering the limited. He has hardly taken stock of this message when his little son, drenched and excited, rushes into the signal box panting that Standish has smashed his way into their house. Dave can't stop what he is doing. The switch fails to work owing to the flood of water, so he has to bang with a sledge hammer on the rail until he succeeds in separating it so that it will throw the freight cars down the incline. This sequence is well pictured, but, of course, the miniature cars are not impressive as they fall over, rather slowly, and never smash or buckle into one another.

Rockliffe Fellowes has the part of Dave, which he plays with realistic feeling, even to the bit where he has to demonstrate the futiltiy of trying to punish a drunken man. Virginia Valli as Mrs. Taylor gives an excellent performance in her battle with Standish, and in other scenes she is sincere and dignified. Of course Wallace Beery is in his histrionic element in enacting the role of the "railroad sheik," whom he makes a thoroughly despicable, unscrupulous scoundrel.

The excellent acting, coupled with Mr. Spearing's comprehension of atmospheric detail and drama, makes this a most interesting picture.—*The New York Times,* July 21, 1924

To vote *The Signal Tower* a place in the top ten films made on the Mendocino Coast is perhaps folly, but that is the feeling one gets reading about it. There is a bit of humor in the above review, in that the New York reviewer criticizes the train wreck scene as being unimpressive because miniature freight cars were used. In fact, according to Clarence Brown, real freight cars were wrecked!

During his long film career, from 1915 until 1980, Clarence Brown was nominated for seven Academy Awards for Best Director. His most famous movies were *Anna Christie* (1930), *Anna Karenina* (1935), *The Human Comedy* (1943), *National Velvet* (1944), and *The Yearling* (1946). Wallace Berry appeared in 138 films between 1914 and 1949. Beginning as a dark villain, by the late 1920s he was a burly softy and a great MGM box-office hit. He was nominated for an Academy Award for *The Big House* (1930). Virginia Valli acted in 40 films, beginning with *Skinner's Dress Suit* (1917) and ending with *The Lost Zeppelin* (1930). She then retired and had a long and happy marriage. Rockliffe Fellowes debuted in *The Regeneration* (1915) and ended his acting career 39 films later in *Rusty Rides Alone* (1933). Between 1924 and 1959, Frankie Darro appeared in 116 films, mostly westerns. His last film was *Operation Petticoat* (1959).

The Signal Tower is available on DVD and YouTube.

(Fort Bragg Advocate, July 18, 1924)

Hollywood Motion Picture Company
Shooting Woods Scenes

A motion picture company of 30 people from the Gerson Pictures corporation of San Francisco and Hollywood arrived Sunday from San Francisco and have been busy all week filming scenes for a picture of the northern California woods, now being produced by the company. For several days this week they visited The Boom and also BoyleÕs camp and shot a number of pictures of woodsÕ life, camp scenes and logging operations

They made their headquarters at Fort Bragg and also took some scenes in the Ten Mile woods. Duke Worne, who formerly directed the filming of a number of pictures in the Mendocino woods, is directing the film.

The company is under the direction of B. Berger, general manager of the Gerson Corporation, with Ernest Smith as camera man. Jane Thomas is leading lady and Richard Hold leading man.—*The Mendocino Beacon*, August 22, 1925

Jane Thomas *(Blum)*

(California State Library)

(San Francisco Performing Arts Library & Museum)

Little is known about the last silent movie filmed on the Mendocino Coast. It was produced by Paul Gerson Pictures, distributed by Aywon Film Corporation, and released on September 14, 1926, but no review or even a plot discription has been found. *In Search of a Hero* was directed by Duke Worne, who had been an actor in five films between 1914 and 1917; he then directed 55 movies between 1919 and 1932. Richard Holt, whose screen name was Ashton Dearholt until 1925, appeared in 49 films between 1915 and 1927. During the 1930s Holt produced five films, ending with *Tarzan and the Green Goddess (1938)*. Jane Thomas appeared in 17 films between 1921 and 1926, the most famous being *The Hoosier Schoolmaster* (1924).

PARAMOUNT PICTURE PEOPLE SHOOT COAST SCENES

A troup of movie people from Paramount Pictures passed through town Tuesday. They had been to Caspar and Elk, where they took a few pictures. They are making a picture supposed to be taken on the English coast, and our coast line is said to resemble the English coast very much. Their main shots were taken around Fort Ross.

> "Quite probably the movies' best ghost story."
> —William K. Everson, *Classics of the Horror Film*

Ray Milland and Ruth Hussey star in this unnerving, atmospheric horror classic set on the remote coast of Cornwall.

Soon after moving into a house purchased at a suspiciously low price, music critic Roderick Fitzgerald (Milland) and his sister Pamela (Hussey) experience unusual occurences: doors open and close by themselves, a strange scent of mimosa permeates the air, and heartwrenching sobs are heard late into the night.

The mysterious activities are heightened when the Fitzgeralds are visited by Stella Meredith (Gail Russell), a beatiful young girl who is inexplicably linked to the house. Each time Stella visits, her life is imperiled by warring spirits trying to reveal secrets of the past.

Long considered one of the most effective films ever made, *The Uninvited* is an unforgettable, hair-raising experience, and one of the first films to deal with ghosts in a serious and terrifying manner.

—*MCA/Universal Home Video*

(*Mendocino Beacon*, October 14, 1944)

Ray Milland, Ruth Hussey and Gail Russell, with view of Elk headlands beyond.
(*Universal City Studios*)

Only exterior shots for *The Uninvited* were made on the Mendocino Coast, and certainly the 'stars' never came here. Most likely the crew who filmed in Elk were on a scouting mission for *Frenchman's Creek,* made a few months later, and Paramount decided to use the footage in *The Uninvited*. Supposedly the cliffs were painted white, but this confusion probably arose because *The White Cliffs of Dover* (not filmed here) was released the same year.

An interesting movie that is damaged by Ray Milland's insipid acting. The film introduced composer Victor Young's haunting melody *Stella by Starlight*.

MOVIE TROUP MAY FILM PICTURE HERE
ACCOMODATIONS SOUGHT FOR CAST OF 100

A representative of a Hollywood Filming company has been on the coasts for some days making his headquarters at Little River inn. His mission is to see if accomodations can be obtained for a movie troupe of approximately one hundred persons to film a picture in this coast section. No definite commitments have been made, and it will likely depend a good deal on his report whether the picture will be undertaken here.

With more and more war pictures being brought out, and with most of these necessitating coast and ocean scenes, the Mendocino coast is getting recognition because of its ruggedness and likeness to scenes on the coast of England.

—*Mendocino Beacon*, May 15,1943

Arturo de Cordova and Joan Fontaine *(Universal City Studios)*

ALBION BLOSSOMS OUT
A CITY OF TENTS
WILL HAVE THREE MAJOR ACTIVIES
THIS SUMMER

Albion takes on the appearance of a circus town, with its tent city which has been erected to house the army of workers which will be employed by Paramount in filming "Frenchmen's Creek."

To those who have read this spicy story, depicting the tale of a French pirate and an English countess, the preparatons are creating quite a bit of interest. Many people have visited Albion the past week to view the preparations.

Some of the local residents visited the castle of the countess and were quite surprised to find a living room completely furnished with furnture authentic to the period. The old fireplace was complete even to flowers on the mantel.

The pirate ship is now at Albion, and when complete with sails will be a replica of the old galleons pictured in the stories of Christopher Columbus.

ALBION RIVER SETTING FOR NEW MOVIE
"FRENCHMAN'S CREEK" TO BE FILMED HERE

It now seems definitely settled that this section is to witness the filming of a picture. It is "Frenchman's Creek," adapted from the DuMaurier story, and Albion river and its harbor will be the principal setting.

Principal headquarters for the cast in which Joan Fontaine will play the leading role, will be Little River Inn. This popular caravansary, however, will only be able to quarter a portion of the 125 members of the cast, and other accommodatione are being sought. It seems probable that quite a number of the players will be taken care of in Fort Bragg.

The whole coast will look forward with interest to the filming of the picture.—*Mendocino Beacon*, May 22, 1943

MOVIE CO. TO SOON START ON PICTURE
DINING HALL BUILT
NEAR ALBION SCHOOL HOUSE

Since the arrival of the work crew of Paramount Pictures at Albion who are preparing the set for the taking of the big picture, "Frenchman's Creek," that community is becoming a beehive of activity. Accommodations for the crew, cook-houses and other temporary buildings are taking shape temporarily. Trucks are busy hauling material and roads and small docks are being contructed. It is expected the picture troupe will arrive here around the middle of June to start filming the story.

One of the units of construction at Albion is a dining hall where the company will be served meals. This is located near the schoolhouse at that place. Several local people have agreed to assist with this service. Mrs. Carl Enochs, who conduced the dining room of Hotel Mendocino, will take over salad making for the luncheheon and dinner periods.

The making of this picture will require at least thirty days and if cloudy days are encountered it may run to 60.

Accommodations for the members of the company have been secured at several points, with a number making their headquarters in Fort Bragg. Joan Fontaine, leading lady, will be quartered in Mrs. Telgard's home at Pine Grove.

—*Mendocino Beacon*, June 5, 1943

One of the Hollywood commentators has this to say: "Paramount searched 500 miles for Frenchmen's Creek, and then, without knowing who owned it, picked the farm of Allan Curtis at Little River."

This is not true, as the old Kent ranch, now owned by Curtis, is several miles north of Albion.

The commentator remarks again the Albion river is being dredged to provide docks and landing places for the pirates' ship. In doing so millions of feet of redwood have been raised which will probably be used later on.

No doubt there are many sinkers embedded in the river remaining from the intensive logging operations carried on in that vicinity for many years.

With the "go ahead" given on the construction of the Albion bridge, an airport being built at its back door, and the filming of this picture, the little peaceful community of Albion will be a scene of much activity for many months to come.

—*Mendocino Beacon*, June 19, 1943

Frenchman's Creek Setting
Creates Great Interest

The Albion river, the redwoods and the sea are the setting of "Frenchman's Creek," being filmed by Paramount. Visitors from the county and farther away are interested in the setting on the coast and week end trips are the order.

Under construction and advanced to a point of interest and beauty are the castle and the old church, the bridge and other features that make up the scenes. Just over the hill from the castle the pirate ship, La Mouette, rises and falls with the tide, never-ending source of interest to visitors. Near is the pirate's cove.

In the castle is a fireplace of the period to which the film belongs and the furniture and appointments are of that period. The castle is constructed of plaster of paris and parts of it are to be covered with ivy. The winding stair is of brick. The church roof is of heavy shakes. These buildings, which by the way have sides only which face the camera, will be left intact when the film is finished.—*Ukiah Daily Journal,* June 21, 1943

OUTDOOR WEDDING
HELD AT "PICTURE CHURCH"
COAST PEOPLE ARE UNITED
IN COLORFUL SETTING

A rare June day on the coast with the blue waters of the Pacific adding charm to the scene, were contributing factors to a very romantic outdoor wedding which was solemnized Sunday afternoon, before a group of invited guests.

Contracting parties were Guy Johnson, mail carrier on the coast route, and Mrs. Lu Celia Robinson Locke.

The ceremony was performed before the set of the little old world church which has been erected by Paramount for the filming of the picture, Frenchman's Creek.

The exterior of the church front, which is a replica of the architecture authentic to the period of the story, has been beautifully decorated for the actual filming of the picture. Flowering vines and shrubbery enhance the beauty of the setting.

The marriage ceremony was read by Reverend Huthnance of Fort Bragg.

Members of the bridal party were three sisters of the bride, who acted as bridesmaids and Shirley Ware of Fort Bragg, who acted as best man for the groom.

The bride was charming in a blue ensemble. A navy blue top coat and navy had were worn over a dress of lighter blue.

Following the ceremony an informal reception for immediate members of the family were held at the bride's home, the property formerly owned by R.M. Bellows, and known to many coasters as the old Eglin place.

Many friends of the happy couple will wish them happiness in their new life together.

A number of local residents were guests at the wedding.

—*Mendocino Beacon,* June 26, 1943

PIRATE SCENES START TODAY
Fishing Scenes Taken
Near Mendocino Woodlands

Director Mitchell Leisen of the Paramount Location Troupe at Albion is all smiles at the success he has been having the past week with the filming of "Frenchman's Creek." The weather has been perfect for technicolor shots and much film has been "canned" during the past week.

The past few days has been spent in the Mendocino Woodlands, east of Mendocino, where a fishing scene has been filmed. The historic coach, pulled by four matched black horses is used to drive Miss Joan Fontaine, feminine star of the story, along the wooded road to a secluded spot along Big River where she meets Arturo de Cordova, the male star, and then they go fishing.

From the coach, Miss Fontaine changes to a row boat, and then she and Cordova row down the river in a beautiful fishing scene.

The backwoods country of the Woodlands is an ideal setting for the picture.

Today, Wednesday, the filming ot the Pirates' landing and fighting on the beach will be started. This sequence of "Frenchman's Creek" will take some time to film and is one of the highlights of the story. These scenes will be taken at Albion.

—*Mendocino Beacon,* July 10, 1943

MENDOCINO FURNISHES
SEVENTEEN PIRATES
YOU WILL SEE THEM IN THE
MOVIES BEFORE LONG

The filming of "Frenchmen's Creek" in nearby Albion took on added interest to the people of this community when seventeen stalwart males of this community answered the call of Paramount and went to Albion to take part in the pirate scenes. The only requisite was a pair of strong arms and ability to row a boat.

Friday the men were taken down for a practice workout before the actual filming took place.

Saturday they were taken down for a wardroom fitting of costumes, authentic to the period of piracy. Long coats, jabots and wrist ruffles, knee breeches and long stockings, wigs of long hair, black, blonde and red heads transformed the men into a motley bunch for make-believe pirates, who will hardly be recognized as peaceful citizens of this community when the picture is shown.

Sunday the filming of the pirate scenes took place, the harbor and ocean at Albion being the setting for the scenes. It was a perfect day for taking pictures. Many local people motored down to view the scene and take snapshots of the pirate crew.

Transportation and free lunch, good pay, blistered palms and sunburned faces, plus a load of fun were recompense for the efforts of the pirate crew.

Who were the pirates? Among the number were John Bishop, Frank Brown, Joe Brown, Gerald Cummings, Clifford Chapman, Homer Drinkwater, Russell Enochs, Carrol Gorden, Johnnie Gorden, Charles Hee, Bill Larkin, Louie Larsen, Vernon Olsen, Bill Pesula, Tom Porteous, Joe Quaill, Harry Schneider, and Edward Silva.—*Mendocino Beacon,* July 31, 1943

SWIMMING EXTRAS MAKE $35 A DAY

Swimmers at $35 per day! Riggers and crew members for the pirate ship, La Marquette, at $16.50 per day! Cornishmen with muskets at $10.50 per day!

Such are the salaries being paid the extras in the filming of Frenchman's Creek.

Who wouldn't be willing to swim the cool waters of the Albion a few times for that price. Even in this day of wartime wages, that ain't hay!

Mrs. Helmi Grimes, who has been acting as recruiter of men for the film company, received a telephone call Saturday evening from Hollywood asking for as many as seventy men to act as extras, twenty of whom were to be swimmers.

Mrs. Grimes was a very busy woman signing up that many extras. There are very few men in the community who are not employed in the daytime at Fort Bragg or at Caspar. The younger men and boys who are available and able to swim have signed up as swimmers. Most men working on the night shift at Fort Bragg are taking part to make up the number.

The foggy weather prevailing the first part of the week was ideal for taking night scenes. Monday, Tuesday and Wednesday the extras were given transportation to Albion to take part in the scenes being shot. Since then the weather has been bright and clear, so filming has been halted for a few days before the scenes can be finished.

Many local people have visited the set to see the men in costume, and many snap shots have been taken of the different groups.

It is a lot of fun while it lasts anyway, and the pay won't come amiss either. $35 a day isn't bad. No siree.

—*Mendocino Beacon,* August 21, 1943

Views of *Navron*, the Cornish castle built by Paramount on the Robinson property south of Little River, for *Frenchman's Creek*.
*Photographs
by Addie Reis.*
Standing on the steps are Bob Bishop, Laing Chambers and Madeleine Harby.

The photograph at left shows the interior detail that could be seen through the castle's open door.

The photograph at right was by Mellis for the *Ukiah Daily Journal*, June 21, 1943, showing the set under construction. In picture are Iva Mellis, Fred and Nellie Leonard.

Views of the pirate ship *La Mouette* and its pirates in the Albion River. *(Reis)* Note swimmers in battle scene: above center.

The full-sized wooden ship was built in Hollywood and hauled up the coast by barge. After the film's completion, the movie company simply left it tied to the dock they had built in the Albion River. Not long afterwards vandals burned it, but supposedly pieces still remain embedded in the river's bank. A few years ago an intrepid amateur historian, unaware of *Frenchman's Creek,* informed the world that he had discovered Sir Francis Drake's 16th century sailing ship.

Pirate chief Arturo de Cordova

Spectators Vernie Brown and Alvin Mendosa next to the stagecoach used at the castle in Little River and near Big River. *(Mendosa)*

The church built next to the castle set in Little River. *(Reis)*

Film crew members eating lunch on the dock built on the north side of the Albion River, looking west. Albion Bridge (Route 1) is at far right. *(Reis)*

Two views of Toni Robinson Lemos, Joan Fontaine's stand-in. (Above: *Robinson Film*—Below: *Chambers*)

Extras playing the roles of English Gentlemen were Joe Brown, Frank Brown, Tony Catherina, Clifford Chapman, Gerald Cummings, George Escola, Don Fenn, Charles Hee, Bill Larkin, Louis Larsen, Tom Porteous, Joe Quaille, Ed Schneider, Eddy Silva. Extras playing the roles of pirates are listed in the July 31st newspaper article on Page 33. Some extras played both gentelemen and pirates. *(Reis)*

FRENCHMAN'S CREEK OPENS IN NEW YORK

"Frenchman's Creek" the Paramount production in technicolor, which was filmed at Albion last year, made its appearance on September 20th at the Rivoli in New York.

Mrs. Gale Lister, nee Virginia Quaill, while traveling on a car in that city was thrilled to see the bill boards displaying advertising matter concerning the opening of this picture. She intended to attend the show on its fourth night. In writing to her parents here, she enclosed a clipping from the New York Post:

""Frenchman's Creek," Paramount's Technicolored adaption of the Daphne DuMaurier tale of a pirate bold and a lady fair—Arturo de Cordova and Joan Fontaine—produced as a budget of almost $4,000,000, arrives on Sept. 20th at the Rivoli; continuous showings, popular prices.

The DuMaurier tale was produced by Buddy DeSylva, Mitchell Leisen and David Lewis (and directed by Mr. Leisen), with much action transpiring aboard a pirate ship, launched 680 miles up the California coast at Albion. Some 250 members of the cast besides the camera crew, technical experts and cooks were housed at Albion. Basil Rathbone and Nigel Bruce, the Holmes and Watson of a weekly radio serial, had to travel 1360 miles each week to make their air program and get back to work on the set. Nearly 2000 props were used in filming the picture."

—*Mendocino Beacon*, September 30, 1944

FRENCHMAN'S CREEK BIG DRAWING CARD
BEAUTIFUL SCENES AT ALBION AND BIG RIVER

The long awaited showing of "Frenchman's Creek" was greeted by capacity houses on Thursday evening. Practically the entire coast area was represented in the crowds that attended the two shows that were presented.

Lines began to form long before the opening of the doors at 6:30 p. m., and extended as far as the Fort Bragg Pharmacy and around the corner.

The crowds waiting to see the second show seemed even larger than the first—double and triple lines having formed of people waiting to get in.

Some Mendocino residents went up early, intending to have dinner there before the first show but seeing the lines forming so early, they went without dinner to make the first show.

The coastal scenes taken in this vicinity are very beautiful in technicolor. The scenes on Big River and Albion River (Frenchmen's Creek) are very lovely.

Many local residents took part as extras in the picture. While they are not clearly shown those taking part could recognize the scenes they were in.

The costuming was very lavish and authentic to the period of the story.

Most people attending thought it was a very fine picture.

—*Mendocino Beacon*, December 16, 1944

The cast and crew of *Frenchman's Creek* stayed at Little River Inn and its owner, Ole Hervila, recalled that Joan Fontaine was not content to be treated as other guests and insisted on caviar, champagne, filet mignon and other items impossible to obtain during World War II. Ole consulted with the film company's location manager, Sid Street, who took the list of hard-to-get items and sent a chauffeur to San Francisco to purchase them. Sid Street then instructed Ole to charge Miss Fontaine double in order to teach her a lesson. When presented with her bill, she called Ole names even he did not recognize. Paramount Studios and Sid Street paid the bill.—*The Finn, The Twin and The Inn* by Mel McKinney

Frenchman's Creek, the 17th century romance about the lady and the pirate, was beautifully filmed in Technicolor and opulently mounted. It was Paramount's (and Hollywood's) costliest investment to that date ($3,000,000) and the costumes alone (which were authentic for the year 1600 and had to be made to order) cost $200,000 for the hoop skirts and pirate coats. The scripting of the film, however, does not age as well as the visual photography. Although the movie is frequently shown on late-night television, it is difficult to consider seriously, its beauty notwithstanding.

Accordingly, because of the film's overall quality, why has it received so much space in this book? Because the locals loved the making of the film! Not only was this the first motion picture made on the Mendocino Coast in 'modern times,' it was a major production, with a castle that could be visited and a sailing ship anchored in the Albion River. In the middle of a war, only a few years after the mills had closed—and in the lingering Depression—*Frenchman's Creek* bought money and excitement to the Coast at a difficult and tenuous time. The numerous local photographers who created the large archive of excellent photographs of the production made it difficult to decide what images could be used and for this reason more space was provided for their work.

FISHING PICTURE TO BE FILMED ON COAST BY WARNER BROS.

Jane Wyman & Lew Ayers Probably In Cast

For some days representatives and agents of Warner Brothers of Hollywood have been on the coast arranging for the filming of a picture whose principal scenes are to be taken in this section.

They now have about 75 busy people in this area, with headquarters at Fort Bragg, where they have taken over all available hotels and other lodgings in this coastal area.

A crew has been busy during the past week taking down the old brewery—at one time a tannery south of Mendocino on the road to Little River. It is understood this is to be reconstructed into a grist mill.

The Mendocino Presbyterian church will probably enter into the picture; possibly the Masonic temple, with its interesting carved figures, and there will be scenes of the bay.

The picture is to be a fishing picture, we understand, and Jane Wyman and Lew Ayes are expected to take part in it. Actual scene shooting is scheduled to start about the first of next month.—*Mendocino Beacon*, August 23, 1947

Lew Ayres Arrives by Special Plane at Little River

Tuesday noon the Little River airport was an active place when one of Western Airlines' big DC-4 planes landed with 51 passengers connected with Warner Bros. new production "Johnny Belinda." Heading the list of stars that landed was Lew Ayres, bedecked in a light suit, felt hat and black moustache. Chas. Bickford, the rough and ready actor, looked quite like the mild-mannered gentleman when he arrived with the plane. Director Jean Negulesco was also a member of the troupe that arrived.

Miss Jane Wyman, the star of the show, will arrive at a later date.

The picture will be filmed on the coast and many of the scenes will be shot around Noyo. As the story has to do with fishing, the Noyo fleet will be used in some of the scenes. It has also been reported that some of the historical buildings in and around Mendocino will be used.

—*Mendocino Beacon*, September 3, 1947

Freak Accident On Monday

In the first accident of its kind, a helicopter on Monday frightened a team of horses pulling a buggy pulling film stars Jane Wyman and Lew Ayres resulting in a near-tragic runaway.

Piloted by Knute Flint and bearing Cameraman Paul Ivanhoe, the Armstrong-Flint helicopter hovered low over a farm to photograph Miss Wyman and Ayres driving up a country lane for Warner Bros. "Johnny Belinda." The noisy rotors startled the horses which Ayres was unable to stop. It was only after they had plunged a quarter of mile toward a steep ocean bluff that they were brought to a halt by Mel Dellar and Lee White, first and second assistant directors. Except for being jostled and frightened, Miss Wyman was uninjured.

—*Fort Bragg Advocate-News*, September 17, 1947

Just a Nichols Worth

by George Nichols

There is a little bit of horse-play in the most serious business, I guess. Jan Sterling, of stage fame, and a principal in the cast of "Johnny Belinda" received her initiation the other day. "Johnny Belinda" finds Miss Sterling in her first movie and she is very anxious to please, not only the director but the public too. When Director Negulesco told her that her first scene would be to walk across the set, stoop and pick up a basket of clothes and then carry the basket off the set, Miss Sterling waited for the "Ready, Camera, Shoot" and then went on the set with all the dignity she could summon. She walked very gracefully up to the basket, daintly reached down and took hold of the handle and lifted . . . then it happened—she lost her balance, stumbled and all but fell down, but didn't release her hold on the basket. You see, the Director had weighted the basket down with lead, and covered it with clothing. Miss Sterling took the ribbing good-naturedly, and is now awaiting her chance to turn the tables on the director.

—*Fort Bragg Advocate-News*, September 23, 1947

Jane Wyman as Belinda McDonald and Bobby-Anderson as Johnny Belinda *(Warner Bros)*

Charles Bickford as Black McDonald *(Warner Bros.)*

Agnes Moorehead as Aggie McDonald *(Warner Bros.)*

Director Jean Negulesco, Jane Wyman and Robert Anderson, on the headlands near the Eaton Ranch, south of Fort Bagg. (*Warner Bros.*)

Local Youngster In Movies

Robert Allen Anderson, 8 1/2 mos. old son of Mr. and Mrs. Axel V. Anderson of Fort Bragg, has chosen a career in the movies.

The little fellow has been selected by Warner Bros. to play a part that he can well fill without too much effort, except to cast his eyes around the lot and wonder "what's all the shoutin' about.' He is on the set every day along with the other actors, and his mother, and a special nurse. His voice is perfect, articulation might be improved a bit, but the Director smiles when Robert sets up a howl.

—*Fort Bragg Advocate-News,* October, 1, 1947

The set for the farm and grist mill, located south of Fort Bragg. *(Reis)*

Like This Section

Jane Wyman and Lew Ayres, principals in the picture that is being filmed on the coast, were contacted at the Little River Inn over the weekend and asked what they thought of the Mendocino Coast. Both of the Hollywood people were very explicit in their remarks—they thought the country was wonderful and liked it very much. In fact, they are planning on returning so they can see more of the country.

Ronald Reagan, also at Little River, is on vacation to this section and he is having a real time. He has gone ocean fishing several times and plans on going after the elusive abalone as soon as Ole Hervilla, owner of the Inn, can find time to take him.

—*Mendocino Beacon*, October 4, 1947

Long-horned cattle, and their trainer, used in grist mill scene. *(Reis)*

Monte Blue Speaks to Assembly

Monte Blue, the world reknowned moving picture star, honored the Fort Bragg High School with an interesting and quite thought provoking speech last Thursday before an assembly.

By way of introduction he said that Fort Bragg has meant a great deal towards. the production of their motion picture, "Johnny Belinda." It is an excellent background and they had received nothing but exceptional praises from Hollywood.

Mr. Blue spoke on the subject of Freedom and Citizenship." During the course of his speech he brought in a summary of his background and some of his interesting experiences while traveling abroad and in the United States.

The audience was impressed with his natural interest in history and the fact that he was present and saw the assasination of President McKinley.

His main point, however, was his intense hatred of Communism. Everything should be done to wipe out this menace to our country.

Mr. Snell introduced Mr. Blue to the audience before he made his speech, and in his introduction he said, "I'm sure the audience will agree with me that Monte Blue is really a big man in more ways than one." After hearing the speech it was quite evident that the audience did agree with Mr. Snell.

—*Paul Bunyan News*, October 6, 1947

Just a Nichols Worth
by George Nichols

...the whole "Johnny Belinda" company is eating pumpkin pie. Ronald Reagan brought back a thirty-six inch pie from Eureka and sent it to Jane Wyman who is on location. Ronnie returns to Washington October 20 for the Congressional investigation.

—*Fort Bragg Advocate-News*, September 30, 1947

Fishing scenes at Noyo.
Left: Stephen McNally; right, Monte Blue. *(Reis)*

Right: Charles Bickford as Black McDonald *(Reis)*

Stephen McNally as Locky *(Reis)*

Just a Nichols Worth
by George Nichols

I HAD NO idea that Stephen McNally, signed by Warners for "Johnny Belinda," is the handsome young man I have seen at church each Sunday. His real name is Horace, and I thought he was a lawyer. Well, he is a lawyer, and graduated from Fordham with a lawyer's degree, and his family, well known in college and legal circles, hoped he would carry on the family tradition. But Steve, as he has been renamed, has stuck to acting, even though his MGM contract didn't do much for him. He had the lead in "Johnny Belinda" on the stage, but in the movie he will play second fiddle to Lew Ayres, who has the lead.

—*Fort Bragg Advocate-News,* October 7, 1947

Local Shriners Fete Fellows of 'Johnny Belinda' Company

Fort Bragg Shriners were hosts to visiting Shriners of the cast of "Johnny Belinda," Warner Brothers motion picture on location here, last Saturday at a dinner at Pine Beach. Following a welcome by C. Louis Wood, Kingfish of the Fort Bragg Shrine club, Harry Goldman introduced visiting Shriners and their ladies to the Fort Bragg group. Monte Blue was master of ceremonies for the evening during a program which included vocal and piano numbers by "Reg" Fulton, son of Mr. and Mrs. Mick Fulton, Pine Beach proprietors. Dancing furnished entertainment for the group following the formal program.—*Paul Bunyan News,* October 13, 1947

Stage Presentation at State Theatre, Fort Bragg.
Left to right: Hal Ogle, theatre manager; Monte Blue, master of ceremonies; Miss Wyman; Pete Paolinelli, projectionist; Ronnie Smith, doorman; and Dan Borzage, accordionist
(Hornzee/Paul Bunyan News)

Jane Wyman Will Present Awards to Old Timers Club

Jane Wyman will present members of the Old Timers club of the Redwood theatre circuit of George M. Mann with awards in recognition of faithful service in their duties on the stage of the State theatre at 8 30 p. m. tomorrow (Wednesday).

Appearing in behalf of George Mann, Miss Wyman will present Hal Ogle, theatre manager, with a watch and diamond lapel button. Ogle receives the awards in recognition of more than eight years service with the theatre circuit.

Ronnie Smith and Pete Paolinelli each will be presented with gold lapel buttons. Both have been employed by the circuit more than two years.

Presentations are being made through special arrangement with Miss Wyman, widely known actress now on location near Fort Bragg with the Warner Brothers company filming "Johnny Belinda."

Miss Wyman and other stars of the movies are staying at the Little River inn during the time they are on location here.

—*Paul Bunyan News,* October 20, 1947

Jane Wyman, Agnes Moorehead, Bobby Anderson and Lew Ayres on High School Hill, Mendocino. *(Warner Bros.)*

Cast with helicopter on High School Hill. Jan Sterling, Jane Wyman, Cameraman, Lew Ayres, Agnes Moorehead, Director Jean Negulesco. *(Chambers)*

"Chow Time" for extras on High School Hill, Mendocino. Waving at camera is photographer and teacher Laing Chambers. *(Reis)*

Filming at the Elmer Strauss house, Mendocino. The building, located on the south side of Main Street, was demolished in 1948. *(Chambers)*

Lew Ayres and film crew between takes, Main Street, Mendocino. *(Reis)*

Ronald Reagan visiting the set of *Johnny Belinda*. *(Reis film)*

Agnes Moorehead, Lew Ayres, Charles Bickford
and Jane Wyman at the Presbyterian Church, Mendocino.

Bobby to Hollywood

Little Bobby Anderson, who was "quite the hit"
with the Hollywood people here to make the picture "Johnny Belinda" is back to work—in Hollywood. On Tuesday, his mother Mrs. Axel Anderson
received a telegram from Warner Bros. producers,
that they wanted Bobby in Hollywood to complete
the picture. His mother and aunt, Mrs. Ward Reis,
were put aboard the Southwest plane Tuesday
afternoon and taken direct to Hollywood.

It is estimated that Bobby will be in the movie
city for at least one week.

—*Fort Bragg Advocate-News,* October 29, 1947

The cast of *Johnny Belinda* in front of the Presbyterian Church, Mendocino.
Jane Wyman, Lew Ayres, Agnes Moorehead, Charles Bickford, Jan Sterling,
Stephen McNally. *(Reis)*

Jane Wyman's exraordinary dramatic gifts are
stunningly displayed in *Johnny Belinda,* the movie
that brought her the coveted Academy Award as
Best Actress.

As Belinda McDonald, Wyman plays the deaf mute
daughter of a gruff farmer (Charles Bickford) and
the niece of his stern but kindly sister (Agnes Moorehead). Because of her disability, Belinda is known as
"the dummy" to the other villagers on Nova Scotia's
bleak Cape Breton Island.

The local doctor (Lew Ayres) senses Belinda's innate
intelligence, however, and teaches her sign language
and lip-reading.

Not all are so kind. Belinda is raped by Locky (Stephen McNally) and she bears a child, called Johnny.
After the brutal Locky reveals that the baby is his,
the story reaches a violent climax when he tries to
take Johnny from his mother's loving protection.

Lew Ayres' sensitive performance, the first-rate
supporting cast and Max Steiner's poignant score
alone set the movie apart as one of the screen's most
memorable experiences.

But it is Wyman's grippingly expressive protrayal
that makes *Johnny Belinda* an entertainment
classic.—*Warner Bros./MGM/UA Home Video*

Two decades after he directed the film, Director Jean
Negulesco said that "making *Johnny Belinda* was the hap-
piest experience of my life. We all loved what we did in it.
This was the only time in my career when all the people
connected with the film—including actors, camermen,
still-photographers, etc.—felt themselves an integral part
of the project."

This sense of accomplishment was a sentiment also felt
by all the locals who took part in the film.

Johnny Belinda was nominated for twelve Academy
Awards, but only Jane Wyman received one, for what is still
regarded as a magnificent performance. Upon receiving the
award she said, "I accept this award gratefully, for keeping
my mouth shut for once."

A recent listing by the *National Review* of "One Hunred
Best Conservative Movies" placed the film near the top.

Except for the return of Warner Bros. to Northern California
seven years later, *Johnny Belinda* would have no contender
for the best film ever made on the Mendocino Coast.

"JOHNNY BELINDA COMES TO NEW YORK"

by Editor A. A. Heeser

The papers announced the opening of "Johnny Belinda" at the Stand last week, so by going to the theatre at 4:40 and standing in line we got very good seats to this production whose filming on our coast section created so much interest.

It is sad and gripping, and you want to be sure you have a handkerchief along to wipe away some tears, for Jane Wyman will make you weep a little in spite of yourself, with her wonderful portrayal of Belinda, all done in pantomime.

The aerial views of Mendocino are good and the Presbyterian Church comes out prominently in all these. And, of course, the wedding scene staged in the church's interior is a big feature, and there, quite recognizable, are the home members of the church choir. The fishing scenes at Noyo are also a prominent part of the picture. The home and ranch scenes I could not seem to recognize and they may have been taken in Nova Scotia. The two widehorn steers that operate the grist mill on a sweep don't belong to any breed of native cattle. It is safe to say that "Johnny Belinda" will have a big run.

—*Mendocino Beacon*, September 17, 1948

CO. RESIDENTS AWAIT RELEASE OF FILM MADE ON COAST

Mendocino county theatre-goers will be interested to learn that the Warner Bros. motion picture, "Johnny Belinda," is being shown in coast theaters and no doubt will soon be booked for the Ukiah Theater.

The picture was filmed at Mendocino in Sept. 1947, and many prominent residents of that city appeared in the scenes and enjoyed the experience immensely.

The dramatic film is based on the Broadway hit of seven years ago.

The Fort Bragg territory is said to have an amazing resemblance to the original locale of the play, Prince Edward Isle, Nova Scotia.

Jane Wyman plays the part of Belinda, an unfortunate girl, deaf and dumb from birth. Steve McNally, an actor in the original play, is the father of her illegitimate son, "Johnny Belinda," a part portrayed in the picture by Robert Anderson, the then nine months old son of Mr. and Mrs. A. V. Anderson of Fort Bragg who spent six weeks in Hollywood to complete the scenes.

Belinda is befriended by the local young doctor, Lew Ayers, who taught her the sign language and otherwise brightened her life.

Other prominent stars cast in important roles in the picture are Agnes Moorehead, Jan Sterling, Charles Bickford, and Monte Blue, who has been in films thirty-seven years.

It is said that Jane Wyman is a strong contender for the Academy Award for her performance in this picture. She won the admiration and respect of the Mendocino people by her charm and graciousness.

The eighty year old Presbyterian Church and the Mendocino High School used as a courthouse will be recognized by county people.

Coast people appearing in the picture are Nettie Nichols, Vernie Brown, Alice Kooyers, Evelyn Lawrence, Stella Nevious, Olive Liefrinck and her lovely young daughters Patsy and Norma Liefrinck. Olive Liefrinck worked in the picture eleven days, Patsy ten, and Norma five.

T.F. Liefrinck was Principal of the Potter Valley High School for some years and the family are well known there and in Ukiah. He was City Superintendent of Schools and Principal of the High School in Mendocino at the time the picture was filmed. Patsy Liefrinck, a blonde, was a junior in high school and her sister Norma, a brunette, was a sophomore. Both are talented musically and belong to the California Scholarship Federation.

Mr. and Mrs. Liefrinck are seen walking to the trial in the courthouse. Mrs. Liefrinck selected to sing in the church choir is the second from the right behind the organ. Mrs. Liefrinck said she would never forget singing "Abide With Me" and "Come Thou Almighty," while Jane Wyman and Lew Ayers looked on.

The Liefrinck family are now located in Healdsburg where T. F. Liefrinck is principal of the High School.

Jewel Gowan, a daughter of Mr. and Mrs. Jud Gowan of Potter Valley and a teacher in the Mendocino Grammar School at the time, comes to the trial riding in a two-seated two-horse spring wagon.

George Finley, son-in-law of Mr. and Mrs. Howard Brook of Potter Valley, acted as a stand-in for Charles Bickford.

—*Ukiah Republican Press*, October 27, 1948

"Johnny:Belinda," Coast Filmed Movie
Bobby Anderson at State on Sunday

The showing of "Johnny Belinda," the movie that was made here on the coast, at the State Theatre on Sunday, Monday and Tuesday, Nov 7, 8 and 9, will unmistakably be one of the big entertainment scoops of all tirne; but to Baby Bobby Anderson of Fort Bragg, who plays one of the important roles—it will probably be just another chance to "car go bye-bye."

(Editor's Note: "Car go bye-bye" is Bobby's term for an automobile ride—his one big obsession in life.)

You see, theatre manager, Ed Smith has made arrangements with Mr. and Mrs. Axel Anderson, Bobby's parents, for Bobby to appear in person on the stage at the State Theatre once each day during the three-day showing of the Warner's picture "Johnny Belinda."

In case you haven't already heard, "Johnny Belinda" was made last fall at Mendocino, Pine Beach and elsewhere along the picturesque Mendocino coast. While the locale is supposed to be Nova Scotia, to coasters that point is unimportant. What is important is that "Johnny Belinda" belongs to "us" and from what we have been told, it's a first rate piece of movie making.

But to get back to Bobby who plays the role of Jane Wyman's son in the picture, Bobby was "discovered" by Warner's talent scout, Joe Berry through a chance conversation with Deputy Sheriff Ward Reis, uncle of the child. Barry told Reis that Warner's were looking for a child of Bobby's age (Bobby was 8 months old at the time) and when Bobby was brought before Director Jean Nugulesco, the response on the director's part was instantaneous. "His nose and forehead look enough like Miss Wyman's to be her child." Nugulesco said in his best Roumanian accent.

Bobby worked with the company here on the Coast for about two weeks and then spent two weeks working at the Warner's studio in Hollywood. Due to his ability to enact his role with a minimum of gurgles and assorted baby noises, Bobby became known as "One Shot" Anderson. Yes, he was even accused of "scene stealing" in one or two instances.

Bobby, now 22 months old, has grown considerably and with him has grown his passion for "car go bye-bye." That's why he is looking forward to the showing of "Johnny Belinda" here in Fort Bragg. Bobby will be able to "car bye-bye" at least once a day for three days in order to be on hand to greet all of his "fans" in person.

Bobby will appear on the stage at the State Theatre at 4 p.m. Sunday and at 6 p.m. on both Monday and Tuesday.

—*Paul Bunyan News*, November 1, 1948

BABY BOBBY ANDERSON

The Fort Bragg Child That Plays the Role of
"Johnny Belinda"

4 p.m. Sunday — 6:10 p.m. Monday — 6:10 p.m. Tuesday

—— STARTING TIME OF "JOHNNY BELINDA" ——

Sunday — 1:57, 4:06, 6:15, 7:26, 9:35 p. m.
Monday and Tuesday — 6:10, 8:19, 10:28 p. m.

The State theatre, Main Street, Fort Bragg, demolished in 1964.

Bobby Anderson, held by his uncle Ward Reis, with theatre manager Hal Ogle, on the stage of the State Theatre.

'Johnny Belinda' Broke Records

Mendocno Coast residents were right proud of their motion picture, "Johnny Belinda."

The picture, which was filmed largely around Noyo last fall, played for four days at the State Theatre in Fort Bragg and broke all house records, according to Manager Ed Smith. Close to 6,000 persons saw "Jolmny Belinda."

"The response was wonderful," Smith said. "I didn't hear one bad report about "Johnny Belinda," and some people saw it two and three times during its run here."

—*Paul Bunyan News*, November 15, 1948

East of Eden — 1954

Warner Brothers
To Make "East of Eden" Here

Don Page, assistant director and Joe Barry, location engineer of Warner Brothers in Hollywood, are at the Little River Inn making advance preparations for shooting scenes for a new motion picture. The locale selected is the city of Mendocino, with some scenes in the railroad yards of Fort Bragg.

The director of the picture "East of Eden" will arrive at Little River Inn next week, as will the leading lady, Julia Harris, of stage fame; and the leading man, James Dean. A supporting cast will also arrive and shooting actual scenes will be started as soon as possible.

According to Page, only principals in the picture will be brought to the Coast, and all extras that are needed will be made up of Coast people.

Actual time of shooting the scenes, andthe length of time the motion picture people will be here is not known at the present time.

The picture "East of Eden" will be directed by Elia Kazan. He directed two well-known pictures "Street Car Named Desire" and "Gentlemen's Agreement."

An old friend of the Mendocino Coast will also be in the company, Ted McCord, head cameraman. He held a like position on the picture "Johnny Belinda" which was filmed on the coast.

Scenes in Mendocino will include street scenes, service station activity, and scene shots in the school gym. Very little was learned of the plot of "East of Eden" but Page did say that the year 1915 would be very important.

Barry, location man for Warners, is quite well-known on the coast. He, too, was with "Johnny Belinda" and made a lot of friends, not only for himself, but also for the company he represents.

—*The Mendocino Beacon,* April 24, 1954

Dr. Preston's house, Little Lake & Williams Streets, Mendocino. Kate's house in *East of Eden*. Burned in 1956. The location is now the Mendocino Art Center. *(MHR)*

Julie Harris on Main Street, Mendocino. James Dean at right. *(Reis)*

'East of Eden' Being Filmed On Coast

Warner Brothers are now shooting Cinemascope sequences for the movie, "East of Eden," at Mendocino. With a personnel of 120, including actors, prop men and technicians, they started filming scenes last Thursday on Main street at the Bank of America. Six days or more will be used in Mendocino and then the troupe will move to Salinas for five days and then back to the studio to finish the picture.

Raymond Massey and Julie Harris are the stars of the picture, although Massey is not present for any of the sequences here. James Dean and Dick Davalos also have starring roles and play brothers in the story. Both are in love with Julie Harris. This is the first picture experience for Dean and Davalos, although both are veterans of the legitimate stage and Davalos has been recently working in television in New York.

Jo Van Fleet, Albert Dekker, Lois Smith, Timothy Carr, Harold Gordon, William Phillips, Betty Treadville are all in the picture. Jo Van Fleet won the Antoinette Perry Award for the best supporting performance of the year in "The Trip to Bountiful." James Dean was a big hit in the New York stage show, "The Immoralist," which just closed. Julie Harris was the star of the New York stage hit, "The Wedding" and recently appeared in San Francisco as the star of "I am a Camera."

The star studded cast is being directed by Director Elia Kazan, who directed "The Street Car Named Desire" and the recent picture shown at the State theatre, "Man on a Tightrope." Over 50 extras have been employed from Mendocino and Fort Bragg. Gail McMath of Mendocino is the understudy for Jo Van Fleet and Robert Wooster and Elizabeth Enochs of Mendocino and Rudolph Urbani of Fort Bragg are among the many local people who are helping Warner Brothers put the show on the road.

—*Paul Bunyan News,* May 31, 1954

just a nichols' worth

by Geo. A. Nichols

The excitement is over and the Warners Bros. trucks and most of the personnel pulled out early Wednesday morning for Salinas where they will continue to film "East of Eden." Excellent weather while the movie group was here made it possible for them to get the scenes they wanted in record time, and they left on Tuesday of this week. Shooting of scenes was never interrupted because of bad weather. Assistant Director Don Page was a very happy person, and promised a return "engagement" as soon as possible.

The troupe had perfect weather while in the coast, and completed shooting ahead of schedule.

The contemplated railroad scene that was to be filmed in the California Western yards at Fort Bragg was postponed and will be shot in the Salinas area, where the huge lettuce fields will make up the background.

The entire coast profited by the film company's stay here. It's like one of the men remarked, "We dropped a lot of money on this coast in the last 10 days, and we're not taking a thing away from you—except scenery—and that's on film."

How true, how true.

*

Speaking of the movie people who were here making "East of Eden," Julie Harris endeared herself to many people while staying at Little River Inn. Last Saturday night one of the waitresses didn't show up, so Miss Harris put on an apron, and waited on tables for the full evening shift. The tips she received, and they were numerous, went to the other waitresses and the cook. And believe it or not, Julie had the time of her life "acting natural."

—*The Mendocino Beacon,* June 5, 1954

*

Received a nice letter from Joe Barry, location man for Warner Bros., who is on location at Salinas completing location scenes for "East of Eden." Joe sent a check for $50 to the local fire department, in appreciation for the cooperation shown the location group by the department.

Barry also asked that the local people be thanked for their cooperation.

"... thank everyone for being so kind to me and

Filming on Main Street. Sitting: James Dean. Walking: Jo Van Fleet. Back of head: Elia Kazan. *(Chambers)*

the company and I thank them all from the bottom of my heart and hope that I will have the pleasure of coming up there soon and seeing them all and working with you all again ..."

That was fine of Joe to write, but then, we all liked him too.—*The Mendocino Beacon,* June 12, 1954

Looking south at the intersection of Main and Kasten Streets. Left: James Dean. Right: Jo Van Fleet. The buildings on the south side of were demolished in 1957 by their owner, Union Lumber Company, to avoid payment of real estate taxes. The land is now part of the California State Park System. *(Warner Brothers/David Loehr Collection)*

Filming at Main & Kasten Streets. Above: Bank of America, now Out of This World. Below: Looking north on Kasten Street. *(Chambers)*

James Dean, Richard Davalos & Julie Harris *(Warner Bros.)*

Richard Davalos, Gail MacMath (Julie Harris' stand-in) and James Dean across from Crown Hall on Ukiah Street. *(Silva)*

(Curry)   *(Helela)*   *(Curry)*

Three views of James Dean sitting on a ladder in what was then the back yard of Dr. Preston's house.
The photographs were taken by two different onlookers. Location is now the Mendocino Art Center.

$1810.91 CLEARED BY LADIES AID
Served Meals to Movie People
on Location For 'East of Eden'

Activities for Ladies' Aid members came to a close last Thursday with a picnic held in Little River at Van Damme park. A summer recess will be observed during the months of July and August.

A delicious picnic lunch was enjoyed by the members and friends who were present. It was a bright sunny day, but a cool wind blowing down the canyon made coats and sweaters feel very comfortable.

The business meeting held after the luncheon hour was held in the recreation hall, with a cheery fire burning in the huge rock fireplace.

The treasurer's report was read and accepted and all outstanding bills were ordered paid.

Friends may be interested to know the report given on the wonderful returns from the luncheon project which was sponsored by the Aid, during the period Warner Bros. were in the community taking scenes for the picture "East of Eden."

A total of 922 meals were served during the five day period they were in the community; 981 meals were guaranteed and paid for at $2.50 a plate, making a total of $2,452.50 paid by Warner Bros. Total expense for meat, groceries and tray rental came to $641.59, leaving a balance of $1810.91 cleared by the project.

This money has been put aside and placed in a savings account, to be used exclusively for furnishings for the new recreation hall, when it becomes a reality.

This was a wonderful opportunity for the Aid to make this sum of money, and while the ladies worked hard during the five day period, they had a lot of fun doing it. The management of Warner Bros. were more than pleased with the meals served and the Aid members feel they were very fortunate to be given the opportunity.

It is probably a unique experience for the film company to be served meals by a church group while on location. They have promised to come again and Aid members are looking forward to a future recurrence of such a project. The wonderful assistance given by Mrs. James O'Donnell and Mrs. Claire Strauss in planning the menus and arranging other details are not to be overlooked in the success of the undertaking. Mrs. Eidsath acted as the business manager, ordering supplies etc., and there was wonderful cooperation on the part of the merchants in delivering supplies at any time; also on the part of members, who worked long hours in the more menial duties of dish washing, setting tables, etc.

Mrs. O'Donnell was presented a beautiful potted rhododendron, a gift from the Aid, as a slight token of appreciation for her work during the time Warner Bros. were in our midst. Mrs. Eidsath made the presentation and com-plimented the "top sergeant," as she was affectionately called, very highly for her assistance and help.

Mrs. O'Donnell voiced her thanks in a few words and later became a member of the Aid.

A moment of silent meditation honoring the memory of the late Dr. R. W. Preston was observed during the meeting hour.

The meeting came to a close by repeating the Lord's Prayer.

A hike up the canyon was enjoyed by some of the group before the outing came to a final end.

—*The Mendocino Beacon,* June 26, 1954

48

just a nichols' worth

by Geo. A. Nichols

Many lines have been written and in all probability many more will be written, about the filming of "East of Eden" by Warner Bros. Gordon Hinrichs, who writes a column in the "Warner Club News" has this to say about Mendocino—

"Cameramen…made the most of long sun-lit days and were able to capture on film in Glorious Warner-Color, some of the grandeur of Northern California's rugged coast line and the charm and beauty of a tiny hamlet which has moved over to let the hustle and bustle of the modern streamlined era rush by."

The writer then paid the women of the Ladies Aid quite a compliment—

"There are many Mendocino memories, but one all the East of Eden outfit will remember will be the lunches the Ladies Aid Society of the town's Presbyterian Church cooked for the crew. This was a project taken on by the women to raise funds to furnish a new addition to the church which the laymen are going to build. If the men do as well with the hammers, saws and squares as the women did with their pots, pans and mixing bowls, it really should be quite an edifice. That home cookin' was certainly delicious, especially those pies."

Up here on the coast we knew all about this all the time, but it's nice to have someone else say it too!

—*The Mendocino Beacon*, August 7, 1954

Film Synopsis

Among the students rushing from classes at the end of the day, Aron Trask (Richard Davalos) and his girl friend, Abra (Julie Harris) are joined by Aron's brother, Cal (James Dean). He follows the couple to an ice house where their father, Adam Trask (Raymond Massey) is excitedly explaining to Will Hamilton (Albert Dekker) his plan to keep vegetables fresh by refrigeration. In introducing his two sons Adam plainly reveals that Aron is the favorite.

That evening, Cal learns from Sheriff Sam Cooper (Burl Ives) that his mother, who deserted Adam years before, is Kate (Jo Van Fleet), owner of a notorious gambling and dance hall. When Adam's refrigeration project fails, Cal, anxious to win his father's affection, enters into a profitable venture with Will.

One night at the amusement park, Cal offers Abra a ride on the ferris wheel. She protests her love for Aron, but pasionately returns Cal's kiss.

At Adam's birthday celebration, Cal makes elaborate preparations to present to his father all the profits from the speculation. However, Adam reprimands his son for profiteering and Cal is further denounced by his brother.

With that, Cal decides to reveal the secret of their mother. Following the meeting with his mother, and discovering Abra's love for Cal, it is a drunken and completely changed Aron who bids Adam farewell before departing to join the Army.

Stricken at the turn of events, Adam is carried home. There, as Abra pleads, Adam finally acknowledges Cal, blesses them both.—*from the East of Eden pressbook*

The time that Warner Brothers spent in Mendocino filming *East of Eden* has been called a week of magic, which it certainly was considering the amount of work accomplished and the resulting cinematic masterpiece. The film received four Academy Award nominations but only Jo Van Fleet was given one. It was voted the Best Dramatic Film of 1955 and also received a Golden Globe Award that year. The Mendocino Coast's greatest film!

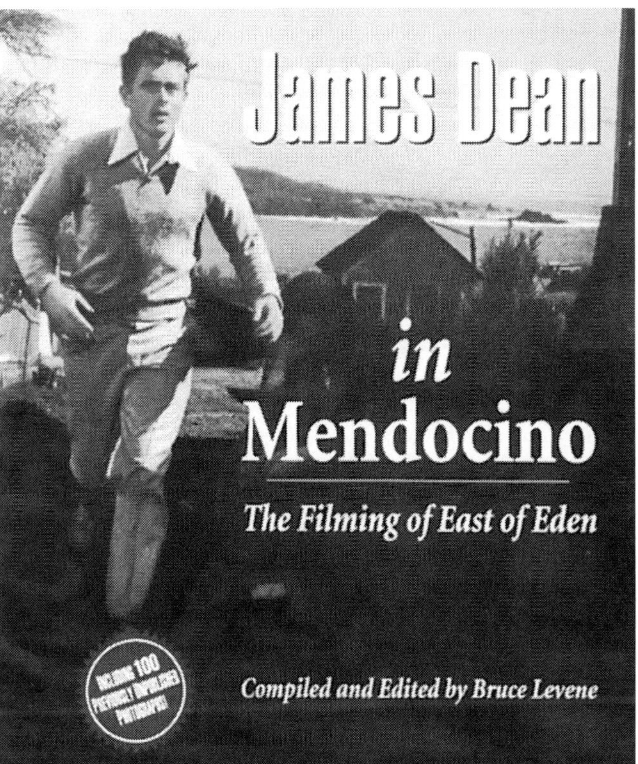

A 72 page in-depth book about the filming of *East of Eden* in Mendocino is available from Pacific Transcriptions.

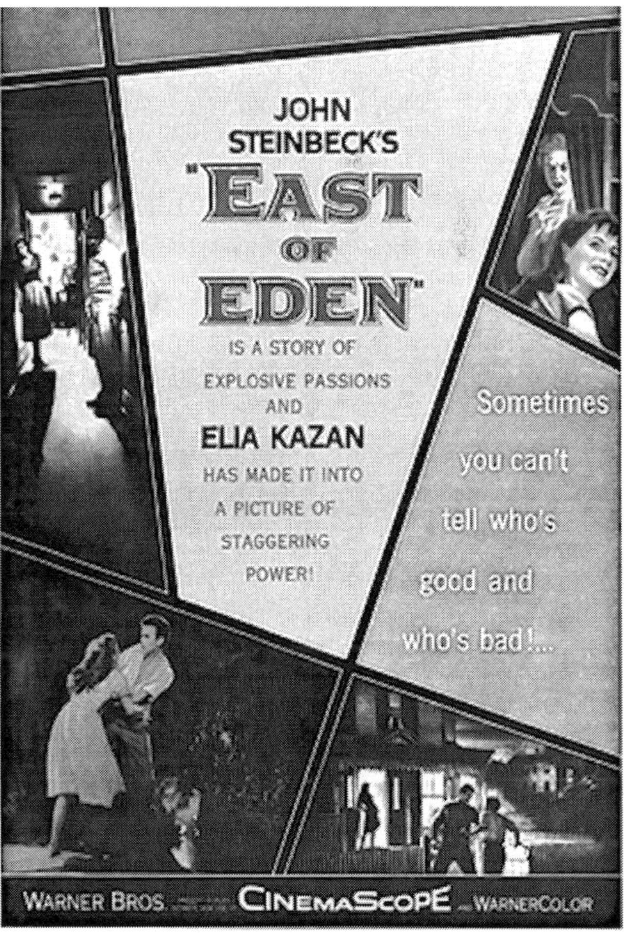

Little Eddie Barff, 7, son of Ed Barff, who lives with his grandmother at Seaside, north of Fort Bragg, is on his way to fame and fortune. He has received a motion picture contract from Top Flight Pictures Corporation of San Franciso and will be used in one of the main supporting roles in the picture "The Secret of Dr. Mesmer" now being filmed.

The picture company was on location in Fort Bragg and "found" young Barff. He was used there and will be used in more filming along the California Coast between San Francisco and Ft. Ross. There will be another month's shooting along the coast, and the young fellow will be taken to the scene of the shooting on week ends, so that his schooling will not be interferred with.

A scene from *The Strange Case of Dr. Mesmer.* At right, kneeling on a dock at Noyo, is Eddie Barff. To his right is French stage star Carine d'Arcy; to her right is Swiss musical comedy star, Ruddy Marrogg. On board the *Petit Bal* is actor Seth Wood, who plays Eddie's father in the film. The *Petit Bal* was owned by Reece Rowe of Fort Bragg and was also used in *Johnny Belinda.* (Photograph probably published in the *Ukiah Daily Journal.*)

After completing the coastal scenes, the company will move to Malta, on the Mediterranean. Young Barff accompanied by his aunt, Amelia Gambell, of Berkeley, will be flown there and will stay for the completion of the shooting. While on location at Malta, Eddie will have a special tutor, so that his education will not be curtailed.

The company plans to make a few more shots around Fort Bragg and Noyo before the picture is completed.

"The Secret of Dr. Mesmer," reported to be a million dollar production, will star Carine d'Arcy, a French star in her first major movie production. The male lead will be handled by Rudy Marrogg, a Swiss musical and comedy star.—*Mendocino Beacon*, August 21, 1954

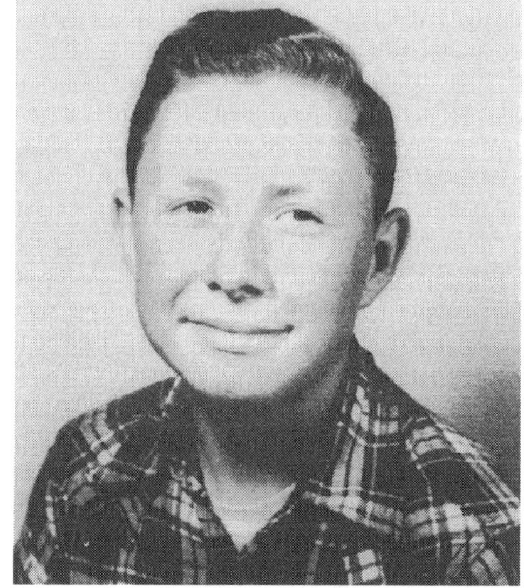

Ed Barff, circa 1954

UNIVERSAL PICTURES, INC. TO START SHOOTING MOVIE
ON SOUTH COAST; 'THE ISLAND OF THE BLUE DOLPHINS'
6 Weeks Scheduled For Filming; To Start Sept. 18

by Olga Cossi

ANCHOR BAY — Universal Pictures Inc. have started work on the filming of "The Island of the Blue Dolphins," a full length color movie which will start here Sept. 18. Officials of the company who have been visiting sites for the picture include James B. Clark, director; Phil Bowles, first assistant director; Robert B. Radnitz, producer; George Webb, art director and Terry Nelson, unit production manager.

Mr. Webb is in the coast area this week making arrangements for work which will be done on the sites chosen such as Anchor Bay Campgrounds beach, Newcomb ranch, Haven's Neck, Island Cove, Cove Estates, Schooner Gulch, and the Jacobsen Ranch, as well as innumerable smaller coves and beaches. Shooting will start Sept. 18 and take about six weeks depending on the weather.

The movie is based on the book by Scott O'Dell and will closely follow the story. Selection of Anchor Bay was the result of a month's search along the coastline between Baja and Eureka. The search for a star for the lead part, that of a 15 year old girl, is still not ended, although officials now have narrowed it down to three potential players. The announcement of the final selection will make headline news in Hollywood.

On location will be a cast of about 20 actors, supplemented by around 50 local persons needed in several scenes. A company personnel of 50 workers will be here during the shooting. Some are expected to arrive this weekend to help get sites ready for shooting. At present, trees are being "planted" on Anchor Bay beach and a village readied on the Newcomb ranch property at the foot of Fish Rock road.

The story is based on a true incident in California history known as "the lost woman of San Nicholas Island." It happened around 1800 when an Indian child was left behind on an evacuated island. She was not picked up until 18 years later when her story came to light. She was buried in the Santa Barbara Mission.

Speaking of the story and movie, officials said, "The Island of the Blue Dolphins" will be for family viewing. We feel that families and children are being fed too much sex and violence. It is our intention in making this type of movie to stimulate but to do so creatively. This story is first of all one of survival, then of a child's learning to trust. Young movie-goers are exposed to far too much mental pap, and this picture will allow them to use their minds and to think constructively." Residents of the area have expressed their appreciation for the type of picture being filmed here and are glad to be a part of such a much-needed movie fare.

The book, "The Island of the Blue Dolphins," was winner of five awards including the Newberry Medal for 1960, the year the book was published. This award is given by the American Librarians Association for "the most distinguished contribution to American literature for children." A similar award was given to the Scott O'Dell novel in Germany. At present, the story is listed as the number one best selling children's novel. The movie is scheduled for release next summer.

Pictured is Celia Kaye as Karana, star of "The Island of the Blue Dolphins," in her hideout filmed last week at Haven's Neck, on the south coast. The 'hideout' is a crude dwelling place constructed by Karana, in which she uses whale bones to form a protective barrier. Filming of the color movie has been in progress for the past two weeks, with four more weeks of shooting scheduled. —*Mendocino Beacon*

Some of the problems faced by Universal Pictures in making the movie involve getting Indian props. Anyone with Indian relics who would be willing to have them used should make this known as soon as possible. Ralph Kerr is taking a list of names for Terry Nelson who will be in charge of the production.

Needed are some 20-foot long boats, double-ended, a few kayaks, and men to man them. This is very important. Anyone interested in acting who can give their time to take part in scenes are asked to give their name to Ralph Kerr now. Types needed are Indians, Aleutian fishermen and Spanish-Mexicans. This includes men, women and children.

—*Mendocino Beacon*, September 13, 1963

barnacles 'round the Bay
by Olga Cossi

GUALALA — Celia Kaye, star of *The Island of the Blue Dolphins*, arrived in the coast area last Sunday and will be staying at Surf Motel during the filming of the Universal Pictures movie here. Miss Kay will portray the lead part of Karana, the Indian girl left on the island when her people were evacuated. The part of her little brother will be played by Ed Rosson who has not yet arrived on location.

Coast sites which will be used in the full color movie have interesting script names. Anchor Bay Beach will be Coral Cove. A forest of trees has been planted on the site. The cliff at the Deltorchio's place at the foot of Fish Rock Road is the location of the Indian village. Haven's Neck is Karana's hideout, a crude dwelling place in which she uses whale bones to form a protective barrier. Lookout Rock will also be located out on the promontory. Island Cove Estates beach is Karana's secret cove. Shooting is scheduled to start Sept. 18 at Haven's Neck.

Terry Nelson, unit production manager, has explained that location sites are closed to the public primarily because Universal Pictures is responsible for the protection of the natural beauty of the property where permission has been granted for filming. Ground cover such as ice plant and other succulents would be destroyed if people were allowed to trespass. In some instances, permission to use sites was granted only because the company gave assurance that the natural beauty would be guarded. The movie will use local people for extras, particularly members of the Indian race who will be contacted on the reservations. The people who have turned in their names for extras will be interviewed at Surf Motel lounge Friday night, Sept. 20, at 8 p.m.

Celia Kaye, with trained magpie *(Universal Pictures)*

Two interesting men who will be here soon are Ray Berwick, bird trainer who will be working with sea gulls which will be used in various scenes, and Frank Weatherwax, trainer of Spike Jr., the lead dog, and the pack of 'wild' dogs featured in the story.

Officials of Universal Pictures and their crews, technicians, workmen, actors, caterers, ete. are being housed along the south coast area, using practically every available bit of housing. The number af personnel has now been estimated as over 80 who will contribute in one way or another to the filming of *The Island of the Blue Dolphins*.

—*Mendocino Beacon*, September 20, 1963

LEFT—Pictured is Tom Mc-Henry, set painter for Universal Pictures as he places a huge rubber "rock" in the hideout of Karana, heroine of "The Island of the Blue Dolphins," being filmed in the south coast area. The rocks cannot be spotted as false—even close-up. Location is on Haven's Neck where the first week's shooting is being done. Mr. McHenry paints the "rocks" to match the natural formations on the point of the promontory.
(*Mendocino Beacon*, September 27, 1963)

RIGHT—Two of the featured players in "The Island of the Blue Dolphins" are Martin Garralaga (left) and Alex Montoya, both popular actors in motion pictures and television shows. Mr. Garralaga played the part of the padre who came to evacuate the Indian village, while Mr. Mon-toya portrays the Spanish sea captain of the rescue ship. This picture was taken at Fish Rock Ranch.
(*Mendocino Beacon*, October 18, 1963)

Point Arena News by Doris York
Movie News

With the arrival Tuesday of 60 more members of the Universal Pictures Company, filming of the full length movie, *Island of the Blue Dolphins* was scheduled to begin Wednesday. Total film personnel in the South Coast area has now reached 80. Though the filming will be concentrated at the Anchor Bay area, some 10 miles south of Point Arena, the 80 persons are housed at all available motels and hotels from Gualala to Point Arena.

The main office is located at Fred Price's Point Arena Hotel. Terry Nelson, unit manager, is a guest here. Most of the hotel's motel units are occupied by movie personnel. A large bus, used to transport personnel to and from the filming locations, is using the hotel parking area as its headquarters.

Young star of the movie, Miss Celia Kaye, director James Clark, producer Robert Radnitz and photographer Leo Tover are guests at the Redwood Motel in Point Arena. Another Redwood Motel guest is James Thorp, who is first aid man for the company. Mr. Thorp was among the first to arrive and he has set up his first aid station in his room at the motel. He accompanies the group to the filming location each day.

An interesting guest at Farnsworth's Point Arena Court is Frank Weatherwax, trainer of six shepherd dogs that will be seen in the movie as a "wild dog pack." Members of the Weatherwax family have served as trainers for the Lassie series.

Ray Burwick, bird trainer for *The Birds*, unable to tame any of the local gulls, went to San Francisco Monday to get 20 tame seagulls to appear in the movie.

Point Arena residents who have seen a strange but friendly bird around their yards recently, will be interested to know that he is a magpie, one of six brought here for the movie. This fellow, who incidentally doesn't talk, has escaped and is visiting around town.

Michelson's Catering Service has its headquarters at the Point Arena Hotel. Ed Michelson has a chuckwagon and will serve lunches daily to the entire company. He brings his service from Hollywood.

—*Mendocino Beacon*, September 20, 1963

Point Arena News by Doris York

A number of our local Indian people have been signed to appear in the movie, *Island of the Blue Dolphins*, currently being filmed at Anchor Bay. Included in the group are Mamie and Raymond Laiwa, Ray and Cindy Laiwa, Leroy Scarioni, Milton, Charlie and Rosalie Ball, Mike Santana, David Smith, Pauline and Raeline Horn, Melvin McGill, Duane Potter, Dennie, Laverne, Reginald, Delbert, Harry, Armand and Pete Pinola.

Robbie Robinson, Stanley Porter and Jerry Homberger will be in the movie and there are others from Point Arena who have been interviewed and expect to be called.

The movie's dogs are living in a pen just south of the Point Arena Court. Usually indoors during the day, they are all outside in the pen every evening. There are nine dogs.

Many of the local people have rented rooms in their homes to help house the numerous movie people who are in the area. Local restaurants are particularly busy at night, providing dinners for the many persons living in local motels, hotels, apartments and private homes.

—*Mendocino Beacon*, September 27, 1963

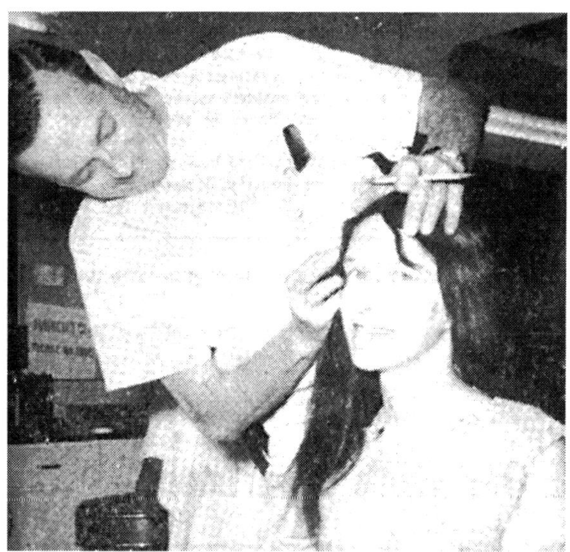

Mardella Stark is being fitted with a wig by none other than Larry Germaine, head of the hair dressing department for Universal Pictures and top man in the business. Extras were painted as redskins, then fitted with human hair wigs. *(Photos and caption by Olga Cossi)*

Much Activity As Filming Gets Underway
By Olga Cossi

ANCHOR BAY—On hand this week for shooting of landing scenes in the *Island of the Blue Dolphins* is Bud Westmore, chief of Universal Pictures make-up department, who will be in charge of the extras playing Aleuts and Indians. Also called in for this week's schedule is Larry Germaine, chief hairdresser for the movie company. A make-up and wardrobe station haa been erected at Anchor Bay on the Norm Pierce property in order to take care fo the large groups of extras used at the Anchor Bay Campgrounds beach where the shooting is taking place.

Celia Kaye, starring in the role of Karana, will be working with Eddie Rosson who portrays her brother in the color film based on the Scott O'Dell best seller. Eddie Rosson arrived at Surf Motel, Gualala, with his mother, Mrs. Rosson this week. He and Miss Kaye will enact scenes where the Indian maiden sees her brother left behind on the island and jumps from the ship to swim back to him. Location of this scene is the northern end of Anchor Bay beach.

Two other Hollywood stars who will be used in the film are Julie Payne, daughter of John Payne, playing the part of a member of Karana's tribe, and George Kennedy, head hunter of the Aleutians. Mass scenes will show the landing of the Aleuts, their stealing of the Indian pelts, the fight between the native Indians and the Aleuts during which most of the Indians are killed. Six manned longboats will be used, each carrying six men.

Tuesday's shooting centered on scenes using a trained seal named Peewee which Karana an her tame wild dog visit at the pool at Coral Cove. The seal was handled by his trainer, James Turk, Eureka. The animal is two months old and was brought up on a formula since he was only a few days old. His performance was excellent in spite of the presence of Spike Jr., the trained 'wild dog' handled by Frank Weatherwax.

Used this week as extras are six children: Pete, Penny, Laverne, Harry and Armand Pinola and Raeline Horne; six Aleut boatmen: Lee Leitner, Richard Bettega, Leeroe Merritt, Charles Migliavacca, Dick Maddigan and William Robinson; various Indians and Aleuts portrayed by extras from Stewart's Point, Gualala, Anchor Bay, Point Arena, and the Air Force base on Eureka Hill.—*Mendocino Beacon*, September 27, 1963

barnacles 'round the Bay by Olga Cossi

ANCHOR BAY — A complete Indian village with eight **grass** huts was the scene of filming of *The Island of the Blue Dolphins* on the Fish Rock Ranch starting Friday. The village had been erected by Universal Pictures Inc. crews to closely pattern the historical basis of the Scott O'Dell novel on which the movie is based. It is located on the flat on the cliffs of the ranch which overlooks Anchor Bay.

The site is the former location of Fish Rock landing which was a busy shipping point for tanbark, railroad ties, cord wood, posts and some grape stakes. Last shipments were sent around 1920.

George Webb, art director, has been in charge of setting the stage for the filming of this full color motion picture. The village will be burned in a dramatic scene featuring Celia Kaye as Karana, the young girl left on the island when her tribe evacuated. Shooting of this scene is scheduled very soon.

This week saw filming of village scenes with Celia Kaye, Larry Domasin, Carlos Romero, Jon Alvar, Julie Payne and Hal Jon Norman portraying key roles. Many extras, mostly Indians, were used for tribal shots.

Shooting Friday was temporarily halted by the presence of two whale boats which had anchored in the bay within camera range of the village Plans were revised in order to continue with the film without including the boats in the background after officials had failed to make contact with the fishermen to ask that they move out of sight for the afternoon.

Peter Saldutti, Hollywood, handmade the sets of Indian jewelry for the men, closely following data uncovered through research in the South West Museum, Los Angeles. The beautiful neckpieces, headbands, etc. were made of abalone shells and other sea shells. Mr. Saldutti also made the medicine man's feathered cape and feather-decorated skirt, and the outfits worn by the Aleuts. Spanish costumes were rented.

Rosemarie Odell, costume designer from Hollywood, made the Indian breech cloths and dresses worn by all tribal players. Burlap was used for these to resemble the fiber cloth woven by the natives of San Nicholas Island. Reserch for all costuming was the same as Scott O'Dell, the author, had used for his story. Several dozen belts, headpieces and jewelry were designed for the woman and children of the tribe. The feathered cape for Chief Chowig and a smaller feathered cape for Karana were created by the tailoring department at Universal.

Larry Domasin, eight, is replacing Eddie Rosson as Ramo in this Universal picture. The young star completed *Fun at Acapulco* with Elvis Presley last March. He has recently returned to Hollywood from Utah where he did a show for the *Death Valley* series. Another movie to his credit is *Dame with a Halo*, which he made last year.

Larry and his mother are staying at Surf Motel for about 2 1/2 weeks for *The Island of the Blue Dolphins*. The young star is the youngest in a family of four boys and three girls. His mother is Hawaiian-Portuguese and his father is Philippino.

Larry and Celia Kaye worked in the cold drizzle last Saturday to complete some of the scenes which take place in the Indian village at Fish Rock Ranch. Shots featuring Frank Weatherwax and his dogs were postponed when the drizzle turned into rain.

Two new feature players took part in this week's shooting, Martin Garralaga and Alex Montoya who portray the Spanish padre and sea captain coming to evacuate the Indian village. Martin in the role of the padre is a natural. He was very warmly robed in his flowing grey costume while most of the cast shivered in their scant burlap outfits. Martin came to the U.S. from Spain as a young man. He was featured in *The Kid from Texas*, and his latest T.V. role is in *The Outer Limits* series shown this month.

Alex Montoya's most recent T.V. appearance was last Sunday morning on Channel 7. Last week he played Captain Arturo Diaz in *Gunsmoke*. He has worked in many western and on the *Loretta Young Show*. In motion pictures, he was featured in *The Magnificent 7* and *Apache Ambush*. He played the lead heavy, a bad guy, in an experimental short, *The Cadillac*, which was nominated for an Academy Award. The show won the American Cinema Editors Award.

Behind scenes, Ray Berwick is working quietly with the 25 birds he is training for use in the picture. At present, he has been concentrating on two magpies who will be Karana's friends on the island. These birds are very quick learners, according to Mr. Berwick who has been in the business 12 years. He will be remembered as working on *The Birds*, filmed at Bodega Bay. Bird training was originally a hobby with Mr. Berwick who is a native Texan.

Another interesting story concerns the very natural and lovely Indian children who are being used as extras in this Robert Radnitiz production. Several of then were standing together after being fitted with wigs and painted a suitable Redskin color. One little voice piped up: "Gee, you know we look like real Indians."

About 50 extras were used as Indians and Aleuts for mass scenes shot at Anchor Bay this week. Manning the Aleutian boat for important scenes with many of the featured players were Lee Leitner, Richard Bettega, Leeroe Merritt, Charlie Miglaivacca, Dick Maddigan and Robbie Robinson, a masterful bit of casting if ever we've seen one! Camera fans were on hand en mass to photograph these "authentic" Aleuts.

Elma Hackett is holding school for the Indian children between calls on location.

—*Mendocino Beacon*, October 11, 1963

Ann Daniel, Rontu and Celia Kaye (*Universal Pictures*)

barnacles 'round the Bay by Olga Cossi

Two exciting days of filming of *The Island of the Blue Dolphins* were completed in the coast area last week, one in Point Arena and one on the Fish Rock Ranch. A special barge was floated at Point Arena Cove so that the camera could take water-level shots of the boat evacuating Celia Kaye and some of her tribe members from the island. The filming started Monday afternoon. During the morning the Indian extras were used at Island Cove Estates for their final scenes,

The barge was tied to the end of the pier so the long-boat could pass close to the camera while scenes leading to the climatic swim back to shore by Miss Kaye were enacted. Alex Montoya portrayed the captain of the boat. Also on board was Julie Payne, playing Karana's best friend. Both featured players try to keep the Indian girl from swimming back to her brother who was left behind on the island. At about 4 p.m., Miss Kaye dove off the boat for the big scene, and was later photographed swimming ashore.

The second exciting scene was the burning of the Indian **vil**lage by Karana, This was staged Saturday morning, starting with setting fire to individual huts called wickiups. Shortly after noon, Celia Kaye as Karana uses a torch to set afire the entire village, a really impressive bit of pageantry. Two local fire trucks stood by to bring the flames under control. The wickiups were rebuilt in part, then the camera shifted to an opposite angle and the village was again set on fire, this time to completely burn.

Wild dogs were used in several shots, with Frank Weatherwax handling his well trained animals which wore, of all things, false teeth! Another interesting point was that because of the rains, and the hosing of individual wickiups after the morning's shooting, Miss Kaye had quite a time setting the village on fire. The huts had to be sprayed with fuel to get a dramatic ,blaze. For smoke effect close to the camera, bee smokers were used. Gum olibanum was burned in these, giving off the odor of incense. The location was closed to spectators because of the danger involved in the day's shooting.

On hand to watch the motion picture progress and to absorb atmosphere was Ann Daniel, 20, Palm Springs, portraying 'Tutok,' the Aleut girl who befriends Karana. Miss Daniel is staying at Surf Motel. She is a sophomore at UCLA and is a theater arts major. Her professional experience was gained as a member of a New York troupe The Second City. This is her first motion picture.

Miss Daniel's mother, Mrs. Frances Holmes, is a teacher at Palm Springs. A brother, Bill Arms, is an artist in Paris where he will have his first showing starting Nov. 1st. A married sister lives in Texas. This is Miss Daniel's first trip to the northern California coast area.

—*Mendocino Beacon*, October 18, 1963

barnacles 'round the Bay by Olga Cossi

Filming of *The Island of the Blue Dolphins* was completed Monday afternoon, when repeated delays in shooting key "wild dog" scenes on Sunday cost the company an extra day on location. Earlier in the week Ann Daniel and Celia Kaye enacted the friendship of Karana, the Indian girl, and Tutok, the Aleut girl, filmed at Haven's Neck. The Aleutian words and phrases used in these scenes by Tutok were taken from **Aleutian Indian and English Dictionary**, by Charles A. Lee, a small pamphlet publislied in 1896; and from, **The**

Celia Kaye as Karana, Carlos Romero as Chief Chowig, and Larry Domasin as Ramo in a scene taken at the Indian Village staged at the Fish Rock Ranch. *(Universal Pictures)*

Aleut Language published by the U.S. Department of the Interior. The pronounciation was not precisely defined in either reference source, yet the sounds were spoken and and accented with authenticity and feeling by the young actress.

During one of the sequences filmed of the two girls, Karana is given a new "hair-do" by Tutok. Later Karana must say goodbye to her Aleut friend when she chooses to remain on the island rather than to go with the people who had killed her father.

The entire Universal crew had a bad case of "go-home-itis" on Sunday, looking forward to being with their familes again even though they had enjoyed their stay here. Terry Nelson, unit production manager, and several crewmen will remain a few days for "mopping up" operations. Mr. Nelson again expressed his appreciation for the friendship and assistance of the residents here who more than made up for any inconvenience caused by the geographic isolation of our cosatal area.

One interesting thing which Universal crewmen saw while they were here was a huge California eagle at Anchor Bay beach. The bird was spotted last Tuesday and was about 3 feet tall with a wing spread of at least 8 feet. The men came upon the eagle which was standing in the stream near where the seagull's cage was kept. When the huge bird flew away a smaller eagle, perched on the cliff, took flight with him.

Special mention should be made of Charlie Brannon and his son Jimmy who provided the catering service for Universal. They served many guests during each day's lunch hour, and did so with a smile. Charlie and Jimmy will be leaving soon, along with most of the crew which was here, for St. George, Utah, where the filming of *Renegade Posse* will begin. Celia Kaye hopes to make a trip to Europe which she had planned before being chosen for the role of Karana. Producer Robert Radnitz flew back to Hollywood as Monday's shooting was shooting was finished. There is much work to be done at the Universal studio before *The Island of the Blue Dolphins* will be ready for release next spring.

—*Mendocino Beacon*, October 25, 1963

"Island of Blue Dolphins," Filmed On Mendocino Coast, Is Opening Attraction

Because the actual locale of the story is now used by the U. S. Navy and is restricted to authorized personnel only, it took more than a month to find a suitable location for the Universal-Robert B. Radnitz color production, "Island of the Blue Dolphins," which is being shown as a one night prevue attraction at the new Coast Theatre in Fort Bragg.

The picture is based on the John Newbery Medal award novel by Scott O'Dell, which he developed from a true life experience of a girl Robinson Crusoe who lived alone for 18 years on San Nicholas Island off the coast of Santa Barbara, California, from 1835 to 1853. She became known in the legends as the Lost Woman of the San Nicholas Island.

After traversing the Pacific coast line for 1,500 miles from Baja, California, to Vancouver Island, Radnitz and director James B. Clark, finally settled on a spot at Anchor Bay. After deciding on the area, they were able to locate the 18 different sites for the story within a square mile. Much of the footage was filmed on the property owned by world-renowned artist Millard Sheets and nearly all the Indians living on the historic Pomo Reservation at Pt. Arena appear in the tribal village sequences. And during shooting on one day, the elements turned in a bravura performance. Within a three-hour span the production company was alternately visited by dust devils, blinding fog, gale-velocity winds, a high surf, two cloudbursts and a hail storm. However, the weather most of the time from there on "was just fine," according to Robert B. Radnitz, the producer.

"Island of the Blue Dolphins" will only be presented two performances, Thursday, Sept. 10, as a special inaugural prevue. However, it will be returned at a later date for a regular scheduled engagement.

—*Fort Bragg Advocate-News*, September 10, 1964

GALA OPENING ATTRACTION!

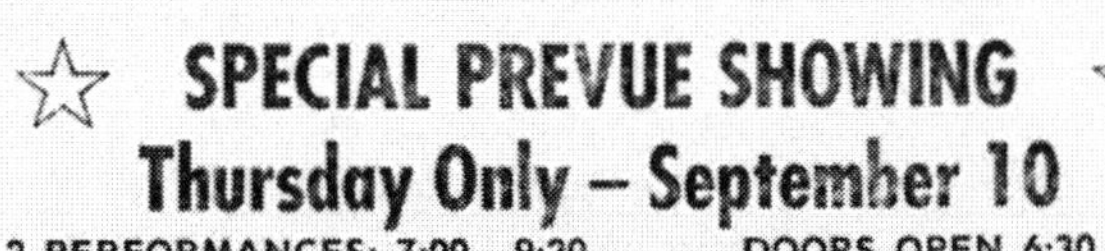

☆ **SPECIAL PREVUE SHOWING** ☆
Thursday Only – September 10
2 PERFORMANCES: 7:00 - 9:20 — DOORS OPEN 6:30 P.M.

A Hollywood Group Of 150
To Film Coast Movie Starting Sept. 9

Again the Mendocino, Little River, Albion area is to become host to a movie colony, which doesn't too greatly perturb us, for we have been there before, with "Frenchman's Creek," "Johnny Belinda" and "East of Eden." So we extend to the producers of this latest production a hearty welcome.

The production of the picture will require a group and staff of 150 from Hollywood, with something over 100 extras. It will require 50 local workers.

Production Manager Jim Henderling visited us Thursday. He has been dividing his time between coast points and Hollywood.

Water scenes involve a wrecked Russian submarine. Either Big RIver or the Navarro will be used for this major scene. But the town is assured a shot from the Heeser Drive.

Photographing of coast scenes will commence here September 9th and continue approximatey until Novembar 15th.

—Mendocino Beacon, July 30, 1965

Motion Picture Stars Arriving For Film Shooting

Shooting is scheduled to begin here today on the filming of a full-length modern comedy, "The Russians Are Coming, The Russians Are Coming."

From now until mid-November, Fort Bragg and the adjoining coastline will be the setting for the accidental grounding of a Russian submarine because its skipper wanted to get a closer look at the United Sltates. The sub gets hung up on a sand bar and the plot unfolds as the crew determines ways of getting away at the same time Americans are mistaking the accident as an invasion.

Shooting of the film will be at various locations along the coast including Fort Bragg, Mendocino, Noyo, Cleone and Westport.

Some of the casting will be done in Fort Bragg with local personalities filling the parts.

—Fort Bragg Advocate-News, September 9, 1965

Movie Makers At Cleone: To Mendocino Friday

Norman Jewison is producing and directing a movie, "The Russians Are Coming," in the Mendocino coast area from Westport to Mendocino.

The film, a comedy, is a present day setting, with Carl Reiner Eve Marie Saint, Alan Arkin, Brian Keith, Jonathan Winters and many others portraying the horror of a Russian submarine crew losing their directions and ending up in New England.

The shock of the small town persons is shown, with everyone being suspicious of one another, and the ends gone to, to make themselves understood. In the end, all find out that peoples of various countries can get along together, and everyone is happy, including Ben Blue, who finally gets up on his horse to be a modern day Paul Revere, shouting "The Russians Are Coming!"

The book, "The Off Islanders", from which William Rose has written the screen play, was written by Nathaniel Benchley. Instrumental in having the film shot here is Robert Boyle, the art director who said that this area is ideal in not being too built up, and that it also has the gorse and moors of Nantucket.

Filming is going on at Cleone on the private Union Lumber Company road, where men with walkie-talkies are stationed to stop production when the huge loaded log trucks go through

It is anticipated that all the filming will be done in this area, with only final clean-up shots to be made in Hollywood. Westport will see the arrival of the movie cameras on Thursday, and the present plan calls for filming to be done in Mendocino, starting Friday.

Filming at the "Whitaker House" on Union Lumber Company's "haul road" neari Cleone, The building was erected as a set for the film.

Carl Reiner, one of the stars of the film, flew to Hollywood this week to receive his eighth Emmy as producer of the Dick Van Dyke show. Also of interest is the arrival of Eva Marie Saint's family. Her husband is Jeffrey Hayden, producer of Peyton Place. Their two children are Darrell, 10, and Laurie, 7.

—Mendocino Beacon, September 17, 1965

Mendocino Goes Hollywood This Week

Movie actors, cameras, trucks, buses and all moved into Mendocino Saturday, to begin filming the sequences here of "The Russians Are Coming, The Russians Are Coming."

The Al Mead home, (the former Chet Bishop home), which in the movie is the home of Deputy Sheriff Norman Jonas (Jonathan Winters) had both interior and exterior shots filmed.

Winters was exceedingly funny to the cast, crew and the gathered viewers in this scene scooting out of the house and into the garage, only to find himself blocked by one of the townspeople. Mr Winters clowned between shots and practice to keep all assembled in a state of laughter. He is a very funny man, in person as well as an the screen.

Monday the scene moved to the Sanko house (the former C. Mathews home) which in the movie is the home of the Rev. Hawthorn (Peter Brocco). Two ladies carreen around in a motorcycle with side car—crash through the fence and into the front steps of the Rev. Hawthorn. All are trying so very hard to be brave and yet warn all the populace that Russians have landed and are taking control of the town.

Filming on Main Street, Mendocino *(Ribeiro)*

Filming at the Sanko House *(Ribeiro)*

The Mendocino Fire station becomes the Glouster Bay Fire Department and Police Station. Lansing Street, Mendocino. *(Ribeiro)*

Muriel's (Doro Morande) kitchen built into the old remedy store on Main street will find her trying to telephone for assistance when attacked by the enemy. Brave little soul, she wards them off with a broom and plumber's friend.

Brian Keith who plays Link Mattocks, the police chief in the film, arrived in Mendocino Monday. He had been in San Mateo with his two year old filly which he plans to race soon.

Eva Marie Saint's family has returned south after enjoying the scenes and weather in and around Mendocino

Among the stars of the play, other than Jonathon Winters are Ben Blue, playing the town drunk, attempting throughout the film to get on his horse.

Ben Blue has had more than three decades of experience and his split~second timing is expertly woven into this film by the producer-director.

Brian Keith, a dour police chief in the film, must cope with events and the hysteria of his townspeople. He is very well known on both the screen and television. One of his recent films was as a star in the Walt Disney production, "The Parent Trap."

Alan Arkin, who appeared one day the fore part of the week on the Fort Bragg radio station, is a newcomer to Hollywood. He has starred on Broadway and is also a composer and folk singer. He is cast as the timorous leader of the Russian landing party.

Theodore Bikel, as the Soviet submarine comander, is cast speaking only Russian and he has to try to make himself understood. Mr. Bikel is a linguist, speaking seven languages fluently, Russian included.

Paul Ford is another of the townspeople, a well-meaning but blundering butcher who attempts to mobilize the citizens.

There are others whose roles will be described as time goes on in the filming of this satire. Nearly all of the players are very cooperative, wanting the local people to know them.

The schedule for the rest of the week calls for "shooting" in Mendocino and Noyo.—*Mendocino Beacon*, September 24,1965

Film Company Busy With Outside Shots These Fine October Days

Filming of "The Russians Are Coming The Russians Are Coming" moved temporarily to Runeberg Hall in Fort Bragg during the rain of Monday.

They have been at Noyo and Mendocino since, however, taking advantage of the fine fall weather.

The Mirsch company moved their filming back to Mendocino on Thursday using scenic Heeser Drive for this location. They are very pleased that the sun is again shining and are looking forward to making up some of the time lost due to overcast skies.

Officials said Thursday that they should be here for several days.

Tessie O'Shea, a music hall comedienne, is being used at the present time. Also in the area is Ben Blue, a long time comedy star. His scenes will run throughout the entire film as he is the modern day Paul Revere, attempting to ride a horse to warn everyone that the invasion has started.

—*Mendocino Beacon*, October 8, 1965

Ben Blue & friend on Heeser Field, Mendocino *(United Artists)*

On Tuesday, filming was done on Main Street, and Wednesday filming was on Heeser Drive until overcast skies shut off the light for these shots of Ben Blue trying to get on his horse.

Jim O'Donnell and Wanda McFarlane were Mendocino's stars on Tuesday as the sequence they were in had to be reshot a number of times because a child did not appear in an upstairs window on schedule. O'Donnell was splicing a rope and Mrs. McFarland was conducting household chores.

Mendocino is being used for nearly all of the village shots, as the homes and business houses here very closely resemble those of the Nantucket coastal area.

—*Mendocino Beacon*, October 15, 1965

"Russian" Sub Launched at Noyo

A submarine was launced in Noyo Bay on Friday. The 140-foot vessel went down the boat ramp with the assistance of a fork lift truck, and on airplane-type trucks. Also assisting was a large wrecker with a cable stretched across the bay.

The submarine, shipped to Fort Bragg to be used in the filming of "The Russians Are Coming The Russians Are Coming," required eight trucks and semi-trailers to bring in the ten sections.

Some two weeks and 2,000 man hours were required to get it assembled and ready for the water. It was moved and assembled under the direction of special effects man Danny Hays and five other special effects men, including Glenn Robinson.

The boat, built of plywood, had 4 1/2 tons of steel on the bottom, is filled with 17 tons of styrofoam and has outside measurements of 140 feet in length, is 20 feet wide and 22 feet high.

Yet to be installed is a 3 1/2 ton, 3-inch practical gun, which it was felt was too heavy for the launching. Four motors will be used for power. All are McCullocch with 100 horsepower thrust. Two are forward and two aft, in specially built wells.

The craft, originally built by 20th Century for the Marlon Brando film "Morituri." Then it worked on "Assault On a Queen" for Seven-Arts Paramount. It was German in design, but Robert Boyle, art director for the Mirisch company, re-designed the exterior to make it appear Russian for this picture.

It is hoped that the seas will remain calm enough that the craft can be floated to Los Angeles, between two barges, when its use is completed in this area.

—*Mendocino Beacon*, October 22, 1965

Ray Welsh (sitting) and Bill (T-Bone) Fredson in row boat help launch sub. *(Ogle)*

Director Norman Jewison filming at the 'Ice House' at Noyo. *(Reis)*

Carl Reiner relaxing between takes, at Noyo Flat. *(Reis)*

Brian Keith, Theo Bikel and Eve Marie Saint at Noyo Flat. *(Reis)*

"The Russians Are Coming"
Shouted Children in New York Blackout!

A few shots were taken Wednesday from the Noyo jetty and the bridge of the convoy taking the submarine out to sea-this was given up for the time being as the weather was pretty soggy and all the crew had to go home to get dried out, on location with "The Russians Are Coming."

The cameras are now at the Witaker house for both interior and exterior shots.

A little unexpected publicity was given in New York during the black out [the famous New York electrical blackout]. Children there were running up and down the streets shouting, "The Russians Are Coming The Russians Are Coming!"

The interesting place has walls which may be moved at will. A stairway that leads up to — nothing. The ceilings of the house are open rafters where kleig lights are placed as well as cameras as the need arises.

The house exterior looks as though it belongs on the coast and had been there many years, complete with flowers, dingy clothing hanging from the clothes line and moss on the pillars of the porch.

—*Mendocino Beacon*, November 12, 1965

Paul Ford and Eve Marie at Noyo Flat. *(Ogle)*

The false front of Gloucester Island City Hall erected at Noyo. *(Reis)*

Russians Need Sunshine, Calm Sea

After two and a half months of shooting scenes in areas of Fort Bragg, Westport and Mendocino, Norman Jewison's "The Russians Are Coming The Russians Are Coming" could be considered to be in the home stretch.

"Considered to be" only because of the element of weather.

What producer-director Jewison, his cast and production crew. headed by Jim Henderling, must have from this point on is sunshine, or a reasonable facsimile.

Most of the "cover" sets, such as the Mirisch-made Whtittaker House at Cleone Acres, various interiors of homes in Fort Bragg and Mendocino and Runeberg Hall are gone. There is nowhere Jewison can turn from now on for interior shooting.

What is left to shoot is the pivotal and probably the most important sequence of all—the confrontation scene at Noyo—when the townspeople of Gloucester Island and the Russian crew of the Soviet sub, combine to rescue a little boy (played by Jonnie Whittaker) who is stuck in the steeple of the Town Hall.

In addition, there is the seaquence where the sub departs the U.S., via Noyo Bay, and the open sea, while accompanied by a flotilla of some 50 small boats and a couple of Air Force jets screaming overhead These are two of the big remaining problems for Jewison and company. There is incidental shooting to be done, but if he were able to get the confrontation and flotilla sequences, the rest might easily fall into place.

"The shooting we've accomplished on the Mendocino Coast so far has been highly satisfactory," says Jewison.

"The country on film is nearly as beautiful as it is for real. The cooperation of the people has been marvelous. We are all high in praise of the community. We feel we've become part of you."

To anticipage when shooting might conclude in ths area would be ridiculous or as ridiculous, say, as one trying to predict the weather.

The company needs sunshine and a calm sea for the submarine to make its exit.

"Anyone who could guarantee us these elements on any given day should be worth a lot of money," says Jewison.

—*Fort Bragg Advocate-News*, November 19, 1965

Film Shooting End In Sight, Coast Praised

It's hail and farewell for "The Russians Are Coming The Russians Are Coming" company to Fort Bragg, Mendocino and the coast.

Principal shooting of the Mirisch Corporation presentation for United Artists release began September 9 with shooting (weather permitting) to conclude tomorrow, Dec. 3.

John Philip Law & Andrea Dromm
(Ogle)

That's a long location in anyone's book. The feel that it was a pleasant location so far as the Hollywood group is concerned, makes it memorable indeed.

Probably Norman Jewison, producer-director of the film, said it best:

"The cooperation of the people here was without precedent."

"I can truthfully say it is the first location I have hated to leave."

"Keep your marvelous country the way it is. Please don't change a thing. I hope we have brought you the same indelible impressions that you've given us. It was pleasant all the way.

"I hope, too, that "The Russians Are Coming The Russians Are Coming" will turn out to be the fine film we hoped for it when we put it before cameras. If it isn't no one in this locality will be to blame, as we received nothing but kind help and cooperation from everyone."

"It's notable that many of the huge cast and crew of the film are considering returning to Mendocino County to enjoy its beauty and friendliness when not under the pressure of work."

"So its goodby for now. The cast and crew of "The Russians Are Coming The Russians Are Coming"willl fondly remember the Mendocino Coast for a long, long time."

—*Fort Bragg Advocate-News*, December 2, 1965

Movie Makers Finish Here, Will Be Missed

This was the final week of filming on the Mendocino coast of the Movie "The Russians Are Coming The Russians Are Coming." Scenes of the submarine in the bay were filmed during the weekend with shoreline shots being made the fore part of the week.

The submarine is being dismantled for shipment back to Hollywood on trucks. The company was unable to ship it between two barges as originally planned due to the weather and heavy seas.

Nearly all of the stars have departed from the area. Still at Noyo on Monday were Jonathan Winters and Brian Keith, who were nearly finished with their parts.

Sheldon Golomb, carrying Cindy Putnam, and Johnnie Wittaker *(Reis)*

Jonathan Winters, Brian Keith & the Gloucester Island resistance *(Ogle)*

The filming of the recent months was interesting for locals as well as visitors. The company welcomed sightseers and had used many of the local people in the filming.

Many of the faces will be missed since they have made themselves so much a part of the area.

The trees planted in the streets and byways of Mendocino have been removed, the false front of the city hall at Noyo will come down and will be removed from the scene.

Several movies have been shot in this area in the past years. However, this is the first that was filmed in its entirety here.

Used extensively throughout the film have been buildings and scenes familiar to all. Many inside shots were made in the old Remedy Store in Mendocino. Other spots were the Al Mead house as well as the Sanko home, the Heeser Drive and many street scenes.

Heeser Drive was used extensively for the filming of the Ben Blue episodes, of trying to get on a horse and finally making it to inform the populace of the invasion. Doing the riding in the film as a stand-in was Lowell Felkins of the Shoreline Riders in Ft. Bragg.

Many local persons have been used in the film including Mrs. Wanda McFarland, Jim O'Donnell, William Robinson, Ches Sandell, Tom Glynn, Mrs. Addie Reis, Fred Rimbach, Joe Gomes, Frank Brown, John Bovyer, Carl Sauer, Ike Jackson, Toni Lemos and four daughters.

Also in the film were Mrs. Stanley and her four children. Pearl Saunders, Agnes Crow, Lew Sawyer, John Costa, Ed Tenney, Dorothy Peterson, Ron Facer, Dave Clayton, Fred Manter, Garnet Carlson, Lillian Larsen, Joe Ponts, Axel Anderson, Mary White, Jim Saunders, Harold Bainbridge, Mio McBernie, Charles Morgan and his mother, Ben Peterson and Harry Docker.

There were many, many others, and each had a very exciting but tiring time while waiting their turn to appear before the cameras.

Mr. and Mrs. Martin Hall worked very closely with the film company.

Many of the older residents of the area can recall seeing sailing vessels in the Noyo bay and have marveled at the sight of a submarine in the peaceful and familiar waterway.

Notable among the many stars in the cast have been Carl Reiner, Eva Marie Saint, Jonathan Winters, Brian Keith, Alan Arkin, John Law, Andrea Dromm Cindy Putnam, Sheldon Golomb, Sidney Clute Philip Coolidge (who claimed to be the mayor of Mendocino), Vaughn Taylor, Milos Milos, Paul Verdier, Gino Gottarelli, C. Baksheesf, Alex Hassilev, Ray Baxter, Nikita Knatz, Doro Morande, Maryester Denver, Paul Ford, andt many others.

Norman Jewison, producer and director of the films for the Mirisch Corporation, will be long remembered as well as will be other members of the staff including Kurt Neumann, Bobby Boyles, Jack Harris, Bob Fender, John Reimer Joe Biroc and many others They have made themselves very popular with the local people and all have invited them back, not only to make another film but just to take time to visit.

This invasion has been a time of prosperity for the coastal area with a good deal of money spent here by the company. Some estimaters have put it as high as one and one half million dollars.

The story of the film is of a Russian submarine coming in too close to land and grounding itself on a sandbar, the landing of a Russian party to seek aid to free themselves. The oftimes hilarious and sometimes scary reaction of the New England townspeople prior to finding out that all that is really wanted is peace and understanding and help. And finally the townspeople realizing that their friends, the Russians, are really in trouble which could become an international incident, and their willingness to assist.—*Mendocino Beacon*, December 3, 1965

Alan Arkin and the Russian sailors say goodbye at Noyo Harbor. *(United Artists)*

Movie House 'Up In Smoke'

END OF AN ERA of movie making on the Mendocino Coast came last Friday morning at Cleone when the Mirisch Corp., producers of "The Russians Are Coming The Russians Are Coming,' set fire to the Whitaker House, scene of many shots in the movie.

The house had been erected by the company on Union Lumber Co. property prior to the shooting of the film. Unfinished, the house was determined to be of less value than the cost of dismantling or moving.

—*Fort Bragg Advocate-News,* December 9, 1965

The burning of the 'Whitaker House' set. (*Ed Freitas/Noyo Chief*)

Coast Premiere Of "Russians" Here Wednesday

The west coast premiere of the comical movie "The Russians Are Coming The Russians Are Coming," filmed in Fort Bragg and along the Mendocino Coast will be held at Coast Theatre here next Wednesday night, June 22, according to theatre manager Neil McBurney.

The coast premiere, which follows the eastern opening by a few weeks, will be a benefit for the Paul Bunyan School for retarded children here and the two showings scheduled for Wednesday night are nearing sell-out status.

Tickets are still on sale for opening night reservations, however. The film will be here through Tuesday, June 28.

The movie has received nothing but rave notices from its east coast openings. It has led Alaskan Senator Ernest Gruening to state that it "implies a profound and salutary lesson" in the absurdity of international conflict. The Washington Daily News and Christian Science Monitor have praised the movie for its comedy and cleverness. Sen. Gruening called the movie "one of the most amusing and entertaining he has known."

The movie previewed in Washington, D. C., for an audience that included Vice President Hubert Humphrey, Ambassador Averall Harriman and other top government officials. It opened in New York City to rave reviews at the Astor, Trans-Lux East and Murray Hil Theatres.

Washington Daily News called the movie "a strong contender for a Nobel Peace Prize," maintaining that the film may have achieved what world diplomats have thus far failed to do "showing the innate absurdity of international conflict."

—*Fort Bragg Advocate-News,* June 16, 1966

YOU ARE CORDIALLY INVITED

TO ATTEND THE

WEST COAST PREMIERE

OF

THE RUSSIANS ARE COMING, THE RUSSIANS ARE COMING

TUESDAY EVENING, JUNE 28TH, 1966

BENEFIT, PAUL BUNYAN SCHOOL FOR RETARDED CHILDREN

PLEASE RESPOND   7:00 AND 9:30

One would expect, considering that the geopolitics no longer exist and that *The Russians Are Coming* was made almost 35 years ago, that the film would be terribly dated. In fact, it isn't and is still as comic and thoughtful as when it premiered. The locals loved the production, in part because the filming took so long, but more so because the cast and crew were so friendly. Perhaps too friendly, for supposedly one local marriage failed to survive the movie company's visit. One of the Coast's best. The film received three Academy Award nominations. Check it out—it's a good one.

Paramount To Make Movie In Mendocino Starting April 22

Paramount Pictures, Inc. will be coming to the Mendocino coast to shoot a scene in the town of Mendocino. The company has made reservations at the Surf Motel in Fort Bragg, according to Vilho Johnson.

Shooting is expected to be on April 25 on the film "William Castle". The production manager for this company is K. DeLand.

—*Mendocino Beacon*, April 1, 1966

Movie Co. Spends 3 Days Shooting Scenes In Mendocino

The Paramount motion picture company shot scenes on Lansing Street, Heeser Drive and Main Street of Mendocino on Monday, Tuesday and up until noon on Wednesday.

The movie is to be a farce on ghosts and will be called "The Spirit Is Willing."

Mr. and Mrs. Martin Hall arranged for local talent to take part as stand-ins and in street scenes. Among those taking part were Mr. and Mrs. Henry Goldsmith, Norman Saari, John Bouvier, Hildegard Wells, Jose Cross, Mrs. Wanda McFarland, Toni Lemos and Tony Resnick.

About 25 persons from the filming capital were here to shoot the scenes for pre-production. A brother of Red Skelton was among the workers.

The group stayed at the Surf Motel in Fort Bragg and had their lunches at the Sea Gull in Mendocino.

A spokesman for the company said that no matter what the weather was on the coast, that it would be duplicated in Hollywood. However, the weather was perfect, with sunshine for the entire filming in the area.

Among the stars to be in the film, none of whom were in Mendocino, will be Sid Caesar.

—*Mendocino Beacon*, April 29, 1966

Critics called *The Spirit Is Willing,* adapted from another Nathaniel Benchley novel, *The Visitors,* witless and stupid. It barely qualifies as a movie made in Mendocino, as only 'street scenes' were filmed here. But at least it provided a bit of employment for a few local residents, although some of them don't seem to remember it.

The film is available on DVD.

The Dunwich Horror — 1969

Horror Movie To Be Filmed in Mendocino

Once again the Mendocino area will be the location for a film production crew, with the wheels set in motion early this week. As in previous productions filmed in this area, local talent will be used in casting.

The filming will be by American International Pictures of Hollywood. Jack Bohrer of American International was in Mendocino Tuesday to scout the area. He found several places suitable for their needs, when taken on a tour by F. A. Nichols of the Mendocino Beacon.

Members of the cast named so far are Peter Fonda and Joseph Cotton who are scheduled to arrive just prior to the actual filming, which is tentatively set to begin the first week of February.

The title of the film is "The Dunwich Horrors."

Director Daniel Haller arrives next Wednesday, for advance casting, and site selection.

Local theatrical producer and entrepreneur, John Breton Storm, is assisting in choosing local talent for parts in the movie of chills and thrills.

Gray, foggy days will be ideal for the.purpose of shooting, according to Mr. Bohrer.

This unspoiled area of the Mendocino Coast is becoming increasingly popular for filming purposes, with many TV commercials made here. Movie making is not new to the residents who remember Johnny Belinda in 1948, and later productions, Frenchman's Creek, East of Eden,and more recently, The Russians Are Coming, the Russian are Coming.

—*Mendocino Beacon*, January 10, 1969

360 Register For Mendocino Movie
Movie Crew Of 75 To Arrive Soon; Shooting Starts February 18

The shooting of a horror movie scheduled for the Mendocino area has the entire coast and surrounding area agog. Hundreds of actors, would be actors, and odd characters are swarming into town.

The script was ready January 14 with the major roles to be filled by Peter Fonda and Joseph Cotton, according to Jack Bohrer of American International Pictures, of Hollywood.

Shooting of the "Dunwich Horrors" is scheduled to begin on February 18.

Seventy-five members of the crew will be arriving before the target date, in preparation for the actual filming.

Four to five weeks is the time estimated for the scenes on the coast to be completed.

Bohrer, who was here last week to scout the area for suitable locations, expected to return Thursday with the director of the movie, Daniel Haller, for final site selection. The setting will be a haunted house, with both exterior and interior to be used.

Drizzling rain and fog are preferred for the background shots, and seas erupting, crashing in thunder on the beach.

More than 360 persons have already registered for the parts available for local talent.

Many of these persons may be disappointed, since there are only six speaking parts for local actors, and two other minor roles wbich have been cast. "There is no need for more to register," John Breton Storm has said. No extras will be needed for the horror movie.

Mr. Storm is director of Mendocino's "The Village Theatre", which now has a play in rehearsal, entitled "Rope."

He has stated that he hopes to announce the names of the local actors cast in the Dunwich Horrors in time for next week's issue of the Mendocino Beacon They are character parts, subject to the approval of director Haller.—*Mendocino Beacon*, January 17, 1969

Local Actors To Appear In Horror Movie

Pranksters, not a part of the script, have entered the scene of movie making in Mendocino. Maybe someone is having fun at the expense of actors and would be actors, who have tried out for parts in the "Dunwich Horrors" to be filmed here, but the pranks could be dangerous.

After the tryouts last Friday a woeful young girl told John Breton Storm "But the director said they'd call me". When he asked her why she didn't check on a call received by phone, a man with a strong accent saying "Come to Albion". She waited in the dark for over an hour.

The following day a young bearded type appeared and said, "My friends tell me you called me." Mr. Storm has called no one by phone. "Ignore the calls unless they emanate from the Gallery Fair and you are certain it is not a prank," he said. "Be certain you know who is calling."

American Internatlonal Pictures of Hollywood will be shooting the movie within the next few weeks, with several street scenes to be filmed in Mendocino, chosen because of its authentic New England flavor.

The site chosen for the filming is a wonderful old farm of New England traditon, complete with outbuildings, south of Mendocino, which shall remain nameless,"to protect the occupant from swarms of sight-seeing and curious visitors."

Prior to last Friday's tryouts, Director of the Village Theatre in Mendocino, John Breton Storm had selected a minimum of six persons for each role available for local talent. There was an air of hushed expectancy as the aspiring actors waited in Gallery Fair. They were seated in the lobby of the establishment and three abreast on every step leading to the second floor.

Mr. Storm called them one by one for the tryout. Director Haller has said that of all of the people brought in for cast selection, they will be able to choose the ones fitting the roles.

Peter Fonda and Joseph Cotton will star.

The production manager is scheduled to arrive this weekend, with the momentum increasing toward actual shooting of the film, with the arrival of the director the following week end. Equipment and crews will be arriving within a few days in preparation for the filming.

Further casting at a later date will call for pretty young women, which should be a boon to the undiscovered starlets in the area.

Incidentally, the Beacon has been informed that neither Mr. Bohrer nor Director Haller speaks with a foreign accent.

Roles for local talent have increased from the number previously announced, to include a farmer, 55, his wife about 50 and their daughter, a country doctor and his groovy receptionist, a librarian, a New England character, about 35, for sheriff, two grocery store men, 65 and 55, a character, about 40 for service station attendant, and a fireman, possibly more.

There is a possibility that a casting office will be set up for final selection from those who have had a tryout. A cross section of the town and nearly communities was present last Friday, from the various business, with local artists, actors and actresses, both amateur and a sprinkling of professionals.

Some parts have been cast. All roles filled will be announced at a later date. The script was ready January 14. Seventy five will be in the technical crew arriving.—*Mendocino Beacon*, January 24, 1969

Storm Delays Movie Making In Mendocino; Schedule Is Now Feb. 25

The recent storms throughout the state have delayed the horror movie in the Mendocino area. The original target date of Feb. 18 for the start of shooting "The Dunwich Horrors" has now been upped to February 25.

Meanwhile, director of Mendocino's Village Theatre, John Breton Storm, has stated "I will be screening young women for parts in the film." Mr. Storm has been assisting in selecting members of the cast for the movie company of Hollywood.

Director Daniel Haller and Jack Bohrer of American International Pictures of Hollywood are scheduled to arrive next Monday, Feb. 10, with the production manager of the film, to complete preliminary arrangement of the myriad details involved.

The production crew and members of the cast will arrive on the Mendocino coast Feb .24, to set up for shooting of film the following day. They will be housed at the Little River Inn and at the Tradewinds Lodge in Fort Bragg,

Some of the street scenes will be filmed in Mendocino, which should create a bit of excitement in the town, which was chosen for its authentic New England setting. The site selected for the major portion of the filming is an old New England farmhouse type of home on a country road, near Albion, South of Mendocino.

Some of the older buildings in Mendocino will probably be used by the Hollywood Company. An estimated 75 wll be the number of the crew, expected to be on location for from four to five weeks, possibly more.—*Mendocino Beacon*, February 7, 1969

Stars Announced For Mendocino Movie

Announcement was made early this week by American International Pictures of Hollywood, that the stars have been selected for the movie "Dunwich" to be filmed in Mendocino and the surrounding area.

Arriving on the coast the first week of April, in preparation for the shooting of film, will be Sandra Dee, Ralph Bellamy, Brandon DeWilde, Sam Jaffee and Lloyd Buchner. The target date of the start of production is April 8.

John Cardos, location coordinator of the Hollwood Company and crew arrived last Thursday night, going into immediate action. Construction was started Saturday on the rugged sea-coast of Little River, with lumber purchased Friday, in Fort Bragg. "We want to do all of our purchasing locally or in the area, if we possibly can," Careos said. "The construction crew will be on location for six weeks," he added.

Arriving with Cardos, in the first contingent from Hollywood, were Rick Jackson and Forest Carpenter.

A huge, pyramid-shaped altar is being built for the scenes of witchcraft to be a part of "Dunwich," the altar to be eight foot high and 16 by 16 feet in size. Twenty foot tall columns will be mounted atop the structure.

Cardos, who worked on the famed Alfred Hitchcock film, "The Birds", is seeking crows for the current production on the coast. The crows are intended to provide "atmosphere", and the plan is to have the birds perched on the ledges and columns of the altar and ceremonial grounds.

If you see a pretty, perky young woman dashing about the coast, with her dark hair in a pixie cut, that will be Sue Arnold, with the all-emcompassing title of secretary, who will be generally assisting in finding props for the production. She is secretary to John Cardos.

Production manager is Jack Bohrer and director os the film is Daniel Haller, who will be staying at the Little River Inn. The Hollywood stars will also be housed there, according to information received.

Construction crew members on the coast have selected the former Merril home on the coast South of Little River cemetery, which commands a fabulous view of the craggy sea-scape and overlooks the altar site.—*Mendocino Beacon*, March 21, 1969

(*Mendocino Beacon*, March 21, 1969)

Filming Starts Wednesday On Mendo Movie

Stars, makeup men, crewmen and cameramen arrived in Mendocino this week and on Wednesday, April 2, the cameras rolled for the first shooting of the horror movie, "Dunwich."

The action for Wednesdays filming took place on the hill south of the Little River Cemetery and was part of a dream sequence. A portion of the cast for this scene was a number of local hippies clad only in their paint-streaked skin. As they danced over the hillsides heavy rain fell, but there was no report of damage to the paint.

The greater portion of the movie "Dunwich" will be filmed in around Mendocino. The altar scene, however, will not be made here, as previously planned. A spokesman for the movie company gave the reason for the decision as the scene, one of sacrifice, called for the use of a number of explosions and lightning effects. Because of the almost constant wind condition on the bluff, where the tower had been built, the safety element had to be considered. It was decided to shoot that sequence on the sound stage in Hollywood.

Stars Sandra Dee and Dean Stockwell arrived at the Little River Inn Wednesday. Also here this week are Production Manager Jack Boyer and Director Danny Hallar.

The rest of the crew and other stars are tentatively scheduled to arrive in the area on Tuesday, April 8. The entire shooting should be done within the next three or four weeks.

—*Mendocino Beacon*, April 4, 1969

H.P. LOVECRAFT'S TERRIFYING TALE OF TERROR AND THOSE WHO EXPLORE THE UNSPEAKABLE!

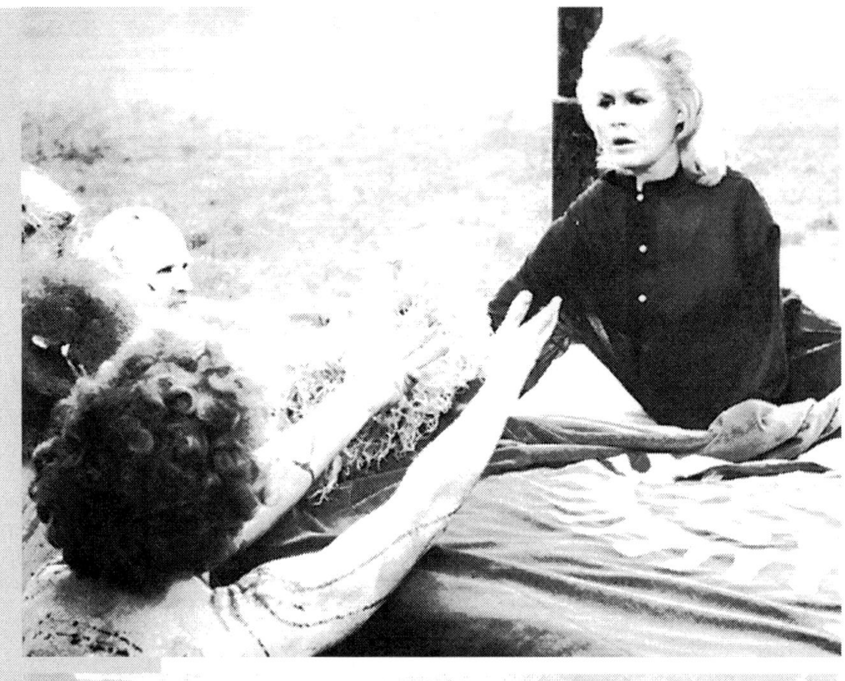

Sandra Dee and others (*American International*)

Sheer horror that will haunt your nightmares as long as you dare to dream!

Sandra Dee stars as the cuddly coed whom a crazed Dean Stockwell pursues for the sake of necromancy. Ed Begley, in his last role, protrays a professor who discovers Stockwell's dirty deeds. An invisible brother, a secret curse, and ancient fertility rites are just a few of the surprises galore in this supernatural treat! Based on H.P. Lovecraft's classic tale, the film is sure to delight horror fans everywhere. Get ready for fun and chills from the master of high entertainment on a low budget, executive producer Roger Corman!—*Embassy Home Entertainment*

If it is possible to adapt H.P. Lovecraft's classic story to the screen, that was not, unfortunately, the goal of this film. Although convincing, even scary at times, overall it is an exercise in futility, with a laughable Dean Stockwell and an ending that makes the whole movie questionable.

Mendocino Coast May Again Be Scene Of Warner Bros. Movie

"Summer of 42" a Warner Bros. movie scheduled for shooting this summer may be filmed on the Mendocino Coast, and a major part of it in the Town of Mendocino. Studio representatives are in the area now, in an endeavor to determine if the local citizens would favor hosting the movie and to enlist the cooperation they will need to create the necessary atmosphere for the 1942 setting.

The story is a simple one, says Production Manager, Don Kranze, and the filming will certainly not be on the grandiose scale of "The Russians are Coming, the Russians are Coming." The major cast consists of three teenage boys and one girl ln her early twenties and these people will probably be chosen in New York. However, atmosphere personnel will be selected locally and while no appointments are being made until May 5, Marlene Hall of Mendocino is talking to people now and lining up interviews for these roles.

A need faced by the movie company is in creating a 1942 setting. T. V. antennas, late model cars, modern clothing of course cannot invade any of their scenes. They need cars and trucks of 1942 or earlier vintage and are asking anyone having such a vehicle to contact Mrs. Hall in Mendocino. They need the cooperation of residents in allowing the removal and replacement of T. V. antennas which they will have done with the promise of replacing worn or rusted parts, and they promise to keep removal at a minimum of 8 to 10 hours.

Other needs of the movie-makers are for housing. During the months of July, August and September, three homes (hopefully overlooking the ocean) will be needed to house the director and his family, a producer, who is a bachelor, and possibly for the young lady who will play a prominent part in the picture.

Basically the story is that of a young man thinking back to his 14th summer, his days on the beach with his young

Two Mendocino girls who are fascinated with movie making in Mendocino are Lucia Zacha (left) and Amy Grasso (right) shown chatting with the stars of "Summer of '42," Oliver Conant, Gary Grimes and Jerry Houser.

*—Mendocino Beacon/*Betty Seagraves

friends, and those elements that went into the growing up days of World War II. Between the childish ideas, and the maturity of manhood, a story unfolds, and the Mendocino Coast may host the unfolding of this picture.

Robert Mulligan will be the director, Richard Roth, producer, Don Kranze, production manager and Mel Efros, 2nd assistant director.

If all the wrinkles can be ironed out, shooting will begin on July 13, or August 3, (depending on coastal weather) and will take about seven weeks. Because of the influx of tourists into Mendocino during Saturdays and Sundays, no shooting will take place on those days.

—Mendocino Beacon, April 24, 1970

Jennifer O'Neill in *Summer of '42 (Warner Bros.)*

Mendocino Movie Draws Large Crowd To Fill Extra Roles

Crowds of would-be actors surged around the Sea Gull Restaurant this week hoping for a part in the forthcoming movie, "Summer of '42" scheduled for filming on the Mendocino Coast this summer.

Casting, although limited, is being done through appointments made by Marlene Hall at the Sea Gull. Mrs. Hall is also helping Warner Bros. line up automobiles of the proper era, 1942 or earlier.

"Summer of '42" will not be on the same scale as the last Warner Bros. production made here, "The Russians Are Coming, The Russians Are Coming," according to Production Manager Don Kranze.

The setting of "Summer of '42" is actually a New England town. However, weather conditions, as well as other considerations, had made the West Coast the choice of the producers.—*Mendocino Beacon*, May 8, 1970

Filming To Start
On Movie July 28

A significant gain for the local economy and a personal sense of participation in the world's most popular form of entertainment will be two of the benefits derived from the filming of Warner Bros. "Summer of '42" in Fort Bragg and the surrounding area.

Filming will begin July 28 with Richard Alan Roth producing and Robert Mulligan directing and will continue for an estimated seven weeks. Jennifer O'Neil, Gary Grimes, Jerry Houser and Oliver Conant star.

Approximately $100,000 a week will be pumped into the economy of Fort Bragg by the motion picture company, which will consist of several score members of the staff, cast and crew.

Mainly, this will be spent for housing, food and for the hundreds of various items necessary for production aspects of the film. Individual purchases by members of the company, who will be buying articles ranging from toothpaste to trousers, will probably swell the total.

Approximately 400 coast residents will be engaged to appear in the picture. In addition to this gainful employment, they will find that moviemaking is enjoyable. Judging by past movie locations, the fun they derive from working in the picture will provide warm and lasting memories.

—Fort Bragg Advocate-News, July 23, 1970

'Summer of '42' Filming
Begins Here July 28

Warner Bros. will be filming "Summer of '42" in Mendocino on Tuesday, Wednesday and Thursday, July 28-30.

Since the film depicts the 1942 era, signs requesting no parking will be posted with temporary traffic restrictions during Tuesday and Wednesday on portions of Ukiah Street, the Woodward-Osborne Alley, Little Lake Road and Williams Street.

On Thursday in addition to the locations listed, part of Heeser Drive and the point at the west end of Heeser will be posted.

Warner Bros. have expressed their appreciation of the excellent cooperation received from ths community of Mendocino, and ask the continued assistance required to meet the necessary traffic conditions.

The company will move from place to place as rapidly as filming permits and posted times will be kept as brief as possible,

—Mendocino Beacon, July 24, 1970

Oliver Conant, Jerry Houser, Jennifer O'Neill and Gary Grimes at the corner of Little Lake and Woodward Streets, Mendocino. *(Warner Bros.)*

Sitting: extra Carrie Honeycutt. Gary Grimes, Oliver Conant, and Jerry Houser. Extras: Dancing—Terry Jones and June Lemos. On sand—Jone Lemos, Arn Williams, Cindy Cowen, Miriam Moilanen—at Ten Mile Beach *(Warner Bros.)*

Gary Grimes and Jennifer O'Neill *(Warner Bros.)*

Coast Landmarks Used in Filming Of Movie 'Summer of '42' Here

A tall water tower, for years a landmark of Mendocino becomes a filming platform where cameras, directors, and related crew take their places while below three young boys enact their respective roles. Then the cameras take their place on the pavement below, the young actors scramble to the tower's top and three pair of bare feet are seen dangling from its deck. From down the street someone calls, "Quiet please, take one."

Over on Main St. a corner dwelling which has served for some time as the workshop studio of Mendocino's Pat O'Brien, suddenly becomes an old fashioned drug store, and the Mendocino Volunteer Fire Department sports a sign reading, "Packett Island Fire Department." Old cars sputter down the local streets and the cameras roll while "Summer of '42" becomes a living image of a screenplay written by Herman Raucher.

A house, which last week was just a residence in Mendocino is now a rented house on a little Island in New England, and three young boys who last month were Oliver Conant, Jerry Houser and Gary Grimes, are now Benjie, Hermy, and Oscy carrying the sometimes hilarious, sometimes tender and often realistic threads of the story.

Directing these three newcomers to the movie world is Robert Mulligan who has to his credit such films as "To Kill a Mockingbird," "Up the Down Staircase," "Inside Daisy Clover" and a number of other well known pictures.

The story, "Summer of '42" is the best one he's read in the past 10 years, says this veteran director, and credit for finding it goes to producer Richard Allen Roth. It deals with the reminiscence of a soldier who looks back to the summer he spent on an island off the New England coast, with the serious business of growing up and with that exerience, so often humorous, so often painful, of a boy becoming a man.

Robert Surtees, Academy Award winner cinematograher is filming the movie which will be entirely filmed on location along the Mendocino Coast.

—*Mendocino Beacon*, August 7, 1970

Rotary View

Mel Efros, of Warner Brothers, cited several reasons for the selection of Mendocino and the North Coast for the filming location of the "Summer of '42" to the Mendocino Rotary Club at its regular luncheon meeting on Thursday, September 3rd, in Preston Hall.

Among the attractions that brought the movie company here, according to Efros, were the splendid scenery, outstanding examples of architecture, community cooperation, isolation of the local sea coast background and New England atmosphere.

Warner Brothers became familiar with this area with the shooting of "Johnny Belinda".

After it was established that the "Summer of '42" could physically be made here and that there was public acceptance by the residents of the area, preparations were begun for the production of the $1,500,000 colored movie last March.

In late May the construction crews arrived to go to work. Last July the main crew came up from Hollywood.

To set up a traveling city, Efros continued, a great deal of coordination is required. Arrangements for lodging, food and transportation were made. Lumber was purchased. Old autos and trucks of the late thirties and early forties were collected locally.

Fifteen to twenty residents of the coast were hired in addition to the 55 persons who came from Hollywood.

New sound and lighting were used.

Between $80,000 and $100, 000 per week has been spent here during the shooting of the motion picture, Efros estimates. The film will be completely photographed on location.

Benefit showings of the completed picture are scheduled for April or May of next year in Fort Bragg.

From what Efros has already seen of the film he is impressed with the finished quality and soft atmosphere of the movie. With the actors considered to be unknowns, along with a slow movement of innocence, both humor and pathos exist.—*Mendocino Beacon*, September 11, 1970

Enthusiastic Crowd At 'Summer of 42' Benefit Performance

The north coast showing of "Summer of '42" drew a capacity crowd to the Coast Theatre in Fort Bragg last Tuesday evening. Every seat was taken from the front row to the last row.

Mendocino and the coast were right at the top with the other stars of the film. Photography of familiar scenes was breathtakingly beautiful, no clashing colors, only muted soft tones with occasional emphasis of jewel-like blues and greens of the crashing sea. The script was poetic, moving and the writer was well acquainted with how the minds of teen age boys functioned during 1942, one of the last years of American innocence.

The audience appearer captivated, responding during the humorous sequences with chuckles to roaring laughter. Absolute dead silence reigned, interrupted by occasional sniffles, during the serious scenes.

The movie, filmed in and around Mendocino last summer was shown one night only for the benefit of the Paul Bunyan Work Training Center, sponsored by Parents & Friends of Retarded Children, Inc.—*Mendocino Beacon*, June 18, 1971

"Summer of '42 brings out the best in director Robert Mulligan — that gift for getting down a specific time, place and atmosphere! His knack for drawing natural, charming and, at the same time, complicated perfomances from young people, and a gentleness and warmth that, when they work, tight-rope their way across sentiment to genuinley touch us."

—*Newsweek*

Suddenly she was there.
Then everything changed.

Hermie want to know all about life and love and war and sex. Especially sex. He and his two buddies spend their summer discussing the future, peering into forbidden books, trying to pick up girls. Hermie is 15 and has a head full of dreams, schemes and terrible yearnings for a certain older woman of 22.

Cast in the form of Hermie's memoir, *Summer of '42* is a warm evocation of youth in a generation on the threshold of change. Robert Surtees' haunting pastel photography, interwoven with Michel Legrand's Academy Award-winning bittersweet musical score, suggests the tone of times past and captures the complex feelings that underlie memory itself. Perfection of detail in everything from clothes to house interiors awakens the '40s so strongly that we not only see but also touch another era.

"We were different then," Hermie says, remembering Bette Davis movies and triple-scoop ice cream cones. Yet director Mulligan also manages to impart a timeless quality to Hermie's summer. What happens to Hermie happens to all of us, sooner or later.

Three highly talented teenage actors (Gary Grimes as Hermie, Jerry Houser and Oliver Conant as his friends) convey both the hilarity of their awkward sexual quest and the genuine pain of growing up. When Hermie is finally united with his elusive "older woman" (exquisitely portrayed by Jennifer O'Neill) in one of the most sensitive love scenes on film, we understand everything he has learned and felt on his path form innocence to experience.

Summer of '42 is set in a gentler, less complicated America. It is about youth, about sexual awakening, about how it is before the first time. Most of all, it is about remembering. "For everything you take, you leave something behind," Hermie says. *Summer of '42* tells us about our own memories, about what we have gained and what we have lost.—*Warner Home Video*

> One of the top ten movies made on the Mendocino Coast, perhaps the most beautifully filmed. If you feel nostalgic, for our past and possibly even your own, the film evokes memories that will warm the heart.

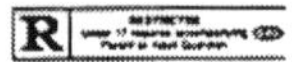

Screen Gems Group Starts Filming Of Television Show in Mendocino

More than 35 persons were scheduled to arrive in Mendocino Thursday morning, Oct. 15, to begin filming a television show for Screen Gems entitled "Doctor in the House."

Heading the list of arrivals will be the series stars, William Windom and Rosemary Forsythe.

Also on hand will be producer director, E. W. Swackhamer; first assistant director Chris Morgan; second assistant directors, Barry Stern, and Mike Frankovich, whose father is the producer and who was the All American football player.

Script supervisor is Larry Johnson; cameraman Fred Jackman, and Rus Kelly, in charge of special effects.

The group will stay at the Little River Inn until departure late Friday.

Arriving on Wednesday will be two truck loads of filming equipment, including a Corvette and a helicopter.

Some of the filming will be equipment from Screen Gems, done aerially. Harry Ackerman is executive producer for Screen Gems.

The show is set in New England, with both Miss Forsyth and Windom playing modern day doctors.

—*Mendocino Beacon*, October 16, 1970

Rosemary Forsyth

William Windom

Only a pilot episode of *Is there a Doctor in the House* was filmed and it did not become a series. The program was broadcast on NBC on March 22, 1971.

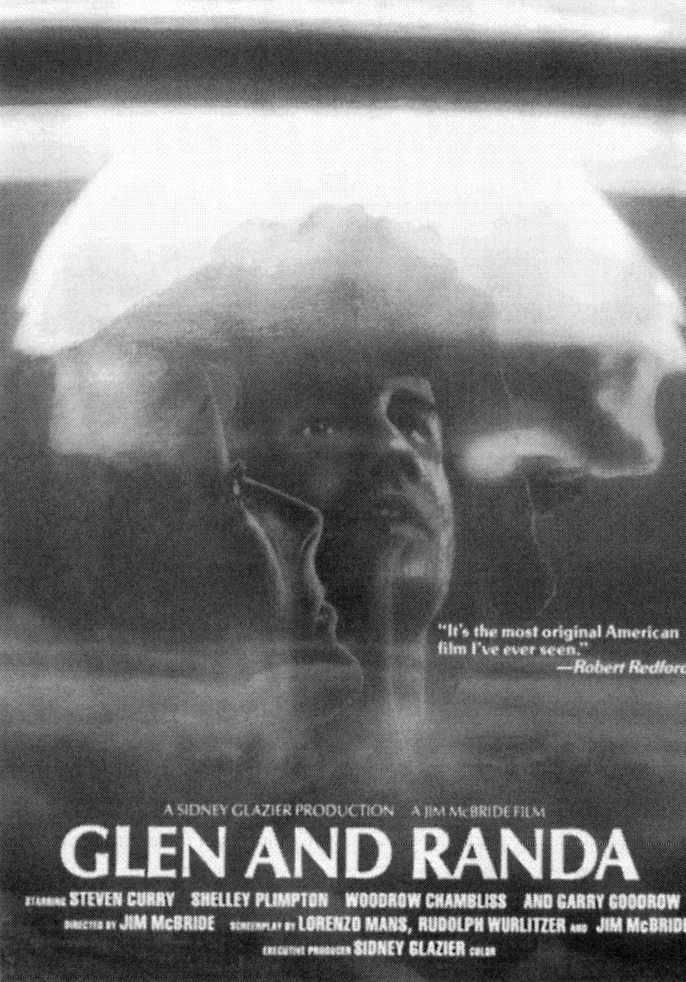

"One of the Best and Most Original Films of the Year!" —*TIME MAGAZINE*

"**Powerfully evocative for the flawlessness of its performance, the excellence of its dialogue and the high quality of inspiration!**"
—**Los Angeles Times**

"**Must rank with '2001: A Space Odyssey' as ONE OF THE GREAT MASTERPIECES OF THE SCIENCE FICTION GENRE!**"—*SHOW MAGAZINE*

"**It's the most original American film I've ever seen.**"—*Robert Redford*

Shelley Plimpton and Steven Curry *(UMC Pictures)*

SYNOPSIS

Perhaps 25 years after a nuclear holocaust has destroyed civilization, two young people, Glen and Randa, set out on an odyssey in search of 'the city'—a legendary place where they believe they will find life as it was. Possessing some of the skills passed down from the former life—they are able to read but unable to understand the meaning of words since the objects they symbolize no longer exist—Glen and Randa accept the remnants of the past without questioning the reasons for them.

Inspired by the grandiose, self-serving falsehoods of a traveling magician, Glen is convinced they will find the city. A Wonder Woman comic book puts a name to Glen's dream—Metropolis.

During their journey, Randa discovers that she is pregnant. As her pregnancy advances, Randa's instinct to find safe shelter annoys Glen, who insists that they press on. At last they reach the sea; they can go no farther. Here they are befriended by an old man, Sidney Miller, who leads them to shelter—a semi-destroyed trailer filled with decaying artifacts . . . television set, refrigerator, etc. Surrounded by these skeletons from the past, Glen attempts to become "civilized"; he watches the long-dead TV and keeps a smokeless pipe in his mouth. Randa and the old man do not share his interests and spend their time playing.

Randa dies in childbirth and Glen and Sidney Miller cremate her body. With a she-goat to suckle the male child, Glen and the old man set sail in a dilapidated boat to search across the sea for "Metropolis."—*UMC Pictures*

The Story

The magician came to camp and gave a show. He even put on a fireproof suit and ignited himself, but there was no applause. Later, when the magician was in his trailer making it with Randa, Glen stayed outside looking at maps. He found one of a place called Idaho, and some picture books about a lady named Wonder Woman who lived in a city called Metropolis that is all shiny and white and where people can fly. He asked the magician about it.

"The city's far, far away, over the mountains," the magician told him. "I was 15 when it was totaled. They was droppin' dead in the streets for years." "Take me to the city," Glen said. But the magician had other business, so just like Prince Valiant on a quest fot the Holy Grail, Glen set out for the city.

The record of the journey is **Glen and Randa**, a primitive, desperate odyssey by the last bewildered survivors of an atomic holocaust, stumbling through the wreckage of a vanished civilization. Neither moralizing sci-fi nor melodrama, despite its fanciful premise, the film is rather like a cinéma vérité doomsday documentary—a parable in newsreel form.

Using a rigorously unadorned style, Director Jim McBride, who was also co-author of **Glen and Randa's** script, conveys a sense of primitive desolation, transforming contemporary landscapes into primeval heaths. Although the film is unsparing in its apocalyptic vision, its dour brutality is frequently alleviated by a cool eye for satire.

—*United Home Video*

Time Magazine, the *Los Angeles Times, Show Magazine*—and particularly Robert Redford—would not, one might suspect, wish to be reminded of the accolades they gave *Glen and Randa* in 1971. But those were different times and perhaps too much criticism 30+ years later is unfair. It certainly isn't the worst motion picture ever made—not even the worst movie made on the Mendocino Coast. In fact, if one gauge of a film's quality is how well the memories are retained, then this unusual endeavor is a screen success.

Glen and Randa was filmed at Schooner Gulch, located between Point Arena and Gualala. No residents remember the filming, nor did local newspapers report the event. A dozen Coast locals were hired as extras and a few received film credits.

Garry Goodrow as "The Magician." *(UMC Pictures)*

Shelley Plimpton, Steven Curry and Woodrow Chamblis. *(UMC Pictures)*

Steven Curry and Shelley Plimpton, *(UMC Pictures)*

THE PRODUCTION OF
"YOUNG GOODMAN BROWN"
By William Phelps

Nathaniel Hawthorne's classic short story about the Pilgrims presented us an era and subject rarely put on short films and provided a challenge in location filming and special effects. — Our first concern was setting the story in a location other than New England. We needed sites within driving distance that would suggest the moods, if not duplicate the geography, of the New England of 1690 that Hawthorne describes. Fox, who is from the San Francisco Bay Area, thought there might be some suitable sites in Sonoma and Mendocino counties, north of San Francisco. After several trips in May, we secured several locations near the coast around the town of Mendocino and a few miles inland. The particular advantage of shooting there was the wide choice of terrain available within a twenty-mile radius. We found lush green meadows, rolling, almost treeless hills covered with wheat that had turned to a brilliant gold, and a variety of forests that ranged from thick pine and silver oak to redwood groves. The variety was critical, as the greater part of the story concerns a journey through the forest, and we wanted to show the woods changing textures and assuming a magical, almost animated quality.

"Witch" is chained to the stake prior to being burned. *(Pyramid Films)*

All the locations (with the exception of the Petaluma site) were within an hour-and-a-half's drive of our base at the Seagull Inn in Mendocino. But this advantage was partially offset by the presence of a morning coastal fog, which would drift as far as fifteen miles inland. This would usually burn off at noon, but sometimes would last all day. When it was foggy on the hilltop scenes, shooting was impossible, as we had developed a consistency of bright sunlight that we wanted to maintain. In the forest sequences, the fog usually worked against us, as it eliminated highlight detail on trees and surrounding vegetation, muddying the background, and not producing the clear day-for-night effect that we needed. This is especially true in the Redwoods, where usually the tall, massive trunks block out all but narrow slivers of sunlight from reaching the forest floor. However, where we had wide shots and dollies in less dense sections of forest, the fog worked for us, as we could not tolerate broad patches of sunlight to burn out the background.

—*American Cinematographer,* March, 1973 (Excerpts)

SYNOPSIS

This film focuses on the Puritan preoccupation with man's inherent propensity for evil. In the opening scenes, the pious minister exhorts his followers; Goody Cloyse, an old woman who had taught Goodman Brown his catechism, anticipates the burning of a "witch." Young Goodman Brown assures his wife, Faith, that his visit to the forest will end by morning. Preoccupation with the world of the evil one permeates even the sun-drenched hilltop. Brown's confidence, reflected in his belief that he can dally with evil and return untainted, is shattered by a sequence of unexpected events: the cordiality of Goody Cloyse and the devil, the unexpected appearance of the pious minister and Deacon Gookin enroute to an unholy rendezvous, the inexplicable and malevolent blotting out of heaven by an ominous dark cloud moving through a windless night, and the pink ribbon of Faith fluttering down through the trees. In despair, Young Goodman Brown races to the unholy communion in the depths of the forest. At the climax of the ceremony, he calls on Faith to resist the evil one. Everything explodes into light. Young Goodman Brown finds himself on the bank of a small stream. It is morning. Dazed, he leaves the forest and turns toward home.

Had it all been a dream? Had he really experienced the demonic faith-shattering events of the past night? In the closing scenes of the film, Brown re-encounters those who had shared his nocturnal experiences: a constable, Deacon Gookin, the minister, Goody Cloyse, and Faith. They greet him unaffectedly; however, his heart is filled with suspicion. Has he lost faith/Faith? The film closes on a note of ambiguity, entirely consistent with the tone of Hawthorne's classic short story.

—Synopsis by Dr. Fred Marcus, Professor of English, California State University, Los Angeles

Extras Toni Lemos, Bob Meuschke & unidentified child. *(Lemos)*

Young Goodman Brown is available on film and video from Pyramid Film & Video, Box 1048, Santa Monica, California 90406

"Bitter Harbor" FBI Story
On TV Sunday

The FBI TV episode entitled "Bitter Harbor" starring Efrem Zimbalist, Jr., will be televised on KABC-TV, Channel 7, at 8:00 p.m. During the filming of the Bitter Harbor, many scenes were taken in Mendocino and the Noyo areas.
— *Mendocino Beacon*, December 10, 1971

Stephen Brooks, Lynn Loring and Efrem Zimbalist, Jr. Stars of *The FBI*.

Local extra J. Christopher Byrne in "Bitter Harbor."

The FBI was a crime drama series based on files from the Federal Bureau of Investigation. It was broadcast on ABC from September 19, 1965 until September 1, 1974. Each episode was 60 minutes.

Two local residents who were hired as extras for "Bitter Harbor" were Peter Paskos and Chris Byrne, who provided the adjacent photograph.

The New Healers — 1972

PARAMOUNT TO SHOOT
PILOT T.V. SERIES IN MENDOCINO

Mr. Wally Samson of Paramount Television will be shooting a pilot TV film in Mendocino on Monday, January 10th.

According to Mr. Samson the group will be on location in Mendocino the entire week, Monday through Saturday. Some thirty local men will be used in the film.

Marlene Hall of Mendocino is assisting with the casting.

The plot involves a group of para-medics and their involvement with members of the medical profession.

—*Mendocino Beacon*, January 7, 1972

The New Healers, a 60 minute drama pilot produced by Paramount Television, was broadcast on ABC on March 27, 1972. Two ex-Vietnam medics and a former nurse join forces to help an aging doctor care for the people of Hope, a rural California community. The program featured Kate Jackson, Robert Foxworth, Jonathan Lippe, Burgess Meredith, Leif Erickson, and William Windom. Produced by Sterling Silliphant and directed by Bernard Kowalski.

Available on DVD.

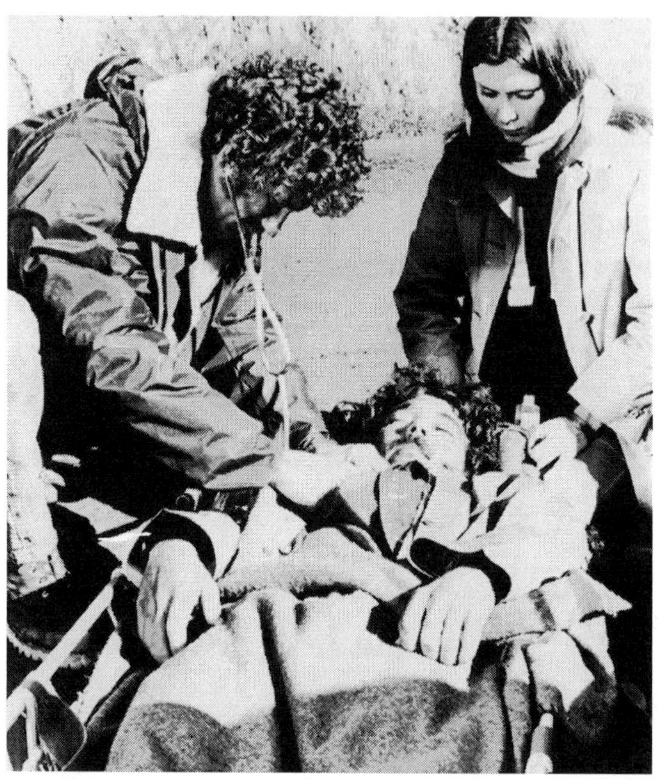

Robert Foxworth and Kate Jackson—Inset: Burgess Meredith (*Paramount Television*)

Slither — 1972

MOVIE SITES

Last Friday a group from MGM was here scouting locations for a forthcoming comedy, "Slither," all about camping and campgrounds. Couldn't have come up with a more timely subject hereabouts. Nothing definite yet about whether or not they will shoot here but they checked settings from Point Arena to Westport. If they do, will be the first couple of weeks in August. Campgrounds? Comedy?

—*Mendocino Beacon*, August 18, 1972

"thououghly infectious, delightfully wacky."
—Kevin Thomas, *Los Angeles Times*
*

Up and down the California coast and into the surreal world of trailer camps, Bingo halls and laundromats, the laughs keep coming in this offbeat road comedy about a group of misfits in pursuit of a small fortune in embezzled cash.

After being paroled from prison, car thief Dick Kanipsia (James Caan) accompanies his cellmate, Harry, home. As soon as they arrive, the house is mysteriously ambushed, leaving Harry mortally wounded. But in his dying breath he gives Dick a clue to the whereabouts of a small fortune. This leads Dick to Harry's former partner Barry Fenaka (Peter Boyle), an embezzler who fronts as a small-time bandleader, comic and mobile home aficionado.

Accompanied by Barry's doting wife Mary (Louise Lasser), the wealth mongers take off in Barry's RV to claim the money. The journey becomes filled with suspense as they are joined by Kitty (Sally Kellerman), a wacky beauty with a penchant for armed robbery — but things really get out of hand when the foursome discover they are being followed by two mysterious black vans.

—*MGM/UA/Turner Home Video*

James Caan and Sally Kellerman are nearly run off the road in exciting chase sequence in *Slither*. (*MGM Pressbook*)

Rear: James Caan, extra Jill Lemos, stuntman Jimmy Double.
Front: extras Kris Williams and Robert Sears. (*Lemos*)

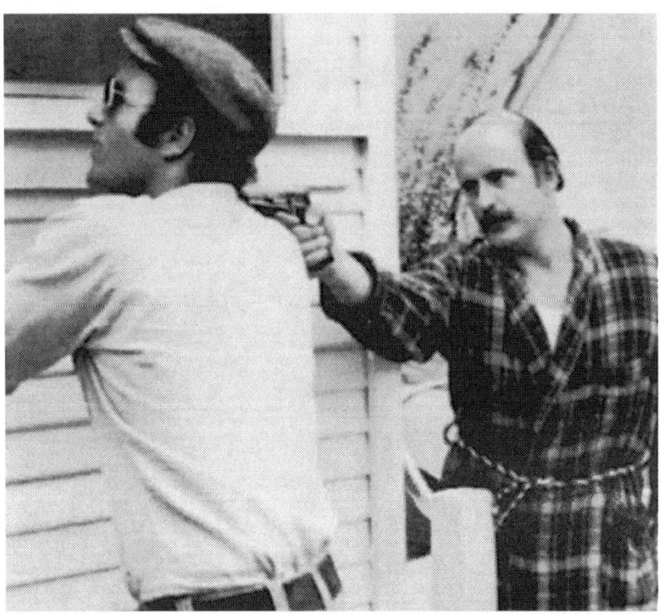

James Caan tries to take a gun away from Sally Kellerman as Louise Lasser watches. *(MGM Pressbook)*

Peter Boyle puts a gun to James Caan's head when he finds him prowling outside his home. *(MGM Pressbook)*

Haunts — 1973

May Britt and Cameron Mitchell *(Herb Freed Films)*

Cameron Mitchell and May Britt *(Herb Freed Films)*

Film Premiere Tonight

The Mendocino Volunteer Fire Department will receive proceeds from tonight's world premiere showing of a locally-filmed motion picture "Haunts (formerly called "The Deadly Veil").

The public is cordially invited to attend.

Show times are at 7:10 and 9:05 p.m. at the Coast Theater, Fort Bragg. Tickets are $5 for adults, $3 for students, and $2 for children under 13.

"Haunts" is rated PG (parental guidance) and stars May Britt, Cameron Mitchell and Aldo Ray.

Many local extras may be seen, including some with speaking parts, according to movie coordinator Toni Lemos of Mendocino.

The film will be shown through Saturday.
—*Mendocino Beacon*, 1977

Haunts

In "Haunts," once called "The Veil," a policeman must stop writing a ticket and catch the Mad Scissorer attacking a victim in the street nearby. Present is a sexually repressed farmgirl who believes she was raped by a goat. Included is Aldo Ray retching over a toilet, Cameron Mitchell with his hair flocked like a Christmas tree.

May Britt is attacked and scissored at in the dark, but breaks free and flees to the house, where Mitchell asks if she's sure it wasn't a rabbit or a deer that tried to kill her.

"Haunts" runs 98 minutes. That's the worst part.—*Variety*, July 27, 1977

Although filmed in 1973, *Haunts* was not released until 1977, one indication of the quality of the film. Some reviewers admired May Britt's performance but this was not enough to prevent the entire production from being an abject failure. Definitely a candidate for the worst motion picture filmed on the Mendocino Coast.

"...And God Bless Grandma & Grandpa" — 1973
aka Evil Town — 1987

New Movie To Be Shot In Mendocino

Once again Mendocino and its environs are to become the background for a motion picture to join such previous attractions as "Johnny Belinda", "The Russians are Coming", "East of Eden", "Dunwich Horror" and "Summer of '42." The latest film feature to come to "Hollywood North" is a suspense thriller dealing with the older and younger generations titled, "...And God Bless Grandma and Grandma."

The operation is being brought to Mendocino by Centaur Productions of Hollywood who said they are anxious to use local people as much as possible. In a call to the Beacon, they indicated a need for about 80 people in the 60 to 70 age bracket plus a few in their twenties.

Shooting is scheduled to start around September 17. Time, date and place of auditions will be announced as soon as they are settled.

President of the corporation, Peter Traynor, said that "...And God Bless Grandma and Grandma" was written by Royce D. Applegate and will be directed by Curtis Hanson. The names of the stars have not yet been released.

Traynor said that one of the reasons for shooting in this area was the cooperation his staff received while scouting the area recently. He said he was highly impressed by the assistance they had received while here.

One of the unique things about this production is that it is financed by Leverage Funding Systems, an investment organization made up entirely of physicians and surgeons, headed up by Traynor.—*Mendocino Beacon,* August 24, 1973

"... And God Bless Grandma & Grandpa"
—Shooting Starts

Shooting on the movie "... and God Bless Grandma and Grandpa" got off to a wet start last Monday. The mystery-suspense-horror film, directed by Curtis Hanson and co-produced by Peter Traynor and William Sklar, is using a large number of local people, many in near-starring roles. Coming from Hollywood for the top roles are Robert Walker, Regis Toomey, James Keach, Doria Cook, and Michelle Marsh.

Among the local people taking some of the more prominent parts are: Lucia Zacha, Bob Donat, Bill Zacha, Jim McKeney, Margo Farrar, Vic Smith, Una Biggs, and Mae Lemos from Mendocino; Thelma Fetters, Greg Spencer, and Harold Peoples of Fort Bragg; R. D. Beacon of Elk; and Dean Creath of Little River. Altogether, locally, the company is using the services of some 50 young people and about 40 older women and 40 older men, all of whom have already been hired.

The company will be working in the area from Navarro to Westport and also a few miles inland during the four to seven weeks that it will take to complete the production.

"... And God Bless Grandma and Grandpa" is basically the story of a small town filled with old people who have found a "Fountain of Youth" and want no interference from outsiders who might discover their unique way of preserving themselves. It sounds like a modern-day Shangri-La.

—*Mendocino Beacon,* October 26, 1973

Four innocent people are trapped in an ever-tightening web of bone-chilling terror when a mad doctor selects them as the subjects of his ungodly experiments!

When they stop for the night in an eerie small town, four travelers — Christopher (James Keach), Mike (Robert Walker), Julie (Michelle Marsh) and Linda (Doria Cook) — unknowingly uncover an insane physician (Dean Jagger) conducting gruesome experiments on the brains of human guinea pigs!

Before they can escape Mike and Linda are brutally murdered by the doctor's sadistic henchmen, now Christopher and Julie have one last desperate chance to get away before the madmen's bloodcurdling experiments turn them into — the living dead!

Little was known about this film until it was unearthed in 2001. It should have remained buried, instead of surfacing as "Evil Town" on vhs in 1987. One reviewer called it "a B-grade ultra-cheap 'Pulp Fiction,' with terrible acting, non-existent gore and flat, talentless direction." (The film had four, that's right, four directors).

"This silly horror film is apparently assembled from pieces of two different projects, including an uncompleted film from the mid-'70s, and spiced up with some gratuitous nudity—but the end result seems hardly worth the effort."

—Cavett Binion, *All Movie Guide.*

There are, however, a few moments of great acting by local extra Margo Farrar—as an evil hypodermic-wielding old lady—who received a film credit (but probably wouldn't want it).

Perhaps the original filming was just a financial scam, as the 1973 *Beacon* article seems to imply.

Definitely the worst film ever made on the Mendocino Coast.

Passengers, Crewmen on C.W.R. see Picture

The filming of scenes from a full length motion picture last month provided a rare sight along the tracks of the California Western Railroad. Passengers and crews of the "Skunk" railroad glimpsed the star of "The Great Elephant Chase" who was, naturally, an elephant.

The movie revolves around a 10 year old boy who becomes separated from his father on a fishing trip. The boy discovers a baby pachyderm escaped from a nearby circus, befriends the animal, and proceeds to have various adventures with the elephant, including meeting a train in a tunnel. In the end, the boy and elephant find the father helplessly drifting down a river. The boy throws his father a rope and ties the other end around the elephant, which stops the boat from drifting over a waterfall.

Larry Lansburgh, 30 year veteran of film making and two time winner of academy awards for animal films, is the producer and director. He and his film crew are from Eagles Point, Oregon, near Medford, where the river scenes for the movie were filmed.

Through the efforts of the C.W.R. and Georgia-Pacific, owners of the railroad, Lansburgh filmed his redwood chase scenes which he needed to complete the film in one week. The film stars—besides the elephant—Slim Pickens, and is expected to be released next spring.

—*The Noyo Chief,* November, 1973

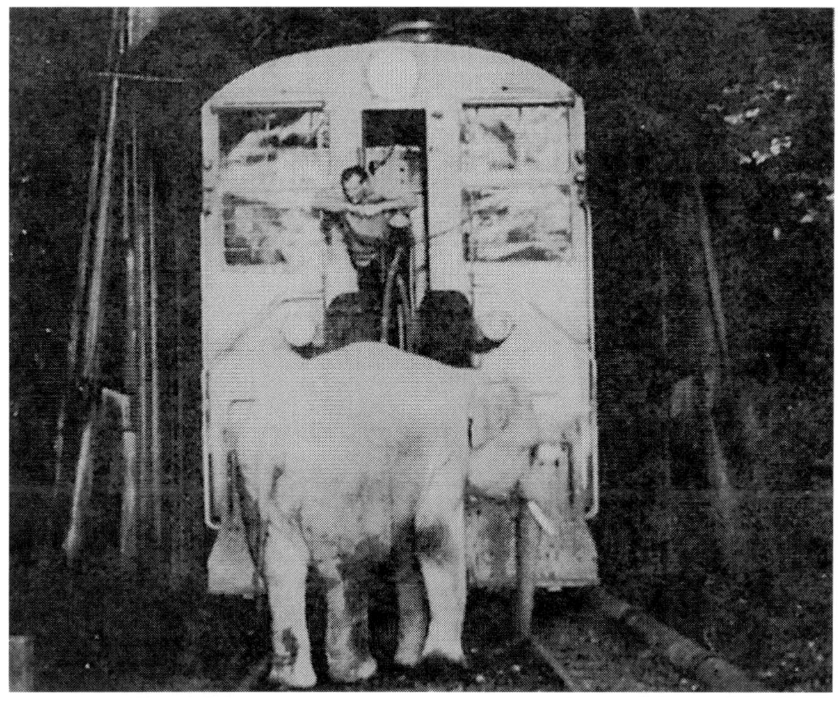

CWR Engineer Walter Lawrence ponders the situation.

Actor Slim Pickens, cameraman, & Producer-director Larry Lansburgh during the filming of "The Great Elephant Chase."

The title of *The Great Elephant Chase* was changed to *The Runaway on the Rogue River.* The film has not been listed in catalogs of educational films for many years. It was the the 9th episode of the 21st season of Wonderful World of Disney

This would be the second time an elephant would appear in a film made east of Fort Bragg (See Page 23).

PILOT FILM

Last week a well-organized and superbly equipped Edgar J. Sherick Productions movie crew worked in beautiful sunshiny weather in Mendocino. Under the direction of Ralph Senensky, they shot footage for "JEREMIAH OF JACOB'S CREEK", a pilot film for a childrens' series for CBS-TV. Much time was spent at the Katharine Merrill residence on the ocean bluff at Agate Beach. This house [where the Helfers lived for many years] was "Abby's House" in the movie and it was decorated to look like a home in Maine.

Everyone will recognize Keenan Wynn who stars as the centuries-old ghost of Jeremiah, and some of you will know Ron Mask, Arlene Golonka, Brandon Cruz, Ouinn Cummings, Pitt Herbert, Eillott Street, Alex Henteloff, Les Lannom, Amzie Strickland, or Tom Palmer, who also have parts in the story.

Francis Nichols, Mae Lemos, Judy Frank, Don Burleson, and Warren Peters had speaking parts in this film and several other local people worked as extras. Filming was also done at the Deli, the Beacon, and the bank [where a holdup scene was shot!].

Another local angle is that movie companies are required to secure encroachment permits before shutting down streets for the purpose of making movies. According to Gene Richmond, who issues these permits, prior permission is supposed to be obtained from all shopkeepers whose shops are located on the streets which are to be blocked.

Further, normal vehicular traffic is not supposed to be held up for more than five minutes at any one time. In this instance I am told that prior permission was not obtained from all the affected shopkeepers, traffic was sometimes held up in town for up to 20 minutes, and North Lansing Street seemed to be completely blocked for several hours one day. Betty Dostal was not the onIy shopkeeper to phone and complain that the stipulated conditons were not being observed.

—*Mendocino Beacon*, March 11, 1976

Keenan Wynn and film coordinator Toni Lemos.

The *Mendocino Beacon* building is Jacob Neck's post office. Extras Mae Lemos (on bicycle) and Francis Nichols (seated on bench).

Ron Masak *(Lemos)*

Extra Judy Frank and friend Judy Sperling inside The Deli, Main Street, Mendocino.

Arlene Golonka *(Lemos)*

A contemporary family, Tom Rankin (Ron Masak), his wife Anne (Arlene Golonka) and their two children move into a dilapidated beach house in the New England town of Jacob's Neck, only to find that it is haunted by an 18th-century spirit, Jeremiah Starbuck (Keenan Wynn). The story is the humorous conflict between the family and the house's ghostly resident, who is only visible to the newcomers and refuses to depart the dwelling.

> The 30-minute pilot episode of *Jeremiah of Jacob's Neck* was broadcast on CBS on August 13, 1976, but the series was never made.

Two views of the camera crew at Shirley's Cafe (Then the Main Street Deli).

Byrd Baker as Uncle Will and Andy Gordon as Andy Delmont.
(*Program Power Entertainment*)

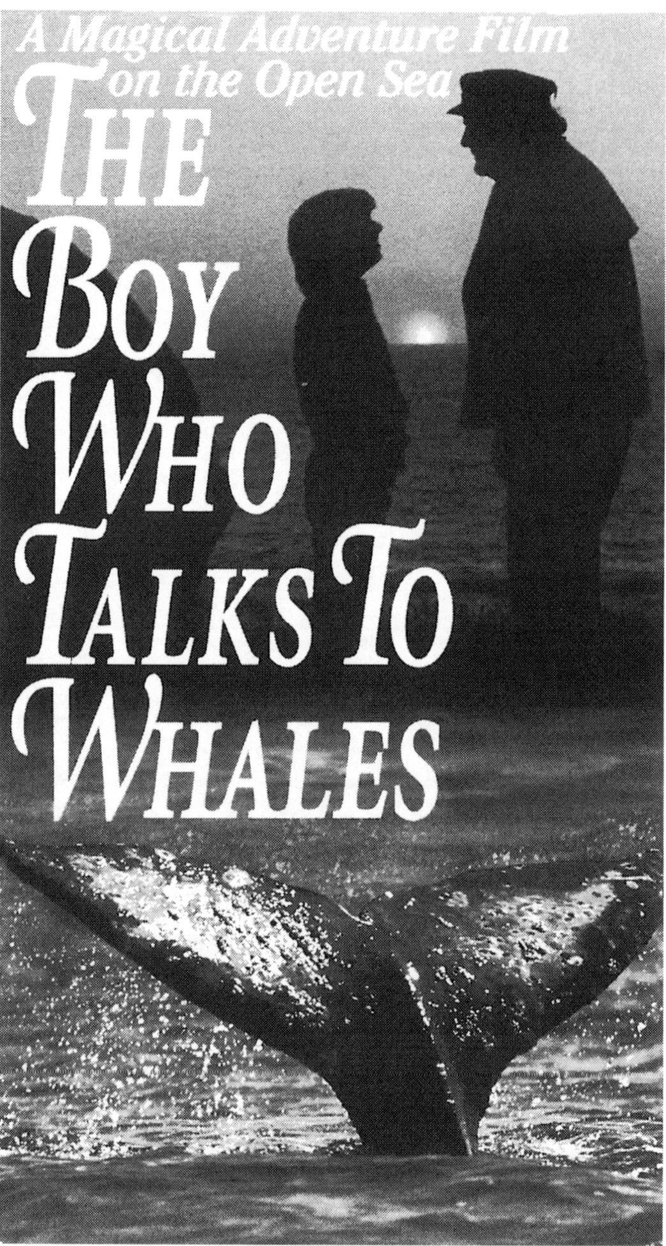

(*Program Power Entertainment*)

15-year-old Andy Delmont has come to spend his summer with his Uncle Will in a small California fishing village. A knowledgeable man of the sea, Uncle Will is fascinated by whales—especially by a gray whale named "Gigi" whom he claims he "talked" to while working at a nearby marine research station. Andy and the other villagers think that Will is crazy for thinking that he can communicate with the whales. But when a dramatic chain of events alters their lives, Andy and Will must head out into the open sea against overwhelming odds in an exciting search for the missing Gigi; and Andy discovers secrets of nature that will change him forever.

Set against the magnificent vastness of the Pacific Ocean and featuring remarkable close-up footage of the fascinating gray whales, THE BOY WHO TALKS TO WHALES is an incredible high-seas adventure and a moving story in the tradition of FREE WILLY. —*Program Power Entertainment*

A Casteel Production starring Victor Jory, Byrd Baker, Andy Gordon and Gigi the Whale. Written and Directed by Ron Casteel. Director of Photography David E. Jackson. Executive Producer Richard M. Davis. Distributed by Carlton Entertainment, Inc. Program Power Entertainment, Inc. No longer available on video tape or DVD, but is sometimes listed for sale on Ebay.

Victor Jory, the narrator of *The Boy Who Talks to Whales,*
at Noyo Harbor.

This movie was originally titled *The Man Who Talks To Whales,* and although Will Brannon is fictional, the character is based on the life of the actor who portrayed the role, Byrd Baker. He was a personal friend of this writer, much-loved and respected by people throughout the world, particularly on the Mendocino Coast. For not only did Byrd speak to whales, he loved them, and during the 1970s he tried to save them from rapacious whaling practices by founding what became known as the Mendocino Whale War. For a few years Byrd criss-crossed the country in his Whale Bus, explaining to and gaining the support of diverse groups of people in his determined, non-violent battle to stop the Russians and the Japanese from killing whales. To school classes and church groups, to anyone who would listen, he gave his talks about how important it was—for those beautiful creatures and for us—to save "God's Whales."

At the time of Byrd's death in 1990, a friend said of him, "He was the most charismatic and caring person I ever met."

The real-life Byrd Baker, with friend Jackie MacAndrew, in front of Byrd's studio on Ukiah Street in Mendocino,
with the Mendocino Whale War Bus and Truck, during May, 1977. (*Cahill*)

"Same Time, Next Year" — 1978

Lights! Camera! Stand-ins

It is 1951 at a northern Calfornia inn.

Doris is a housewife from Oakland on her way to a religious retreat. George, an accountant from New Jersey, is on his way to do a friend's income taxes.

George and Doris are happily married with three children each, both faithful to their respective spouses—until now.

"Same Time, Next Year" is the story of their 26-year affair, during which George and Doris face some problems and many changes.

Alan Alda and Ellen Burstyn have the lead roles in this romantic comedy by Bernard Slade which opened on Broadway in 1975 and is being filmed at Heritage House, Little River, for Universal.

Stage producer Morton Gottileb is co-producing with Walter Mirisch. Director is Robert Mulligan. Filming began February 1.

Stand-ins for the stars are Sandra Hahn and Bob Avery, of Mendocino.

Toni Lemos helped find local extras. They are:

From Mendocino—Jean and Warren Peters, Jerilyn Self, Chatter and Jack Bishoff, George Halter, Pam and Charles King, Art Lemos, Susan and Tim Todd, and Susan and Tim Aguilar.

From Albion and Little River—Kay Burkard, Jan Bradshaw, Lu Robinson, Agnes and Rolph Stormer, June and Norman McMillan.

From Fort Bragg—Harvey Mace and son Lan, Joe Thomas, Marge and Henry Goldsmith, Helen and Peter Ferbrashe, Caroline and John Bailey, Darcia Grover and Aria and Jim Evanoff.

"Same Time Next Year" is set in a cottage at the inn built by the studio, close to tbe bluff of a small cove.

—*Mendocino Beacon*, February 16, 1978

George (Alan Alda) and Doris (Ellen Burstyn meet at a seaside resort and begin a love affair that lasts for 26 consecutive years. *(Universal City Studios)*

As the years go by, George and Doris change with the times during their marathon love affair. *(Universal City Studios)*

"Same Time, Next Year"

by Bob Avery

A few of us locals have spent the past two weeks working with the film company on location, and if the film turns out to be as good in total as the parts we have seen then we will be able to say with pride that we had a small part in the production.

If it doesn't turn out so well (a highly unlikely prospect) then we can at least say that we had the good fortune of spending our time with a very pleasant and talented group of people, that we learned a lot, and were paid fairly for it.

It has been a remarkable experience, certainly for me, and I hope for the rest of the local people also.

I have been repeatedly impressed with the willingness of every person involved with the shooting to overlook our layman's ignorance and to answer virtually every question in detail and without complaint.

Consequently I have been able to absorb a lot of information about some of the hows—and whys—of movie-making, some of which may hopefully show up as improvements in our local theater productions.

The best part of it, though, has been the people. The producers have assembled some of the best talent available to make this picture, and working with them has been a privilege.

Robert Mulligan, the director, is the classic image of "The Director," from curled Stetson to safari jacket, slender and taut—and he is the consumate boss.

Movies, I think, are the director's medium, and his word is law. He decides when, what, and where—and he bears the responsibility for all the people, equipment and content.

The film in the cans at the end of the day is the result of his direction; and he must see that all the elements combine as smoothly as possible to produce the best pictures in a minimum of time. It must be an ulcerous occupation.

Fortunately for this production, Mulligan is a shrewd and clever man who recognizes the abilities (and limitations) of his crew, and uses them.

He has a sense of humor, and just the right balance of tolerance and temper.

He also knows this area, having spent a summer here directing "Summer of '42."

Altogether he is just aloof enough to maintain his control without jeapordizing his humanity. I like him.

Apparently his crew like him too, because it is a pretty smooth operation to watch. If they don't like him, then they must respect him enough to at least do what they do well . . . and fast.

Richard Mulligan, director *(Lemos)*

Right in there with the director is the cameraman, Robert Surtees, consulting, advising, and never excluded fron the fundamental work.

Now in his 51st year with the industry, Surtees is the acknowledged master. He has seen it all, and you can't fool him . . . he knows!

He can tell the intensity of light with his eyeballs as well as any fancy meter, and he doesn't miss a detail. With him, you can bet every frame will be right.

And assuming Mulligan's direction is correct, how can they miss? Surtees has three Academy Awards for his camerawork, something like 47 nominations in his lifetime, and if he wins another for his current nomination (for "Turning Point") I understand he will be the only cameraman in history with four Academy Awards.

He deserves it. He is a fine gentleman with a great sense of humor, and he's damn good at his business.

All of them are experts, and all of them are good people. I wish I could tell you about each and every one, because all of them are the substance of every inch of film.

But Universal employs up to 80 people on this location, and I trust those I omit will understand, as much as I think you should know them too.

So what about the stars—the glamor? Where do they fit in to all this?

Don't worry, folks, it's all there still, at least as far as this picture is concerned.

Alan Alda and Ellen Burstyn are the stars—the focus of all this activity—and it has been the wisdom of the powers that be to maintain the "image" for this production.

Alda and Burstyn are generally not seen until it is time to be seen, when all the lights are set, the camera is positioned and the sound tested.

Then they arrive on set in their own vehicle, step in and do what they are supposed to do. When they are not "on camera" they are separate—in their own room, corner, or back to the dressing rooms—until it is time for them to be "on" again.

This procedure, I understand, is not standard in the industry any more. But for this film in this location the star "distance" is mantained, and the stars remain a certain mystery.

In those few minutes when I have had the chance to chat with them it has been a rather awkward conversation. In one sense I would love to talk "biz" with these two fine performers, or get to know them; but in another sense I don't want to intrude with nonsense that they have surely heard a thousand times before.

So, you wind up not saying anything—afraid to be a dummy, maybe—and perhaps that's part of why they remain apart.

Alan Alda and Ellen Burstyn at Heritage House, Little River. *(Lemos)*

In all fairness, Alan Alda and Ellen Burstyn seem to have a good time together: lots of jokes, laughter and pleasure in their work. They are very good at their craft, and I suspect they would be fun to talk with.

I don't know if the separatism is their idea or not, but it really doesn't matter. They are the ones you will see in the final product. It is their show, and they are the ones you will remember, and if it helps, they seem like good folks.—*Mendocino Beacon*, February 23, 1978

Ellen Burstyn was required to be eight months pregnant for a scene in "Same Time, Next Year." She complained to director Robert Mulligan about the weight of material she was carrying to achieve the necessary effect. To this the director replied, "Carry on."

*

Alan Alda is required to age 26 years in the course of the film. He stepped out of his dressing room grey-haired, wrinkled and jowled through the miracle of studio make-up, causing one of the camera crew to remark, "Man, you're getting older." "Know anybody who's getting younger?" Alda retorted.

This warm, touching film received three Academy Award nominations. A sequel planned for 1992 failed to materialize. A Coast top ten movie.

Mendocino backdrop for Davis

A gesticulation of the irrepressible Bette Davis on location in Mendocino. Between scenes she makes her point clear with crew members of "Strangers," a CBS television feature co-starring Davis and Gena Rowlands.

Chris-Rose Production Company arrived here two weeks ago from Hollywood for the Mendocino Coast scenery because it's the East Coast of the Pacific. The filming should be wrapped up sometime next week.

"Strangers," the story of an embittered New England mother whose daughter returns after a long estrangement, will be aired sometime in the spring or fall '79 season. This is the first major work produced by the screenwriter, Michael DeGuzman.

Locations at 600 Kelley Street, Main Street and Mendosa's Market in Men-docino as well as Noyo Harbor and Fort Bragg Library provided backdrops.

About 50-80 Coast residents earning $30-a-day, played stand-ins or extras. Betty Barber of Mendocino doubled for Ms. Davis; Judy Frank was the stand-in double for Gena Rowlands.

Extras include Donny Salo, Renee McDonald, Krishan Timberlake, Louis Spencer and Joan Spencer, all local residents.

"People have been very friendly. We are glad we're here," said production manager Ric Rondell.

Motion Picture Development coordinator Toni Lemos, of Mendocino, accompanied the director in conducting local auditions for Mendocino school students.

—*Mendocino Beacon*, December 7, 1978

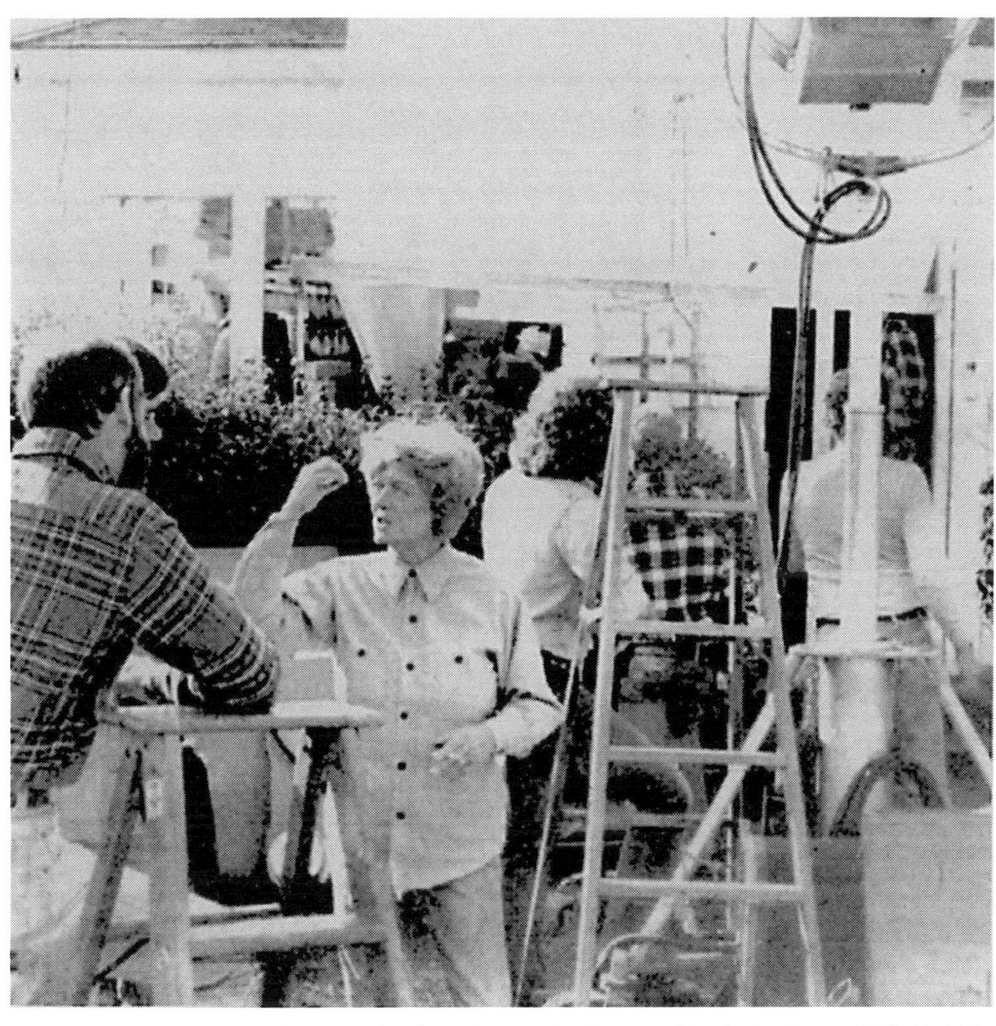

Bette Davis and Director Milton Katselas discussing scene in *Strangers*. *(Mendocino Beacon/Holly Hefele)*

Bette Davis & Gena Rowlands *(Lemos)*

Bette Davis dancing with Donald Moffat. *(Lemos)*

Movie Company donates $500 to MFD

This week the Mendocino Fire Department was presented with a check for $500 from the Chris-Rose Production Company upon completion of their television movie "Strangers," starring Bette Davis and Gena Rowlands, that was filmed on the Mendocino Coast.

The company had utilized the fire department facilities during the past four weeks.

There is a drive under way by the department to expand its service to the Coast by the purchase of new fire and rescue equipment. This money will go toward the drive.

The donation expresses the Chris-Rose Production's appreciation to the many people of the Coast for their courtesy and co-operation.

Three children were chosen to play the parts of Bette Davis' neighbors in the film and will be taken to Hollywood to complete interior scenes. They are Krishan Timberlake, Renee McDonell, and Donnie Salo.

Other local people who were featured in minor parts were Kris Williams, John Zunino, Don Fosse, Grail Dawson, Jill Fosse, and Steve Jordan. In addition some one hundred other extras were chosen to perform in the background.—*Mendocino Beacon*, December 14, 1978

Bette Davis won an Emmy Award as Outstanding Actress for her powerful portrayal of an embittered widow. The great actress was truly at her best in this made-for-television tearjerker, and Gena Rowlands, as her daughter, kept up the pace with Davis scene for scene. *Strangers* was broadcast on CBS on Mother's Day, May 9, 1979.

The scenes at Noyo were supposed to be a July 4th celebration—but the actual filming took place in December, when the Mendocino Coast was cold and damp. Between takes, Davis and the cast would warm themselves in front of portable stoves.

Bette Davis and Gena Rowlands (in background) on set of *Strangers* at Noyo.

Extras Rhonda McDonell, Stella Salo, Myrna Shandell and Bette Davis (*Lemos*)

Renee McDonell, Donnie Salo, Bette Davis and Krishan Timberlake (*Lemos*)

Rick Lemos and Gena Rowlands (*Lemos*)

Movie Making on the Coast
by Diana Desroches

"Beneath the Darkness" is the proposed title for a movie being filmed in the Fort Bragg area. The crew has been at work here for the past three weeks.

"Fort Bragg was chosen for its scenic values," said Martin B. Cohen, location producer. "Not only is the scenery beautiful, but within a ten mile radius you have ocean, river and forests. This is ideal for filming our movie."

"Within 20 minutes, people, trucks and motor homes can be at the filming site. This allows more time for photographing and costs less since the crew is paid for travel time. Also, close sets allow easy communication with a walkie-talkie."

Cohen created the idea for the movie though he was not the writer. It was originally set in Oregon but the Fort Bragg area was chosen for the filming because of its natural beauty and convenience.

The plot of the movie has a cannery company attempting to increase the salmon catch by developing a new breed of salmon that grows rapidly. These salmon have been given chemicals to induce the rapid growth.

Some of the fish are accidentally let out of a storage tank and get into the stream, where they are ingested by a Coelacanth. Coelacanths are a fish believed by some to have lived a million years ago. They never passed the evolutionary stage. When some of these salmon are ingested by the coelacanth it creates a sudden evolutionary cycle. It starts a mutation in which it becomes a humanoid—neither man nor fish.

The humanoid lives and breathes underwater. It has features of men—a skull, brain, the ability to live on land for short periods of time and can think. It also has a tail and fins. The humanoid wants to mate with humans. The story continues

Director Barbara Peeters set up next shot.
(*Fort Bragg Advocate-News/Jeff Boice*, November 16, 1979)

as the humanoid progresses on its evolutionary cycle. Cohen says people concerned with the environment will be interested in the movie.

Doug McClure, Ann Turkel, and Vic Morrow are the main characters in the film who have starred in other movies and television series. There are about 30 members in the crew and about 15 actors starring at different times.

Many local people have been hired as extras. Directors of theatre groups in both Mendocino and Fort Bragg suggested local actors to participate. Many families, children and church groups are taking part. In some of the carnival scenes, as many as 200 extras were required.

Cohen said, "It is very convenient to have Boy Scouts, letter groups and community activity groups participating with a donation going to the group for their specific needs.

"If the filming schedule is to be changed it is hard to call 200 individual persons. With these groups—another "head" delivers the message. Not only by word of mouth, but radio and community cooperation were means of providing extras for the movie."

A carnival scene was filmed for four nights at Dolphin Cove. You will recognize the locations in the movie such as Dolphin Cove. "This is unique," said Cohen. "Often a movie will be filmed in a certain location where they want it to appear like some other place far away."

Cohen added, "The film will be shown all over the world, but most importantly all over the United States." It will be a good advertisement

Ann Turkell, Doug McClure and Tony Penya examine bizarre creature.
(*Fort Bragg Advocate-News/Jeff Boice*, November 14, 1979)

for this area—and such features as Dolphin Cove—where tourism, fishing and sightseeing are year long and an important part of the economy.

Many other Fort Bragg sites were used in the film—near the Wharf Restaurant, outside the harbor, the hospital, the Pudding Creek area, etc.

There are ferris wheels and merry-go-rounds in the carnival scene. A car was run off the Pudding Creek logging road bridge as part of the movie, and a boat, the "Bucko", was blown up in the water. There is a creature who is half salmon and man in various sets.

The rain this past week did slow progress some. Luckily, director of photography David Lacambre is from Paris where it rains frequently and enjoys filming in the wet weather. He has a special French camera which helps him photograph in the rain.

Several local boats were chartered for the movie—"Captain Cook," "Beverly Jean," and the "Glomar." Boats owned by Dale and Bob Armitage were also chartered for the film along with boats owned by the stars themselves.

The most unique invention and boat chartered was the "Glomar," built and devised by John Milnoti, owner of the boat "Captain Cook." The "Glomar" is a flat boat used as a camera platform on both land and water. It splits and folds up and can be taken from place to place.

"The Glomar is handy—especially when being used for filming where it can travel on land or water easily from location to location," commented Cohen.

"Many people have helped in different ways to help make the movie," said Cohen. "The manager of the Coast Theatre has allowed us to review parts of our film on their large picture screen. Though we have a smaller machine to audit the film, it is far more advantageous to show it on a bigger screen. This way if we have missed something in a scene it will show up better, and also helps us be sure we have gotten what we want after each set," said Cohen. "The manager of the Coast Theatre has also given us much helpful advice to aid in the filming."

Two producers are helping make the movie. Roger Corman is the executive producer in Los Angeles. He is also the owner of the Los Angeles movie company—New World Production Co.—which is making the movie. They make six to eight pictures a year. Martin B. Cohen is the location producer. He is concerned with the actors and

The Humanoid (*Fort Bragg Advocate-News /Jeff Boice,* November 9, 1979)

directors. He is also concerned with the artistic end of the movie and seeing that costs are kept within budget.

In about three more weeks the movie crew will go home to Los Angeles. Down will come the fantasy sets where local adults and children mingle enjoying hot dogs and Cokes when not being filmed. Also no more free rides on the Ferris wheel and carousel or balloons for the children as they take part in the carnival scenes.

Many local residents came to observe the filming and to see how a movie is made. Local actors were able to apply their talents and interests as "extras" in a "real" movie. Though it will seem quiet after "movie making" ends, they want to have the movie previewed here in the spring.

—*Fort Bragg Advocate-News,* October 31, 1979

> *Beneath the Darkness* was retitled *Humanoids from the Deep.* It contains violent horror, unintentional laughs, near-x-rated scenes of rape and nudity—with a finale definitely not for the squeamish!

Coast acts up in 'Beneath the Darkness'

By Diana Desroches

Many local children, teenagers and adults recently received an insight into film making. They not only were able to observe the process, but were participants as "extras" in "Beneath the Darkness," just filmed in the Fort Bragg area.

The movie director is in charge of the set. Although it is unusual to find a female movie director, Barbara Peeters fills that role here. She has many responsibilities and decisions to make while filming the movie, such as the angle of the shots and the different camera lenses to be used during the scenes.

Barbara works hand and hand with Daniel Lacambre, director of photography. There is also a first assistant director who directs the actors and a second assistant director working with the "extras." There are light technicians, stunt men, photography assistants, "grips" (handymen), make up people, a sound man, etc.—all working together.

Barbara explains that way back in June she and others began scouting the area as a film site and choosing location sets. Sample filming of the area was taken back to Los Angeles. Local boats had to be scheduled for charter. Actors from both Mendocino and Fort Bragg read parts for the film. About a dozen local actors were selected for actual "speaking parts" in the movie.

Viewers will recognize familiar businesses in the movie—The Noyo Ice Company, Grader's, Schnaubelt's and dock boys pushing ice off the back docks of Caito Fisheries. They will be able to pick out local boats—the "Charmaine," "Caito Bros.," "Nip and Tuck," "Tara Dawn," etc.—many scooting back and forth along the harbor. There will be several shots of the Mendocino coastline, the town of Mendocino, the Noyo Mooring Basin, Dolphin Cove, Mendocino Coast Hospital, Pudding Creek bridge, Footlighter's Theatre, etc.

Children and adults—as "extras"—mingled in the carnival set at Dolphin Cove riding the ferris wheel, carrying stuffed teddybears, eating free hotdogs, popcorn and Cokes and running away from the creature who toppled over cake booths and ran through shooting galleries and onto the merry-go-round. Both young and the old watched frightened as the other creatures broke docks and ran through the panicked crowd.

Grandmothers and teenagers dug into their closets for their nicest outfits and pretty long dresses as they toe-stepped to the Footlighter's band. The Footlighter's theatre was the hall setting of the "75th Noyo Salmon Festival"—adorned with crepe paper, helium balloons and other colorful decorations. As "extras," the crowd watched appalled and disturbed as actors fought in the theatre parking lot.

Several young local persons assisted by helping out with special effects—such as creating thunder and lightning. The Fort Bragg High School Band paraded through the carnival. One local high school girl, Bonnie Taylor, interested in becoming an actress and stunt woman got a chance to learn from the stuntmen as she participated. Also divers from the Coast Guard helped on the set.

Many humorous and unexpected things happen on the set. One was when teenagers preparing to disco dance discovered they were going to be stepping to ragtime music by the Footlighter's band. Quick prompting and rehearsals helped them learn unfamiliar steps. Another was when the dock broke prematurely, dunking three surprised stuntmen. At one point it was necessary to ask the crowd if any men were wearing size-12 shoes that they would temporarily trade with Doug McClure. Luckily one man had had just the right thing—a new pair of size 12 brown, leather, western boots. The movie crew and "extras" had to chuckle after several rehearsals of a fight scene when the Footlighter Theatre door came off in Vic Morrow's hand. The "hardware men" were quick on the scene to put the door back on.

About 1 a.m., after many hours of filming, the hungry crew breaks for "lunch". The "extras", too, join in the elaborate buffet style lunch. Interested persons get a chance to talk with the stars and crew, get autographs and study the camera and sound equipment.

The creature was designed by Rob Bottin, who designed many of the costumes for "Star Wars". The suit weighs 65 pounds. Though one local girl was prepared for the creature to come after her, she became very frightened and hurdled a carnival booth. Another creature was also sent in after her. She then put up a strong resistance as she began to scream. The green, yellow, and black creature covered with wet hair, fins, legs, and a large protruding brain is indeed frightening. His flailing arms, large bobbing head, sunken eyes and several long teeth created a hysteria in the crowd as "extras" ran from the creature.

A very tense moment in the film making was when the creature was set on fire as he jumped off a ramp. Stuntman Jack Tyree was covered with a special gel with only a protective covering on his face. After he stepped into the costume, this fire-resistant gel was applied on the costume, too. It was not only a climactic point in the movie, but a tense moment on the set while an anxious crew and observers watched him bravely execute the stunt without injury.

As Barbara points out, there are many important segments and persons in the filming process in order to make the movie. Jeff Boice, manager of the Coast Theatre, has been working with the set, photographing "stills" to be used by the movie company for advertising. He has also taken photographs that will actually be used in the film. He has also assisted by allowing the crew to use the theatre's large picture screen to view the "rushes"—several days filming. Barbara points out, "We are fortunate to choose a filming site where so many people are interested in acting, movie making and wanting to take part."—*Fort Bragg Advocate-News,* November 14, 1979

Another Movie to be filmed here

Mendocino, the scene of a number of motion pictures in the past, has again been chosen as the background of a movie to be made in February by Aspen Productions of Los Angeles.

The mystery story will be filmed between Tuesday, February 12, and weather permitting, March 14.

Shooting locations include several spots along Lansing Street, School Street, Point Cabrillo Road at Caspar Beach, and the intersection of Capella and Williams Street. Heeser Drive will also be a scene of action as will the Comptche/Ukiah Road and Little River Airport Road intersection and one scene will be shot at Point Cabrillo Drive near the lighthouse.

A scene at the Justice Court called for painting that building a "weathered" white. Permission for that action was taken at the last Mendocino Historical Review Board meeting. Representative Toni Lemos attended the meeting and must return later for a decision as to whether the court building will remain weathered white, or if another coat of painting will be required.

Mrs. Lemos also appeared before the Mendocino Services District for permission to have P.G.&E. extinguish certain streetlights during the filming of some scenes. The lights will be out only during actual shooting of the night scenes, which require special lighting effects due to their "mysterious nature," and the P.G.&E. representative will be on hand to turn the lights off and on. Permission was granted.

Permission for road encroachment was also sought, and given from the Board of Supervisors and the State of California.

On Thursday, February 28 a fire scene is scheduled near Caspar Beach. Fort Bragg Fire Department will assist with this scene which will not be on a county road.

Aspen Productions has requested, and received, permission to control traffic. Those controls, however, must be limited to five minute intervals.

—*Mendocino Beacon*, January 31, 1980

Cameras roll again in Mendocino

Almost as if by magic a Mendocino bank became a mortuary, a real estate office became a coffee shop, fences sprang up and instant forests appeared. Almost overnight the town of Mendocino became "Potters Bluff."

Tuesday the cameras started rolling on the Richard R. St. Johns presentation of Ronald Shusett's production, "Dead & Buried." This is a terror suspense thriller from the creators of "Alien."

Because of the success of "Alien," publicity people tell us, the exact plot of "Dead & Buried" is not being revealed to the public. "But," we are assured, "those extras walking around out there are not zombies."

While not listed as science fiction, nor supernatural, the movie does delve into surrealism because, "It is about a place that could not actually exist," we are told.

St. Johns announced that the Aspen film, budgeted at nearly $6 million, will shoot for five weeks on location here, then move to Goldwyn Studios in Hollywood.

Starring in "Dead & Buried" are James Farentino, Melody Anderson and Jack Albertson. Farentino is already on location, the other stars are not expected here until later.

Three speaking roles as well as some 15 background extras have been cast for the picture by Toni Lemos of Mendocino. She is the county movie coordinator working with the production company.

Mrs. Lemos earlier appeared at the Board of Supervisors, the Mendocino Historical Review Board and the Services District Board meetings for necessary approvals for the filming.

Filming will continue in the Mendocino town area this week and most of next. Some scenes will be shot in the Caspar Beach area late next week, weather permitting.

One of the reasons the Mendocino coast was chosen for "Dead & Buried" was the need for a fog-atmosphere in the picture.

The movie will probably be released early in 1981.

—*Mendocino Beacon*, February 14, 1980

The building next to the Justice Court in Mendocino is Buckaloo and Associates, a real estate agency. But in Potters Bluff the building has become a cafe. Above are members of the construction crew of "Dead & Buried making the transition.—*Mendocino Beacon/Betty Graubard*

An Open Letter To The Good Folks Of Mendocino

We, the folks from Aspen Productions who are here filming a picture called "Dead & Buried" want to thank you for the kind hospitality that you have shown us. We would also like to apologize for any inconveniences that we may have caused you. We don't want to disrupt your way of life or in any way upset you. We are just here to do a job making a movie, which is the only work we know. We really are not bad eggs and would like to get to know all of you better. So please, if you have any problems, or if we are in any way needlessly disturbing you, please let us know and we will try to rectify the situation. Just try to bear with us and before you know it we'll be gone. s/Aspen Productions—*Mendocino Beacon*, February 14, 1980

Jack Albertson and stand-in Skip McClaren at Caspar Beach. *(Lemos)*

Left: Filming at Portuguese Beach, Mendocino *(Wagner/MHR)*

Filming at Caspar Beach. *(Wagner/MHR)*

Mendocino Coast extras await a very earthly horror on the loose. *(Avco Embassy Pictures)* Identified: Left of car: George Halter, Behind car: Bob Avery.

Jim Cruttenden, Tim & Susan Aguilar, Jill Lemos *(Wagner/MHR)*

Melody Anderson and James Farentino enjoy a happy moment, not knowing what lies beneath the surface of peaceful Potter's Bluff.
(Avco Embassy Pictures)

Michael Pataki and James Farentino prepare to exhume the body of the mysterious stranger whose death sparks *Dead & Buried*.
(Avco Embassy Pictures)

Hearse at Catholic Church and Mendocino graveyard scenes.
(Wagner/MHR)

A well-made gory thriller about bizarre murders in a small New England town, with even more scares when the corpses come back to life. Probably best not to watch it late at night.

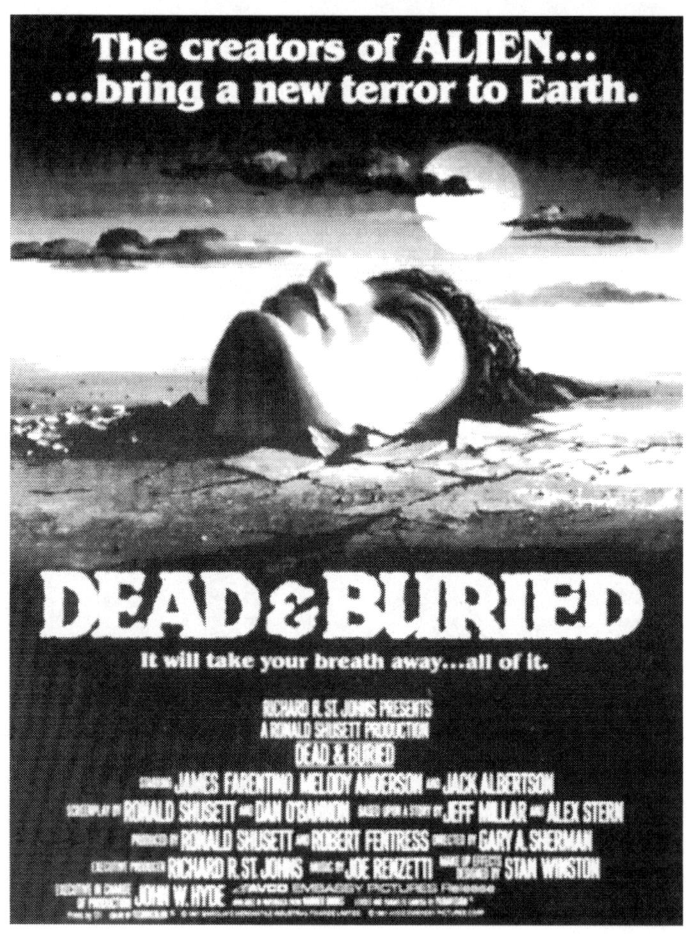

Cujo — 1982

The Movies Return To Mendocino

Cujo, a rabid St. Bernard written about in a recent Stephen King novel, will be the subject of Mendocino's next movie production starting in early October.

The tentative 10-day shooting schedule has been set back for the second time in the Sun Classics production, directed by Peter Medich, this time due to the sudden illness of production director Jack King who entered the hospital recently. King was replaced by Neil Machlis. Shooting schedules, according to Sun Productions representative Debra Lawson, have not been finalized.

The 1981 best selling King novel revolves around a family and its St. Bernard which follows a rabbit into a cave only to be bitten by a rabid bat causing a variety of suspensful happenings.

Exterior shots will be filmed in Mendocino utilizing a facade constructed in front of the Mullner Mansion overlooking Mendocino Bay. The facade is a replica of the Nielson Mansion in Santa Rosa where most of the interior shots will be filmed. Some interior shots will be filmed in Petaluma also, according to Toni Lemos, county movie coordinator.

The book takes place in Castle Rock, Maine, calling for exterior shots of the mansion on the coast. According to a source at the site of the construction, the facade will be 100 feet wide by 26 feet tall. Construction on the Victorian replica began Sept. 10.

After the facade is finished, the landscaping consisting of shrubery and a sodded hillside will be done before the shooting begins, he said.

Lemos said the Evergreen Cemetery will be used in some night scenes and portions will be filmed outside St. Anthony's Catholic Church, Pine Beach Inn tennis courts, and the Shell Station—to be disguised as a bus station.

Because the cast has not been hired, Lawson said, she could not confirm that locals will be hired as extras for the movie.

Though earlier quotes in the *Press Democrat*, taken from the permit hearing before the board of supervisors last Tuesday, estimated $500,000 would be spent in in Mendocino County, Lawson said many of the decisions concerning expenditures have not been made.

A Santa Rosa contractor, Jack Funk, was used construct the facade; local businesses, such as Baxman Gravel in Fort Bragg, were subcontracted to do the work.

—*Mendocino Beacon*, September 23, 1982

Shell building on Lansing Street becomes Greyhound bus station. *(Mendocino Beacon)*

Scene at bus station being filmed. *(Mendocino Beacon)*

All The Town's A Stage

By Rob Fowler

"Cujo," a suspense movie bcing filmed in Mendocino this week, "is about fear," said producer Dan Blatt of Sun Classics Productions in an interview with the Beacon this week.

"The bare essence of the film is how a nightmarish fantasy of a child became a reality, and what one mother will do to save her child," hc said, giving praise to the Stephen King novel of the same name on which the movie is based.

The film begins with a scene of sleepy Castle Rock, Maine, recreated by Lansing and Ukiah Streets in Mendocino. The one-minute shot, which took a crew of 50 workers all afternoon, night and morning to film, sets a "once upon an evening" atmosphere to the movie. The inside shots will be filmed later in Santa Rosa.

Castle Rock or Mendocino, the scene is easy to picture, a family moves to thc country to escape the city. But their escape is to a house with a memory of mass murder lurking in the closet (ironically filmed in front of the home of Mendocino's most recent major crime).

Because of the haunted house reputation, the youngster begins to see "monsters in the closet," Blatt explains. But when a dog is bitten by a rabid bat, the monster episode becomes real.

"In the real world there are monsters—criminals," Blatt said. "They have to be confronted like Cujo. This is a story about what a mother will do to save her child."

The mother is played by Dee Wallace, who recently gained much attention as the mother in the blockbuster "E.T." She and Blatt teamed up previously for "The Howling."

"Wallace is terrific," Blatt said of his star. "She worked hard in E.T., but this will be a different, greater role for her. She is asked to perform a tremendously wide range of emotions in this movie."

Wallace will be co-staring with Daniel Michael Harly, who appeared in "Ryan's Hope," as well as having been a regular on "Chicago Story." Dee's son is played by Danny Pintara who has been cast in television commercial roles thus far.

Dee's real life husband, Chris Stone, played Dee's husband in "The Howling," but in this movie he portrays "Steve Kemp" the other half of an affair she is trying to break off.

The movie is directed by Peter Medak whose history is as interesting as any movie. As a 19-year-old he left Hungary for England when the Russians entered the country. He entered the movie business there and has since directed a list of movies which includes "The Ruling Class" with Peter O'Toole, "Negatives" with Glenda Jackson in 1969 (his first movie), "Joe Egg" with Albert Finney, "Changling" with George C. Scott, and "Zorro" with George Hamilton.

Art Direction is by Guy (pronounced Gee) Comtois. The director of photography is Anthony Richmond, whose past work includes "Don't Look Now," starring JuIie Christie and Donald Sutherland.

"All of those men are great artists in their own right," Blatt said.

Blatt's credits are extensive. "The Howling," "Raid on Entebbe," "I Never Promised You a Rose Garden" and an award-wining CBS special "The Children Nobody Wanted," stand out as his major achievements. He was in Mendocino once before filming "Jeremiah of Jacob's Neck" in 1976.

Asked about the uncommon Mendocino County Movie Ordinance, which was formed in between his works here, Blatt said he couldn't speak for other film agencies regarding any alleged hinderance, but said, "We're very happy to be here. But this is your town. If you have rules, we feel like we should abide. This experience has been a positive one. We hope you would want us back when it's over."

He commented that local film organizer Toni Lemos, "has been very good to work with."

The shooting is scheduled to continue through Saturday, Oct. 9, at which time the crew will look to the Santa Rosa area for filming in the Neilson Mansion there, which the recently constructed facade above the northern bank of Big River duplicates Those indoor scenes, he said, should take about 7-8 more weeks.

The release date of the film is undetermined.

Filming occurred Thursday and Friday nights and resumed on Lansing Street Monday as the town received a redecorating job to look like Castle Rock.

"Castle Rock Motors," "Castle Rock Volunteer Fire Dept," "Welcome to Castle Rock" and a Greyhound Bus sign were all new to the town this week.

Filming on Monday afternoon attracted a healthy crowd on Lansing Street as locals and tourists took advantage of beautiful weather to gather on the fringes of the makeshift outdoor studio. The patient were treated to a good look at the complications of making a short segment of a film.

The scene showing supporting actors William Sanderson, Kaiulani Lee (the "Helen Jamesian" leader in "The World According to Garp") and Billy Jacobi driving up to the bus stop (portrayed by the Shell building), holding a depressing conversation on the walk to the bus and a short goodbye hug.

The scene was practiced several times before the final shot with the camera positioned on a track for steady manueverability.

Just before the film was rolled for the final take, a manager requested audience participation through silence and the actors were on their way.

—*Mendocino Beacon*, October 7, 1982

Facade erected on Mollner House located on Crestwood Drive, east Mendocino. (*Lemos*)

Cujo on to Santa Rosa; fireworks fizzle

Filming of "Cujo" by Sun Classics Productions was slated to end yesterday, Wednesday, after several staff changes canceled a previously scheduled fireworks display and forced the crew to extend its business in Mendocino four days longer than scheduled.

Filming this week included several shots at the facade built in front of the Mollner Mansion north of Big River, and the Catholic Church. Some scenes of actors driving around town were scheduled to be shot Wednesday.

Sun Classics Production Associate Mario Iscovich said problems with obtaining fireworks also contributed to the downfall of Friday night's scheduled fireworks display on the Mendocino Headlands. The event was rescheduled for Tuesday evening, but a heavy fog again stopped the production.

Iscovich said the scene will either be scrapped or done somewhere in Santa Rosa where the group expects to begin seven weeks of filming on Thursday.

Producers called a meeting Wednesday morning to announce staff changes after three days of filming had been completed. Installed as director was Louis Teague, whose previous credits include "Lady in Red," "Alligator," and "Fighting Back."

The company dominated the Jackson Street and Crestwood Drive area in East Mendocino while filming mansion scenes, but Iscovich commented he has received no complaints from neighbors, and said of Mendocino "this is one of the better sites we've filmed in."

Traffic blockage occurred Monday and Tuesday on Lansing St., while the company filmed a scene in which actors boarded a Greyhound Bus in front of the Paperboy. He said complaints were expressed from drivers forced to detour, but he and producer Dan Blatt both considered the public participation "great."—*Mendocino Beacon*, October 14, 1982

Your most horrible fear is the one that comes true.

What's the scariest thing you can think of? A fanged vampire? A moldy, centuries-dead ghoul sprung to life? A demonic slasher who can't die? Chances are the things that frighten you most are not from filmdom's Hall of Horror but from everyday life. Things like a child's fear of the dark. The loss of a job. A car spinning out of control on a rain-slicked street.

Cujo is the story of an everyday family coping with its own everyday fears, until suddenly those fears coalesce and materialize as a living nightmare: a slavering, flesh-ripping beast of horror. Now the family must summon every ounce of its strength and cunning to battle that terrifying entity . . . to the death.

Says Stephen King, the best-selling author whose novel provided the basis for *Cujo*, "I like to scare people and people like to be scared. That's what I'm here to do." And that's exactly what King does, time and time again. It's likely that more Jujubes, nachos and popcorn have been spilled in fumble-fingered fright during King movies than any other films.

So get ready for *Cujo,* an irrestible movie force. But first, get a good grip on your popcorn.—*Warner Home Video*

Dee Wallace in a scene from *Cujo. (Warner Bros.)*

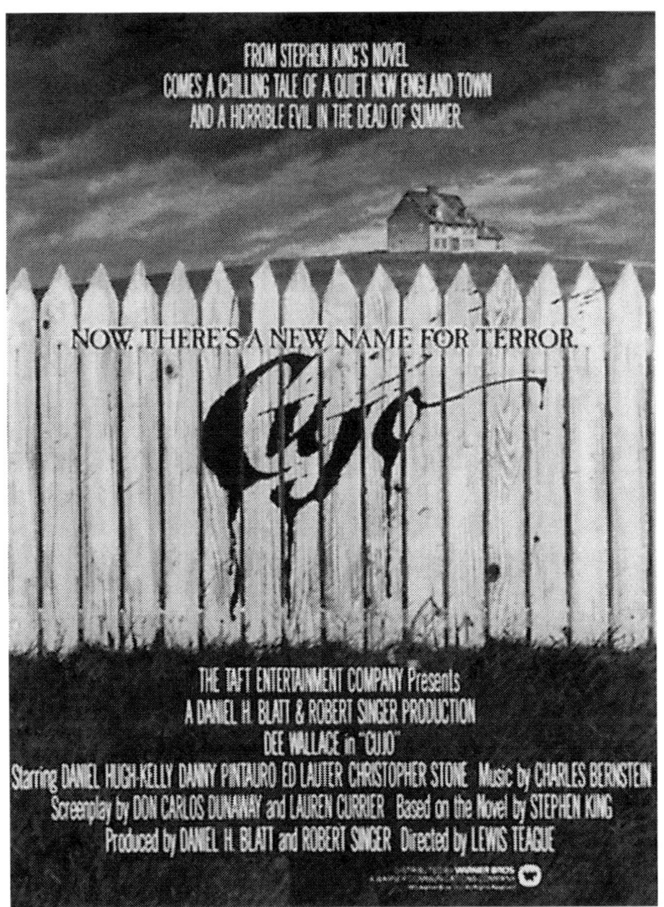

This harrowing tale of a woman and her child trapped in a car while being attacked by a rabid dog is not a film viewers ever forget. *Cujo* is considered a cult classic by horror movie lovers.

Video Disc Filmed Locally

Movie making on the Mendocino Coast has seemingly returned in force. Recently residents of the town of Mendocino were treated to the scene of film crews and actors for the filming of "Cujo," and just last week several South Coast locations were used for the filming of "Treasure."

The movie will also be shot in New York, New Orleans, the Grand Canyon, and Oregon. The story is about a girl who loses a horse when her father dies and spends 15 years looking for it.

Sheldon Renan Productions, the producer of "Treasure" found out about the South Coast through Ken Rosen who acted as local coordinator on the project.

Many different locations were used over a period of several days. The OZ house in Point Arena was used one night for a masquerade party scene in which the whole Gloriana Opera Company from the Mendocino-Fort Bragg area acted. According to Si Kroll of OZ, other filming was also done at OZ's suspension bridge.

A local cemetery and Gualala Point were also filming locations. Camera man Dennis Matsuda dangled out of a helicopter to film Leilani White of Manchester riding Virginia Sorensen's stallion Galafas along the beach at sunset.

White, with her long black hair, served as a double in the scene for the star of the film, Dory Dean.

With all the local excitement many residents are understandably anxious to see the film in the theater, but the film is not planned for theater distribution at all. The film will be made into a video disc to help promote new video disc technology.

To that end, a contest will be run with the film. A gold plated horse with a safe deposit box key inside, worth

Leilani White, Producer Sheldon Renan, Dory Dean & Cameraman Dennis Matsuda.

$150,000, will be buried in one of the filming locations. Movie viewers will be able to use their video disc equipment to find clues as to where the treasure is.

Due to be completed in about a month, the video disc's release is set for June, and three other similar discs are planned for the future.

—Independent Coast Observer, November 12, 1982

(Photographs by Eleanor White)

Dory Dean, star of *Treasure*.

Stunt double Leilani White of Manchester, Northern California Women's Bareback Riding Champion, riding Treasure (Galafas).

**Somewhere is a Horse of Gold.
A Treasure of $500,000 waits for you!**

A Prize of Over $500,000... Watch this magnificent film. Find the hidden clues. Then, solve the puzzle and lay claim to the most fabulous buried treasure of modern time!

Shot on location throughout America, with an original stereo soundtrack, TREASURE: In Search of the Golden Horse is both a spellbinding fantasy film and a challenging puzzle. In this program are all the clues you need to locate a buried treasure worth over $500,000!

The Film...

TREASURE: In Search of the Golden Horse is the story of a girl whose father and Arabian stallion disappear. Also gone is a solid gold statuette of her horse. She searches across America, following obscure trails, mysterious maps and clues from curious strangers. Join her in her search, because it is up to you, the viewer, to find the golden statue. . .and claim the $500,000 prize!

The Puzzle...

Within this program are *all* the clues you need to locate the golden horse. It is waiting for you, somewhere in the continental U.S., in a place open to the public twenty-four hours a day, seven days a week. Inside the horse is the key to a safe deposit box that contains the $500,000 prize.

TREASURE: In Search of the Golden Horse does not require that you travel the country in your search—you can unravel the clues in the comfort of your home and make one trip to claim your prize! Start today— the golden horse and the $500,000 prize goes only to the first person to solve the puzzle. Be sure to refer to the contest rules that appear at the end of the program.

—*Intravision/Vestron Video*

Treasure: In Search of the Golden Horse is an unusual movie, in that it was never intended to be shown in theatres or on television. When filming began in 1982, it was to be used as an example for the then new video technology, the videodisc, which allowed one to jump to any part of the movie with great speed—the predecessor of today's interactive CD-ROM. But before the film was completed, funding ran out and the project was shelved. The following year a book was published by Warner/Intravision, the film completed, and a videotape placed on sale. The contest was announced and the reward money put in an escrow account. The buried treasure had to be found within five years, otherwise it would be donated to a national charity. Naturally the contest generated a fair degree of publicity and treasure seekers around the world tried to use the clues, solve the puzzle, and find the Golden Horse (actually gold-plated brass)—which held a key to a safe deposit box containing $500,000. But although the clues and cryptograms contained in the movie enabled one to crack the codes, no one succeeded. So in August, 1989 an executive of the Big Brothers/Big Sisters of America Foundation was told where to dig for the Golden Horse and the money was awarded to that organization.

Obviously, *Treasure: In Search of the Golden Horse* cannot be judged like other motion pictures, as its purpose was quite different. Judged by the videotape alone—which is not really fair—it certainly would not have been a theatrical success, but the film contains some beautiful camera work and Dory Dean's acting is quite good. Some sequences using local extras are very interesting. The book, videotape and videodisc are long out of print.

Racing With The Moon — 1983

Love story may be filmed on coast
by Rob Fowler

A 20th Century Fox 1940's love story could be the next movie filmed in Mendocino, county officals said this week.

County movie coordinator Toni Lemos of Mendocino said Monday she was awaiting word from director Richard Benjamin on the company's decision on the location of the (tentatively titled movie) "Racing with the Moon."

Benjamin was given a tour of the Mendocino coast last Monday by Lemos' daughter, Jain Lemos, and was reportedly pleased with the area but, Lemos said, the company has been searching for locations as far north as Canada and budget decisions were not expected to be finalized until later this week.

Should Mendocino be elected as the site, filming will begin in April or May.

Benjamin, the star of several movies for televison and cinema, was reportedly interest-
in the California Western Railroad station and several pre-1940s constructed homes suitable for both interior and exterior shots in the script.

Mendocino's now famous movie ordinance was drafted three years ago when residents complained of inconveniences from companies which filmed in the streets and at night allegedly without regard for the community.

The ordinance regulates the filming only in public places. After the adoption of the ordinance some community leaders complained that revenue was being lost because the ordinance was detracting filmmakers from the county.

No word was available on what permits would be needed for "Racing with the Moon."

—*Fort Bragg Advocate-News,* February 9, 1983

Steam engine wanted for film

Old Engine No. 45 may be running down the California Western Railroad tracks sooner than expected, but it won't be going more than a few yards past the depot.

Twentieth Century Fox will be filming "Racing with the Moon" on the Mendocino Coast from April 25 to May 31, and the director, Richard Benjamin, wants to use the steam engine for final movie scenes.

That's the word according to Toni Lemos, Mendocino County film coordinator.

An inspector from the Federal Railroad Administration is expected to examine the engine early next week to determine if it can be put back to work, Lemos said.

"If it can be fixed up enough to use I'm sure they will do it but the decision is entirely up to them," Lemos said.

It would cost approximately $112,000 to completely renovate the engine, according to Henry Foltz, California Western Railroad general manager.

Lemos said how much money the film company might contribute toward repair of the engine has not been mentioned. "I'm sure they will do whatever is reasonable," Lemos said.

Plans would not likely include getting the engine completely fixed up, but painted and operational to the point of appearing realistic in the film.

"They will paint it at least and prepare it for display," Lemos said, "to preserve it for the community after the filming."

Scenes in which the engine would be used are at the conclusion of the movie when several young boys go off to fight in World War II.

The steam engine would be seen pulling out of the CWR station.

A contribution from the film company could be a lot of help for a group currently organizing to repair and operate the steam engine, which was put out of service in 1980.

The group is now in the process of forming a nonprofit entity to raise money for the restoration of the locomotive.

A preliminary public meeting was held last night by the group at the Chamber of Commerce office.

The locomotive has several problems, some of which occurred when the engine was derailed on its approach to the Skunk Depot in 1980.

Besides the damage from the derailment, the boiler systems needs quite a bit of repair work.

In May of 1959, an article on the Skunk line was published in National Geographic, giving the attraction quite a bit of notoriety.

It was in 1964 that CWR purchased a steam engine and several old passenger cars to use on the line, and it became the first railroad to convert from a diesel to steam powered engine.

For 15 years Engine 45 took passengers through the redwoods on a trip from Fort Bragg to Willits. Business was so good another engine designated No. 46, was purchased in 1968.

But with the derailment of No. 45 and boiler problems with both 45 and 46, the engines were retired to a spur line south of the Georgia-Pacific roundhouse, where they sit today.—*Fort Bragg Advocate,* April 1, 1983

Old Engine No. 45, with Director Richard Benjamin (dark jacket) at 'Skunk' terminal.*(Lemos)*

Movie plans outlined by director

by Rob Fowler

"We've found a new home," said "Racing with the Moon" director Richard Benjamin describing his crew's newfound affection for Mendocino Tuesday night as the moviemaker unveiled plans for the coast's next movie.

"It was as if (author) Steve Klobes saw Mendocino first and wrote about it," Benjamin said describing his amazement over how well the Mendocino Coast matched the beautiful surroundings described by the Santa Cruz-reared Klobes screenplay for the film—being billed as a tender romantic comedy set during the second World War.

In a well-received and often humorous informal gathering at the Kelley House in Mendocino Tuesday night, the internationally-known director/actor replayed his and Mendocino movie coordinator Tony Lemos' fateful drive around the area in search of scene locations.

With script in hand Benjamin posed what he considered to be troublesome scenes, beginning with an episode at a secluded pond, an ocean bluff scene and dance in the Redwoods. Each time, to his amazement, Lemos turned a few corners and presented him with exactly what he had imagined in the script.

Then he thought he'd stumped her by mentioning the need for a 1943-era train and, you guessed it, the once tattered Skunk steamer is now being dressed up like new for the movie and future display.

The movie will offer many on the coast a glimpse of what things were like in the 40s, and several local residents will be transported back via participation in the script.

At least 80 high school-age youths, styled in the haircuts of the-40s, will be needed for a scene to be filmed at two campuses. People used as extras on the sidewalks will walk by vintage-1940's Chevrolets parked on streets repainted with the once-prevalent white line down the center instead of today's yellow.

The story revolves around two 17-year-old boys sort of going to high school in the west coast town of Point Muir (which is actually the coast) just before their induction into the Marines.

One of the youths, Hopper (Sean Penn), casts his eyes upon the girl of his dreams dancing in the woods and falls in love during the often confusing and uncertain six weeks preceeding his departure to a war zone.

Without giving away too much of the script, Benjamin said Hopper, the son of the town's grave digger, suspects the girl is rich and belongs to the family which owns the "mansion on the hill" where he courts her.

Early on in the movie, however, it is discovered by the viewers that she is instead the maid's daughter, and for reasons to be pondered, she fails to make it clear to her new love.

Penn is currently on display across the country in the movies "Bad Boys" and "Fast Times at Ridgemont High" and played the role of Tim Hutton's best friend in the movie "Taps."

—*Fort Bragg Advocate-News,* April 27, 1983

Elizabeth McGovern & Director Richard Benjamin on Main St. in Mendocino. *(Paramount)*

Elizabeth McGovern & Sean Penn in romantic scene, Mendocino Headlands. *(Paramount)*

Sean Penn, Nicholas Cage and extras in Red Cross scene at Cotton Auditorium, Fort Bragg. *(Paramount)*

Filming begins next week

Most of the filming in Mendocino for "Racing With the Moon" will be done during a three-day period next week and will require some traffic blockage.

Movie officials spelled out the tenative schedule to begin Monday morning, May 2, with shooting expected to be completed in Mendocino by Wednesday.

The most uncomfortable time for residents, directors said, will be early Tuesday morning when traffic will be blocked at times on Main Street from the Mendocino Hotel to Pepperwood Potters. Congestion is expected to be reduced to a minimum by 10 a.m. that morning, about the time most shops are opening.

Parking will be most disrupted during this time, as the 40s-era scenes require early model cars to be displayed along the sidewalks.

"It won't took good to have your 1981-car parked next to our '38 Chevy," director Richard Benjamin explained.

Foot traffic will be disrupted slightly during the filming, but, as one shop owner explained, the congestion caused by people watching the movie-makers will deter shoppers the most.

One official said a shuttle bus will be offered in Mendocino Tuesday for residents forced to park away from their destination. No specifics were available on its route at press time.

After Tuesday the filming will move to the block surrounding Mendosa Brother's store on Lansing St., with shooting confined to a more condensed area, it was announced.

The moviemakers are not exactly asking for any of this free. They have refurbished the Skunk Train, donated to Mendocino Community Library and School District and rented school-grounds at rates which would make bed and breakfast owners more than envious.

Approximatcly $400,000 was donated to the libraries and more than $2000 has been donated to the Middle School project while an undisclosed sum was spent stoking up the steam engine

The tentative shooting schedule for Fort Bragg, expected to be released today, is centered at Laurel Street between California Western Railroad and the Franklin Street intersection.

There will bc some rerouting of traffic to allow filming of the Green Parrot—a movie theater in the film—to the Treasure Cove to keep newer model cars out preserving the early '40s look.

—*Fort Bragg Advocate-News*, April 27, 1983

Stepping Back in Time

With the help of about 30 townsfolk, Mendocino stepped back in time this week to help foster a 1940s love affair.

Spectators lined the streets this week watching the repetitious but somehow fascinating process of putting "Racing with the Moon" on celluloid.

Moviemakers, headed by director Richard Benjamin, began production on schedule Monday shooting backyard scenes at tbe corner of Carlson Street and Heeser Drive.

The movie's star, actor Sean Penn, spent the day practicing high hurdles as he repeatedly ran through a scene in which he escapes the jaws of a dog by beating it over a fence.

He caps the scene by turning to gloat victoriously at the giant animal but in a later scene in the movie, a stand-in was given the pleasure of having his pants ripped off by the dog who gets the last laugh.

Tuesday about 30 extras from Mendocino and Fort Bragg turned Main Street into a bustling walk through the 1940s. Old cars lined the streets and extras casually walked by framing a scene where Penn races across the headlands to steal the attention of co-star Elizabeth McGovern.

The series of scenes shot that afternoon began with Penn standing at the edge of the headlands overlooking Mendocino Bay. Binocular-clad he appears to be looking for a Japanese submarine which a nearby sign warns could be lurking off the coast.

Upon scanning the horizon he spots McGovern stepping out of a bus on Main street in front of the public library (Savings Bank of Mendocino).

In this early segment of the movie he is still forming a friendship and nervously paces in front of the building until she exits and he can continue pursuit down the street to where the "North Coast Bus Line" comes by to pick her up.

It was clearly evident at day's end that the filming of a movie can require patience by eveyone involved. Repeated rehearsals keep people occupied, but for many of the extras the days was spent sitting and waiting,

Betty Barber and Grail Dawson had good things to say about their experience as extras, but pointed out they stood on a street corner for over eight hours before being called to a modest performance.

"Our moment of glory was brief and obscure," said Dawson the next day. "It's a painstakingly slow process, but it is fun to be the observer."

Dawson earned his keep by stepping out of a car in the background of a scene, opening the door for Barber who got out with a bag of groceries. Look for it in the movie.

Barber, once a stand-in for Bette Davis, described the experience as "being a cog in a machine."

"You keep wishing they'd let you know what the machine was doing. Here you see the scene being made, but it's hard to get the big picture," she said.

Extras on Tuesday had just as long a day but it was filled with repeated walks down an unfamiliar Main Street which was transformed to meet the script and the era.

Aside from the most noticeable change at the Savings Bank, several shops agreed to change signs such as Zacha's Bay Window Gallery which became "Ida's" beauty salon, Dr. Hahn's office which turned into Baily's Drug Store, and tbe Shell Shop which became Luzato's Shoe Service, the latter completely remodeled inside to look and smell like a shoe shop.

Tbe extras, who were paid from $45 to $50 as well as earning a dinner of New York steak, started changing their appearance at 6:30 a.m. with the help of award winning designers hired for the production and were out on the streets by about 7:30 a.m.

"I think more attention is paid to detail in this wardrobe, not just because it is a period piece," said Amanda Avery, who has been an extra in two other Mendocino movies.

"This is a better crew than the other movies I've been in. Maybe these people feel more secure in their jobs. I'm impressed with most of the townspeople too. A lot of cars have been stopped, but the crew is good about letting people through. In other movies it wasn't that way."

"You have to come out here with a patient attitude because you're a human prop and you havc to rcmcmbcr that."

Two other extras from Mendocino, Abby and Janet, who had been walking up and down the street as background for hours were also impressed with the friendliness of the production people.

"The people we've worked with have been really nice, both in the dressing areas and on the streets," said Abby.

"They're very practiced at being cordial," explained Janet. "We've seen them put up with all kinds of s..., and they're handling it."

Another local, Cammie Conlon, said the filming was slow, but some of that was due to the ability of the crew to keep the streets open. "If they closed the streets to traffic," she said, "they would be out of here real fast."

Reactions from local bystanders to the filming were overwhelmingly positive despite traffic tie-ups.

Spectators, both locals and visitirs, who were interested enough to stand and watch the process said they didn't mind the obstructions. Persons who did mind probably didn't stay long enough to be interviewed.

"We've never had a complaint with a movie coming here," said a local couple as they watched an almost hidden from view scene being prepared.

"It brings in a lot of money and I think we can live with it."

Another couple from Healdsburg had been surprised by the fillming and said their stopover in Mendocino had turned into "a reminiscing thing."

"I was just 12 years old in the 1940s," the woman said, "but seeing this brings back some of the memories of bobby socks, haircuts and suits. For us this is a day back in our past and it's not in the way of anything we're doing."

Not everyone was pleased with the movie filming. Some business persons voiced complaints over the use of the sidewalk in front of their shops which they said hurt business.

One resident was less than impressed with the quality of the entertainment provided bythe moviemakers and termed it: "The same as always, the invasion of our town." Questioned further, however, he said he really didn't care that much about the tie-ups and upon hearing of donations to the community took a fairly neutral stance as he continued to look on.

Also, at least one employee of the Mendocino Savings Bank said it was necessary to explain to some customers that the bank wasn't going through its since-abandoned plants to move across town and no, this is not the library.—*Mendocino Beacon*, May 5, 1983

Richard Benjamin, Carol Kane and Nicholas Cage on Laurel Street., Fort Bragg. *(Paolinelli)*

Moviemakers Transform Laurel Street

Laurel Street took on the look of 1943 "Point Muir" Wednesday as shooting began in and out of local shops for Pararmount's "Racing with the Moon."

Coast residents and tourists took to the street watching with fascination as cameras, screens, and electricial hookups were put into place for morning and afternoon shooting inside the Green Parrot.

Those taking a night walk out on the town Thursday were treated to watching filmipg at the Paramount theatre between the "Barber Shoppe" and "North Coast Cafe."

The marquee, constructed by Santa Rosa Signs and featuring "My Favorite Blonde" as well as lighting by camera gave the spot an attention-catching glow.

Once ready to start Wednesday, observers saw extras walking back and forth in front of the Green Parrot and cars—one driven by Fort Bragg's Red Burke—driving past the ice cream shop and turning around to pass by it again.

That was just for background, as the shooting was going on inside, where the Parrotts new interior was garnished with a candy counter, brightly dressed counter workers and Christmas decor.

The new Coca-Cola window design on the Parrot was painted by Rick Sacks of Caspar. The little boy and girl sipping sodas, however, was removed.

Some people found even the lot where lunch was served interesting, with tables set up cafeteria style surrounded by a bus and trailers, "Cinzano" umbrellas propped up to shade food and a North Coast Bus Line Co. older model bus parked in the alley.

Everyone's got to eat.

Watching as the crew set up Fort Bragg residents Jo and Will Kelsey were fascinated witi the "movie people."

"We've lived here when other movies were filmed, but we've never come down to watch before," remarked Will Kelsey

Both Will and Jo were particularly struck by the attention to detail they have heard is going into this picture. Will is a history buff and has been involved with Kelley House in Mendocino.

He said that on Tuesday a painter sprayed some type of covering on the face of the Paramount "to make it look older because it was just freshly painted.

"Another guy came over and sprayed something else on it and it all ran together. You wondered what they were doing but look at it this morning. It looks just like it's two or three years old."

An example of just how much planning is taking place can be seen in the filmmakers' anxiousness to see an ABC documentary that will show how bowling pins were picked up manually before automation. A bowling alley scene will be shot for "Racing with the Moon" and the action needs to be authentic.

Reminiscing on younger days was easy for Jo Kelsey as she watched young cast member walk back and forth from the lot between the Advocate-News, City Hall and the set.

"Seamed stockings—one girl didn't know how they were worn I guess because instead of having them straight and centered in the back of the calf she had it twisting around her leg like this," she said, showing how girls in her youth did not wear their "hose."

Keeping the lines straight was important, she said.

"We had big, high pompadours, and that was during rationing when you could get only one pair of shoes and they usually were fabric," recalled Loretta Mayhew.

She remembered checking her stockings reflected in store windows as she passed for crooked seams as well.

Something became obvious after talking with various observers—everyone's a director. But most were unfamiliar enough with the game that they avoided armchair quarterbacking.

People noticed the smallest points, many of them possibly things that won't even be seen in the movie.

For instance, as the men who marshall the late '30 model cars moved an auto back to where somebody in charge wanted it, a few folks on that southside sidewalk noticed the car was blocking the theater's Fire Exit.

One lady asked a man with a radio if anyone cared about that. He replied it wouldn't be seen in the shot.

"I heard they painted the street white," said Jim Fite, who left City Hall just long enough to see that the tale was slightly exaggerated and only the yellow center line had been painted over.

Another question which many people had concerned was how close the ticket theatre booth was to the street.

The theater facade was put smack up against the building there and the booth protrudes well into the sidewalk.

"You couldn't very well take a chunk out of the building," explained movie publicist Bruce Bahrenburg.

As well, set coordinators told him some theaters of that period —such as the Acme in Syracuse, New York— had booths which stood out from the building.

Meanwhile, other Laurel businesses were changed as well. Posters advertising Nehi soft drinks adorned the windows of the Laurel Deli which in Point Muir is the "North Coast Cafe."

And The Copy Shop became the "The Optimo" selling cigars, tobacco and soft drinks.

Many people said they wished the theater could stay. They liked its looks.

The filming activity also caused an increase in traffic along Franklin St. as people came in their cars to see the excitment was all about.

Filming in Noyo Harbor will follow Saturday night and shooting on the Skunk Railroad line will be May 28 and June 6 at the depot, with schedules subject to change.

—*Fort Bragg Advocate-News*, May 20, 1983

Green Parrot and State Theatre
to live again in movie
by Cindy Friday

In the nostalgic eyes of Lena Paolinelli, the Green Parrot is a location made for a lightly romantic movie like "Racing with the Moon," now being filmed in Fort Bragg.

Paramount began filming the movie about two weeks ago, and the Green Parrot is only one of many locations being used for setting the scene in the film's fictional town of Point Muir.

Improvements have given the Green Parrot a new look. Walls have taken on lighter color and have been "antiqued," a Paramount painter explained. The bar has been refinished, windows repainted, and some floor tiles have been replaced.

Regulars past and present might miss the organ which has been removed. It will not be returning, says Lena, owner of the Green Parrot.

Lena recalled that the little known Fort Bragg ice cream parlor was started in 1929 by Ray Ware. It wasn't until Jan. 1, 1947 that Lena and her husband "bought the fixtures and the utensils."

Lena and husband Pete worked together in the fountain at the same time Pete worked as a projectionist for the old State Theatre, a position he had held since the 1920's, or around 40 years. The theater was closed in the early 1960s.

As well he worked at the Liberty and at the old Rockport Theatre, according to news articles.

As a projectionist Pete worked in the days when highly flammable nitrate film was shown on hand-crank projectors, and people learned what was playing at the silent films and talkies by handbills.

"In 'The Russians Are Coming, The Russians Are Coming' (made in 1966 and starring Alan Arkin and Jonathan Winters), he worked with developing film to make sure everything they took came out," says Lena.

"He worked with Jane Wyman in "Johnny Belinda" (filmed here in 1948)," she proudly recalls. Wyman won an Oscar for best actress in the picture. Wyman is currently in the starring role of popular television show Falcon Crest.

Showing off a picture with Pete and Jane on the stage of the State, she notes Jane was accepting an orchid corsage.

"She was so nervous she was tearing the orchids. Can you imagine, a movie star being nervous?"

The theatre front being erected in front of Treasure Cove (across the street from the Green Parrot) is an amalgam of the State Theatre which was built in the '30s and operated here in the '40s and other theatres of the '40s period.

A spokesman for "Racing with the Moon" explained the Laurel Street facade will look like a "neighborhood theatre but more baroque—complete with a marquis, glass cases and posters.

The old State sat on the College of the Redwoods parking lot at Pine Avenue and Main Street. The succeeding Coast Theatre on Franklin Street was built in 1964.

A picture painted some 25 years ago by Dot (Racine)

The Green Parrot Ice Cream Parlor, with its famous sign. *(Paolinelli)*

Johnson and given to Neil McBurney, former manager of the State and Coast Theatre, has been used along with other records by movie researchers to create the movie theater's facade in "Racing with the Moon."

Lena thinks the remake on Laurel looks quite a bit like the original State.

Though the old theaters are gone, the Green Parrot remains.

For the last five years, Lena says she has closed it for one month periods in summer and fall to vacation to faraway places.

Her hiatuses have taken her a to nearly 20 countries—including China, Japan, Italy, Greece, Spain and Turkey.

"I walked the wall in China. Maybe you ought to include that. Not everybody does that," she suggests.

"It had been the kids' hangout until I started closing and people started going other places," she reminisces.

The fountain of the Green Parrot. *(Paolinelli)*

Filming on Laurel Street, Fort Bragg. *(Paolinelli)*

In "Racing with the Moon" the "hangout" is exactly what the place will become again, according to Associate Producer Art Levinson.

"Many people have fallen in love here, got married, and now their children and grand-children come in," she says.

For now, the fountain "is more or less something to come to," she says, indicating she's not really interested in drumming up business.

In past days when the place was far busier, Lena's family worked there—"when cokes were five cents."

Leaving her travels and turning to talk of local history, Lena notes this is not the first time the Green Parrot has been in a movie.

A group of students from the University of California Los Angeles, headed by director Jim Scaiffe, filmed "Scarlet Ibis" in Fort Bragg in February of 1977.

Lena recalled they used only the eatery's bar "and someone coming in through the door." She has no idea what happened to the movie after the group left.

But she recalls no changes in the restaurant were made for that movie, the Green Parrot having appeared pretty much as it was, unlike "Racing with the Moon."

The lights which have been added to the Green Parrot are from Ma's Laundromat, she adds.

Interestingly, Lena will have to apply for a permit if she wants the neon Green Parrot sign to remain hanging after the movie is completed, said City Building Official James K. Fite.

Though the green glow welcomed pleased customers years ago, its re-hanging qualifies it as a new neon sign. Fort Bragg's sign ordinance prohibits the installation of new neon signs, he said.

Some people say they like the parrot sign better than the Golden State Ice Cream recently taken down, Fite understands.

"People like it up there," agrees the Green Parrot's owner.

Perhaps the best thing that can be said about the unique sign is tht it will be on film for all to see upon the movie's realease, and for Coast residents it has been a nice reminder of the past.

After filming is over the Green Parrot soda fountain, Lena insists, will be once again open for customers.

—*Fort Bragg Advocate-News,* May 18, 1983

Extras Kevin Fraser, John Schweikert, Scott Hamilton & Jeff Walsh.
(Lemos)

Extras Harry Rothman and Lee Edmundson.

LOCALS in the MOVIES
"Racing With The Moon"
Bonnie and Biage Quattrochi: extras

Bonnie: We'd let Toni Lemos (local coordinator for films) know quite a while ago that we'd be interested in working on a movie. We'd almost forgotten about it when she called us. We had no idea of the amount of work that went into making a film.

Biage: I didn't mind the haircut they made me get, and the clothes were something. In fact l told 'em, don't pay me, just let me keep the shoes!

Bonnie: But those clothes put 10-15 years on the women! It was dressing like my mother used to dress ... we had a 6:30 a.m. call on the day this picture was taken, and had walked about five miles ... we were as tired as we looked.

Biage: The deal was pretty good though—$45 a day and the meals were unbelievable. Petit fours and steak .... I feel very fortunate to have had this type of exposure to the process of the film business. It's another part of life we never would have known ... we've done three days now and we're looking forward to doing another.

Jim Lamb: stand-in

It's not such hard work. The waiting around is harder than the doing of it. As a stand-in—well, first the actors do a rehearsal for the cameraman with the director. We watch. Then they call in the Second Team (that's us—they're the First Team). We stand on the marks, walk through the motions, get measured. They set the lights, make sure the technical aspect of the scene works. Meanwhile the actors don't have to exhaust themselves.

The money's a real gain. And it's a chance to be extremely close to the production of a film. To be there. I'm learning a lot and the food's good. The night shots late in the week are the hardest because I work from 6 a.m. on weekends at my regular job. So I've been learning about endurance ...

Judy Christian: extra

I've enjoyed it, except for a bad hour sitting in an old bus with fumes rising. But other than that, great. The money's good, the people are nice, and it's a change from any job I've ever had in this area.

Lee Edmundson: extra

I was hoping for a job as a stand-in. In terms of money and also experience-wise the stand-ins have the best deal, I think. But then, the extras actually get to be seen on screen ...

I think it was great. Not only fun but incredibly educational. I went to see "Bad Boys" the other night and I had a whole new insight into how they got certain shots, a new understanding of the work that goes into "the magic of cinema." The TEAMWORK that's involved! No bull, no temper tantrums, just focused hard work. It's a lesson in professionalism for me as an actor, as a director, as a technician ..

Sue Zipp: extra

The Paramount people are really incredible. They've all been doing it for 18-20 years, and they're tight, together, and NICE. Watching the cinematographer and the director was like watching the Bobbsey Twins in action. The costumers were wonderful, cheerful, and very thorough.

I did it for four nights. The first night was great fun. There we were in this bus with half the seats gone, and lights and cameras set up in the bus, the crew were there—we had lotsa laughs. The next night was Saturday and there was more pressure to wrap it up early. A lot of us were very tired. But nobody ever freaked out. A very few people from Hollywood were on little ego trips—me biggie, you extra—but most everyone else was great. It'll be nice to write home to Mom about it ...—*Arts & Entertainment,* June, 1983

Sean Penn and Nicholas Cage on the Skunk tracks in Fort Bragg. *(Paramount)*

Artfully directed by Richard Benjamin, *Racing with the Moon* is a film so tender, so insightful, so full of heart that you'll never quite forget it. This is the story of Henry "Hooper" Nash (Sean Penn) and his buddy Nicky (Nicholas Cage) enjoying their last boyish exploits before they enter the marines. Elizabeth McGovern portrays Penn's mysterious girlfriend. What ensues is a tender, bittersweet tale of lost innocence and the trauma of growing up too fast. The result is a magic moment, brilliantly captured within the emotional crosscurrent of America's most dramatic time—*Paramount Home Video*

Although *Racing with Moon* certainly is an overly sentimental love story, as a reflection of its times the film works exceedingly well. The Coast people who worked in it liked their jobs and the film has become a viewing favorite.

Sutters Bay — 1983

A 30 minute comedy pilot broadcast on CBS on August 15, 1983 that starred Granville Van Dusen and Linda Carlson, a couple who leave New York to start a new and less complicated life only to discover that there are other problems afoot in their new community. The story is set in a small American town, Sutters Bay, and depicts comical incidents in the lives of the residents. The pilot episode, however, relates a serious matter when the school teacher, Emma Frye, protests being fired because she is single—and pregnant.

The principal actors were Susan Kellermann, as Monnie, the waitress at the Koffee Kup Diner; Dennis Burkley as Sheriff Ward; Alice Ghostley as Elfreda, the telephone operator; Granville Van Dusen as Jeff Hamner, editor of the Sutters Bay Advocate; Linda Carlson as Barbara Hamner, Jeff's wife; Frank Cady as Doc Medford, the town physician; and Meg Wyllie as Margaret Pierson, Jeff's assistant. The producers and writers were Mort Lachman and Sy Rosen, the director was Bill Persky.—*CBS Entertainment*

Granville Van Dusen and Linda Carlson (*CBS Entertainment*)

Sutters Bay was filmed at Noyo and Mendocino, apparently very fast and with no local media attention.

CBS films locally for new TV series

Camera crews were on location in Fort Bragg and, along the Mendocino Coast this week filming the opening segments for a new CBS television series staring movie actress Angela Lansbury.

The show will premier sometime this summer or fall on a CBS Movie of the Week and then become a weekly series. Although the movie and series will be filmed in Los Angeles, the Mendocino Coast footage is expected to be used each week to open the program.

The program is set in "Cabot's Cove, Maine," and Lansbury portrays a school teacher who also writes murder mysteries.

The first show for the movie is entitled, "The Murder of Sherlock Holmes," about a person dressed as the detective at a masqurade ball who is murdered. Arthur Hill also stars.

The latest filming was done Tuesday in front of the Blair House on Little Lake Street in Mendocino where Lansbury was filmed picking flowers and washing the windows of the house, which will represent her home in the series.

Jessica Fletcher (Angela Lansbury) inspects her flowers in the Blair House yard. *(Wagner/MHR)*

Amanda Avery of Mendocino worked with the cast as a stand-in and Rolf Stormer of Albion was Hill's double during an opening scene where Lansbury is traveling down the street in a Mercedes.

Other locations used were a "field trip" on the Mendocino Headlands, which used several Fort Bragg and Mendocino persons over 18 years old, a school bus scene at Cotton Auditorium, a Noyo Harbor scene and a bicycling club scene using several local women as members.

—*Mendocino Beacon*, May 17, 1984

Murder mystery filming continues

Mendocino—Local filming continued on the new CBS series "Murder, She Wrote," last week as film crews were in the Mendocino and Fort Bragg area taking shots for an upcoming episode.

The crews are expected to regularly return to the coast during the year for various shots.

This week local residents Bud Kamb, Cathy Hansen, Lew Harris and Rolf Stormer were used in several shots as stand-ins for the actors. Likewise, Alan Simon and Lawrence Bullock performed non-speaking roles as two deputies.

The episide, to be shown in the next few months, is titled "Hit, Run and Homicide" and features Van Johnson. Neither he nor the series star, Angela Lansbury, were on the coast for the filming, however. The episode involved a mechanical car which appears to operate without a driver.

A helicopter was used for the scenes over the Point Cabrillo Light House, Noyo Harbor and the town of Mendocino.

Two weeks ago a segment was shown featuring coastal residents Art Williams, Pam Hudson, Scott Wells and Doug Nunn.

—*Fort Bragg Advocate-News*, October 10, 1984

Toni Lemos, local film coordinator; Ann Campbell, executive director, Mendocino Histori-cal Research; Angela Lansbury; Jack Lemos, Mendocino Historical Research trustee—in front of Kelley House. *(Wagner/MHR)*

Film crew enjoyed local cooperation

by Martin Hickel

The 85-plus member cast and crew of "Murder, She Wrote" was busy Monday transforming Fort Bragg's Noyo Harbor into "Cabot Cove," the mythical Maine setting of the weekly television mystery series.

Scenes for two new episodes for the fall season, "Joshua Peabody Died Here, Possibly," and "Sticks and Stones" were filmed along the coast before the company was scheduled to fly out of Little River Airport on Wednesday.

Appearing in the productions are Angela Lansbury, who portrays mystery writer Jessica Fletcher and is the leading actress in the series, and John Astin, Chuck Conners, William Windom, Tom Bosley, Meg Foster and a number of other actors.

Additionally nearly 80 production crew members were involved in the filming.

The Universal Studio production occupied the town of Mendocino last week, providing an added attraction to vacationeers and locals alike, although some complaints were heard about the mock-highrise construction site erected on the Mendocino Headlands.

The construction site was being removed Tuesday with the area expected to be restored to its natural setting by yesterday.

"Talk about method acting, we had some extras show up who were already on their way down to protest the project anyway," said Brian Brosnan, location manager for the shoot.

In the sequence, which required digging a large hole and erecting a cyclone fence, a high-handed developer is blocked from putting up a building "out of character" with Cabot Cove; a clear case of life imitating art, Mendocino-style.

But in general, Brosnan said, the company has received great cooperation from the community. In return for the use of their premises for location shots, the studio made donations to a number of service groups and organizations including the Mendocino School and Fire Districts, Albion and Little River Volunteer Fire Departments, Fort Bragg Fire Department, Mendocino Recreation and Park District, Crown Hall, the Mendocino Presbyterian Church, St. Anthony's Church in Mendocino and the Kelly House.

"We don't want to give the impression that we just descend on the people here," Brosnan said. "We want them to know that what they're doing is just as important as what we do, more so in fact, because this is their home."

"I think it's wonderful they come here," said Jill Fosse, one of a number of stand-ins hired by Universal.

"A lot of us need the work, and they do pay well. I heard some merchants were complaining about the traffic, but I think we can use the money," she said.

Other local stand-ins for the stars were Pat Turner, Ken Turner, Bob Canclini, Jim Lamb, Peter Russel and Mervin Gilbert. In addition, locals were employed for set work and as extras in several crowd scenes.

—*Fort Bragg Advocate-News,* August 1, 1985

Filming on Main Street in front of the Mendocino Hotel. *(Wagner/MHR)*

Angela Lansbury and extra Jill Lemos Fosse. *(Wagner/MHR)*

Angela Lansbury, with guest stars Theodore Bikel and Heidi Bohay. *(Wagner/MHR)*

Another chapter finished
for 'Murder, She Wrote'
by Katherine Lee

"Quiet on the set!"

"Action!"

The camera rolls.

Somewhere in Cabot Cove, Maine, Jessica Fletcher, a bag of groceries clasped in her arms, and "Doc" Hazlett, are strolling along the sidewalk chatting when they come along Sheriff Tupper sticking a piece of paper under a windshield wiper on Doc's car.

Thinking he's just received a parking ticket a picqued Doc lays into the mild-mannered sheriff while Jessica quietly stands by and watches.

Enter handsome passerby, who recognizes Jessica as a long-lost acquaintance.

"Cut!"

Angela Lansbury, William Windom, Tom Bosley and guest star Leslie Nielsen relax.

Mimicing the scene in "Dead Man's Gold" they've just played, Lansbury and Nielsen make exaggeratedly surprised faces at each other and burst into laughter.

"Murder, She Wrote" was back in town.

Today is the last of 10 days actors and a Universal Studio film crew of 80 have spent in the Mendocino-Fort Bragg area shooling exterior scenes for the nation's number one rated television mystery show.

Filming for two episodes, "Dead Man's Cold" and "Obituary For A Dead Anchorman," has taken the highly mobile team to Noyo Harbor in Fort Brag, Mendocino and the Headlands, and back roads between the two towns. Interior sequences have already been completed in Southern Celifornia, according to Toni Lemo, Mendocino's liason to the film industry.

Both episodes will be aired in two to three months. They've make a total of six episodes filmed on the coast to date.

In addition to Nielsen, guest star of "Dead Man's Gold," Chad Everett and Abby Dalton journeyed to the coast for their roles in "Obituary to a Dead Anchorman."

A total of 150 locals have played background parts. Seven coastal individuals auditioned and were chosen for speaking parts in "Obituary For A Deadman," the story of a news program similar to "60 Minutes" but named "Scrutiny."

Kathy O'Grady plays the sole female reporter. Harry Rothman, Steve Jordan, Chris Byrne and Lindy Peters all play reporters. Peter Wells plays one of Tom Bosley's deputy sheriffs and Donovan Holtz plays a bartender.

Lawrence Bullock was selected for a silent part also as a deputy sheriff.

—*Fort Bragg Advocate-News*, September 16, 1986

The Masonic Temple becomes the Cabot Cove Courthouse. *(Wagner/MHR)*

The Mendocino Fire House becomes the Cabot Cove Fire House. *(Wagner/MHR)*

Filming on the Mendocino Headlands *(Ribiero)*

It's a wrap, movie makers go home
by Katherine Lee

The cast and crew of "Murder, She Wrote" are back in sunny southern California today, having completed filming in the Mendocino, Fort Bragg area Tuesday.

Noyo Harbor was the scene of the last shoots, after which Angelea lansbury, the series' endearing star, departed with her husband, Peter Shaw.

Both experior and interior scenes were filmed for two episodes, "Deadman's Gold" and "Obituary for a Dead Anchorman," which should be aired in two to three months, according to Toni Lemos, Mendocino's liason with Universal Studios.

Wednesday, a small group of the production team remained on the coast, seeing to the final details of what has become an annual event. This was the third year "Murder, She Wrote" has visited the coast.

"Everything went well," Mary Wehrle, production coordinator, said Wednesday afternoon. "Other than a bit of rain, we had no major problems."

For over a week, the fast-moving production crew shifted their trucks and equipment to a variety of locations locally, transforming familiar scenes and buildings into their East Coast, Cabot Cove counterparts.

In Mendocino, the windswept Headlands, Main and Lansing Streets served as backdrops for both episodes. The Masonic Hall became the Cabot Cove courthouse, Panache the mayor's office, and Circa the Lady of Fashion Boutique Store.

Exterior and interior scenes were filmed at the Hill House for both episodes. And Mendocino's Blair House, Jessica Fletcher's home, made its annual appearance with a freshly planted flower garden and (spray-painted) green lawn.

In Noyo Harbor, the "Suzy Q" was used in "Deadman's Gold," and a scene was filmed in the Tradewinds cocktail lounge.

Stars Lansbury, Tom Bleley and William Windom were joined by 20 co-stars and supporting actors and actresses.

Co-starring in "Deadman's Gold" were Leslie Nielsen and Robert Hogan, who plays a recurring character in the series.

Featured actors and actresses were Julia Mongomery, Wendy Kilbourne, J. Eddy Peck, Grant Goodeve, John Laughlin, Ian Ruskin and Sean McClory.

Handsome Chad Everett lead the cast for "Obituary for a Dead Anchorman," which included Kathleen Lloyd, Mark Stevens, Robert Pine, Robert Lipton, Abby Dolton, Rogan Hogan, Richard Paul, Eric Stern and Frank Annese.

Local celebrities landed parts in "Obituary" as well.

Kathy O'Grady, Harry Rothman, Steve Jordan, Chris Byrne, Lindy Peters, Peter Wells and Donovan Holtz all won speaking parts of at least one sentence. Lawrence Bullock played a silent role as one of Tom Bosley's deputy sheriffs.—*Mendocino Beacon*, September 23, 1986

Angela Lansbury and extra Marci Fosse *(Lemos)*

Sign erected on Mendocino Headlands for one episode.
(Wagner/MHR)

"Murder, She Wrote" is going into its fourth season and six of the episodes have already been shot in and about Mendocino. Now two more episodes are to be filmed here, back-to-back, three days each, for a total of six days.

In addition to Angela Lansbury, Tom Bosley and William Windom, stars who will be here are Ruth Roman, Gloria de Haven, Kathryn Grayson, Dody Goodman and Julie Adams. There will be six one-line bit parts for lucky locals who are chosen and quite a lot of $50-a-day extras will be hired from our community.

Mitch's Barber Shop will be a beauty shop, the Chocolate Moosse will be the travel agency, Alan Sussex says his new building will be the Mayor's office and work is to be done at Blair House, Russian Gulch Park Headquarters and down on Main Street.

—*Mendocino Beacon*, September 24, 1987

***

Shooting of two new segments of the TV serial "Murder, She Wrote" began last Friday with an all-day session at the intersection of Ukiah and Lansing Streets. Mitch Ortiz' barber shop was trimmed in pink and became "Loretta's Beauty Parlor" for the day. Across the street the Savings Bank became the "Cabot Cove Court House." The weather and the people of our community cooperated and the movie work went on very well.

I was interested to learn that the MHS marching band would play a part in one of the "Murder, She Wrote" segments and that Bob Ayres made arrangements so that the money they earned will be used to pay for a field trip for the 20-member band.

Final shooting was a night scene at Alan Sussex' building on Main Street Wednesday.

Some 40 locals were employed as extras at $50 per day and six who had a line to speak were paid more. Businesses were compensated for possible loss of income while the movie work was going on. Lee Geoble's security men kept things under control, foods like prime rib and lobster tail were purchased to feed the workers, local inns did alright while providing quality accommodations, and so on. If the much discussed "multiplier effect" operates the very considerable amount of money pumped into our little town changes hands seven times before moving out to other areas. It all helps our economy.

—*Mendocino Beacon*, October 1, 1987

The Mendocino High School Marching Band became the Cabot Cove High Band. Shown are Band officers: Jonathan Wax, president; Lily Parsons, secretary; Jed Ayres, vice president. Compensation received from Universal Studios paid for an extra field trip during the school year. (*Mendocino Beacon*)

Television series crews return to coast

They're back!

Crews from Universal Studios returned to Mendocino for a week of shooting the television series "Murder, She Wrote." Many of Mendocino and Fort Bragg's homes and businesses are transformed into Cabot Cove, Maine—home of mystery writer Jessica Fletcher each spring. This year is no exception.

Filming began last week on the Mendocino Headlands with the *Beacon* Building, Blair House, The Wharf, Russian Gulch State Park and Hill House also serving as backdrops for the series.

Since the television series began filming locally several years ago, estimates are that more than $2 million has entered the local economy. More dollars are generated in the area through the hiring of area residents, and through return trips to the area by individuals associated with the production.

First Assistant Director Allen DiGioia said the crews have employed more than 150 local residents during the week, many of those "background artists" or extras. Additionally, actors and crews spent Sunday roaming the streets of Mendocino in search of souvenirs and gifts for those they left in Los Angeles.

"I think the word is out (on Mendocino)," DiGioia said, "And it's good." He said the production enjoys their trips to Mendocino not only because it is a welcome relief from being in the studio, but also because of the ease with which they are able to work with the community.

"People here are very cooperative," he said. "It's easy to get locations, people....There will be many more productions here."

"There are a lot of names given through channels about a location, either good or negative. Mendocino has a good reputation. People only have positive, good reports."

Director Walter Grauman says at least one more season of "Murder, She Wrote" will be filmed on location in the area, and agrees there is no better place to be working on location.

"The exteriors... local talents... local color... It's all conducive to good film."

Pat Turner, who is filling in for local casting coordinator Toni Lemos, said one of the benefits reaped from the local filming is continuing to work with the "Murder, She Wrote" production company.

"This crew, the group... there's a comradarie, a niceness," she said. "Many of these same people are all working together again and they all work extremely well together."

Local residents and tourists in town for the weekend followed the crews from location to location to seek autographs, a photograph, or simply a glimpse of one of the cast. In addition to "regulars" Angela Lansbury, William Windom and Ron Masak, other actors including Jean Simmons, Richard Anderson, Shelly Fabares and Ken Howard were on the set at one time or another.

The episode is a two-hour special which will air near the change in television seasons. No specific date has been given yet.

Crews left early this morning to return to Los Angeles and complete taping of the segment.

—*Mendocino Beacon, April 20, 1989*

Extra Brian Gandy and casting coordinator Pat Turner at Noyo Harbor. (*Dailey/Mendocino Beacon*)

Stars for a day
Behind the scenes of a hit series
by Linda Dailey

So, ya' wanna be in pictures. Well, let me tell ya' sweetheart, I was. And, on one of my first times in front of the camera, I blocked Jean Simmons.

Yes, I was one of more than 150 local residents used as an extra during the recent filming of the television series "Murder, She Wrote."

The episode filmed here ends the fifth season Angela Lansbury has starred as sleuthing mystery writer Jessica Fletcher and includes a constellation of other guest stars as those tangled in the web of intrigue woven by scriptwriters,

The two-part episode, entitled "Mirror, Mirror" will air May 14 and 21. Jean Simmons plays another mystery writer, Eudora McVeigh, on a trip to Cabot Cove to see Jessica. She is followed by, among others, Shelly Fabares, Richard Anderson and Ken Howard, as well as the Cabot Cove "regulars"—William Windom and Ron Masak.

Along with the stars come those who make the series and the stars what they are—the production company. There are about five people working behind the scenes for every person seen on screen. There's the director, his assistants, their assistants, the cameraman, his assistants, the soundman, his assistants, the trainees, the costumers, the makeup and hair artists, the background artists or extras, the properties crew, the electricians, the stars' personal assistants, their stand-ins, coordinators for this and that. And they all come along on location.

Saturday morning. 0900 hours. The offices of *The Mendocino Beacon.*

Instead of writing in the office, today I'm playing like I'm working (in addition to working on this story). I'm an extra in a scene which involves a mob of reporters descending on Eudora outside the offices of the *Cabot Cove Gazette.*

Earlier in the week Jack Lemos came by to show off the building. It was good, but, well, the entrance to the real newspaper office was judged to be too difficult to duplicate in the studio. Another entrance is used and Gallery Mendocino becomes the newspaper and the newspaper office becomes home to a delivery service.

The curtains and other exterior niceties have gone into place also during the week. By Saturday morning, why, it's Cabot Cove. There have never been so many plants outside the *Beacon* Building—or people.

I've come early, dressed as I would would be in Dallas or at any other metropolitan or city newspaper—suit and long coat, pad in hand and camera bag over shoulder. Normal attire.

Pat Turner, who is coordinating local casting while Toni Lemos is recuperating from surgery, is looking for all her extras. Throughout the day she will count us again and again and round us up like a hen closely watching over her chicks. We fill out forms and exchange information.

Meanwhile, some of the stars have filtered into the area surrounding the set. Susan Maeder walks by as she leaves her dressing room. The local actress scored one of four speaking parts to be included in today's filming. She will be portraying a reporter. We joke about how she stole a part made for me.

"They wouldn't let me talk anyway, Susan," I assure her. "What would they want with a reporter with a Texas accent anyway?" This is Maine and everybodys supposed to sound like a Yankee.

"I've got to go to makeup," she says. We dash past the post office and around the corner to the makeup trailer. Inside it's cramped,

'Founders Day' in Cabot Cove. (*Wagner/MHR*)

but makeup artists and hairdressers are busy at work on the female actors while waiting for the men to make a first appearance.

"I'm so nervous," Susan confesses. Hairspray and brushes are flying. "Break a leg," I wish her as I leave the mist of hairspray behind.

"Reporters! Reporters!" Someone is calling the extras over to the prop trailer in front of the *Beacon*. Some of us are reporters. Some of us are curious townspeople. There are already lots of curious townspeople on the other side of the cameras and lights.

Although I came prepared with my own notebook, camera and tape recorder, phony credentials, tape recorders, steno pads and other paraphernalia is distributed.

An Indian galloping down Kasten St., just prior to throwing a lance at the mayor of Cabot Cove. (*Wagner/MHR*)

There happens to be an equal number of male and female reporters, however, many of the fake credentials have men's names. I become Thomas somebody.

Costumers check out each person for authenticity. "On or off?" I ask Marci Olivi, the women's costumer, as I show her my coat. "On. Definitely," she says. Radford Polinsky, the men's costumer, is distributing ties and jackets to some of the more casually dressed extras who are to be reporters for a day.

It's showtime.

Allen DiGioia, the first assistant director, assembles us in front of the *Gazette* offices prior to shooting the scene to explain what we're doing.

Eudora is leaving the newspaper offices, he tells us. She is a mystery writer who has involved herself in solving a murder.

"You're all trying to get the story," he explains. "Crowd around just like real reporters do. The whole nine yards. Let's have lots of electricity. You're newshounds."

While Eudora is leaving, she is met by her New York publisher Lew Bracken/Richard Anderson. He arrives in time for the pack to scent him out and follow him to a nearby taxi with a barrage of questions

So here we are, acting. Cinema Verite was never so vrai.

"Reporters aren't neat," says director Walter Grauman, noting a neatly knotted tie. "He looks too well-kempt." The extra he addresses obediently loosens his tie and runs his fingers through his hair.

Susan Archuletta is another of the female reporters wearing a male name on a credential.

"This is an easy way to make some money, not only for the townsfolk, but the store owners, too," she says. "This demystifies everything. This big part of the world, for a change, comes to see us. It's fun."

Most extras agree and say they wish the movies would come to Mendocino more often. It's a clean industry that puts money back into the economy. "So traffic is blocked for a couple of days. Big deal."

"This is upbeat," says Archuletta. "It's a circus-like atmosphere,"

"A slow motion circus," adds Brian Gandy.

Although we've been in front of the cameras for what seems like forever, we're just getting started, Lighting and sound as well as camera positions were checked. We ran through the scenes and Mario marked our spots on the bricks. Now we're ready to rehearse a couple of times,

"Ms. McVeigh.... Ms. McVeigh," Susan Maeder, Harry Rothman, Judy Frank and Steve Jordan bark. They are the talking reporters, We get as far as Eudora responding, when I block out Jean Simmons,

"But, but," I move. We break and go back inside the foyer of Gallery Mendocino. "Allen," I ask, "I was supposed to stand here." I point at my tape spot. "Don't worry," he say. Mario gives me a new piece of black tape.

It's almost noon and we've done a couple of different camera shots. We go in and out of the camera shot as the entire scene is shot at four different angles.

We have lost all track of time, but we're finished in front of the *Beacon*. The circus packs up and caravans to Russian Gulch and the Cabot Cove Sheriff's Office.

We stand and wait. We see Angela Lansbury pass by on her way to do a scene with Jean Simmons. Ron Masak is singing and telling jokes, We tell our life stories to other extras or ask questions about this whole process or Hollywood life of members of the production company.

We try to recall Jean Simmons' cinema history and that of the other actors on the set, We all draw an immediate blank, except for Shelly Fabares and Richard Anderson—"The Donna Reed Show" and the bionic people.

Stomachs are growling, Rumors of lunch. We eat our choice of London broil or fish with vegetables, salad, dessert, at about 3 p.m, We get an hour for lunch.

Waiting. Waiting. Waiting.

Shortly after 7 p,m, the reporters are "waiting for the story to break" and for darkness to fall,

Walter Grauman tells us we will get coffee and doughnuts outside the sheriff's office while we're waiting for something to happen. Two of our number will speed to the local bakery for coffee and doughnuts for everybody.

No reporter I know has ever gone looking for food while waiting for a major story, except if it's over in the next room and free. "But, hey," I remind myself. "Welcome to television."

Shelly Fabares is: the celebrity we pester in this scene, She waits with us, as does Grauman. They reminisce about the early days of television. Those extras who were in Mendocino during those early days fondly tell of one television, one station and bad reception.

(By the way, Jean Simmons was Ophelia in "Hamlet." An award-winning role for her. The list of other films in which she has starred is endless, but perhaps one we may all recall is as Miss Sarah Brown in "Guys and Doll." Who could resist Brando?)

It's 8 p.m. The coffee and doughnuts have arrived as has the darkness. We run through the scene a couple of times. By 9 p.m. we're finished,

We leave as the crew is breaking down the lights, the magic. We say goodbye to some new friends with hopes to see them again, hopes to see ourselves on the small screen.

—*Mendocino Beacon*, April 27, 1989

Three old salts as extras at Noyo Harbor: Photographer Bill Wagner, Historian Wally Smith and Pete Kendall. (*Universal Pictures photographer*)

The Blair House — Jessica Fletcher's home in *Murder, She Wrote*. (Wagner/MRH)

Noted mystery writer Jessica Fletcher, a widow who lives in a small coastal town, Cabot Cove, in Maine, has a knack for solving puzzles, which comes in handy as she often finds herself in the middle of a real-life murder investigation.

264 episodes of *Murder, She Wrote* were broadcast between September, 1984 and May, 1996. Several two-hour movies were made after the series ended. Only nine episodes were filmed in Mendocino, beginning with the pilot, THE MURDER OF SHERLOCK HOLMES. Supposedly, the series end was to be made in Mendocino, but this did not happen.

The Mendocino Coast episodes were:

Season 1:

1 & 2. THE MURDER OF SHERLOCK HOLMES

Debut 2 hours. Filmed April, 1984. Broadcast September 30, 1984. Jessica is caught up in a costume ball when she unexpectedly spends more time with her publisher.

3. DEADLY LADY. Filmed June, 1984. Broadcast October 7, 1984. A multimillionaire, swept off his yacht during a hurricane near Cabot Cove, turns up in Jessica's backyard.

8. HIT, RUN AND HOMICIDE. Filmed September, 1984. Broadcast November 25, 1984. A car with a mind of its own, runs down the former employer of a brilliant electronics inventor.

10. DEATH TAKES A CURTAIN CALL. Filmed September, 1984. Broadcast December 12, 1984. Defecting Soviet ballet artists decide to leave just as the body of the KGB officer assigned to them is found. USSR Rostov Ballet in Boston.

Season 2:

2. JOSHUA PEABODY DIED HERE . . . POSSIBLY. Filmed July, 1985. Broadcst October 6, 1985. Excavation at the site for a new hotel turns up what may be the remains of a Revo-lutionary war hero who didn't die naturally.

10. STICKS & STONES. Filmed June, 1985. Broadcast December 15, 1985. After a woman is electrocuted in her bath, Cabot Cove is flooded with poison pen letters.

Season 4:

7. IF IT'S THURSDAY, IT MUST BE BEVERLY. Filmed July, 1987. Broadcast November 11, 1987. When Deputy Martin becomes a widower by murder, the investigation turns up some surprising activity.

10. INDIAN GIVER. Filmed July, 1987. Broadcast November 11, 1987. A resident of Cabot Cove threatens the Native American who claims to own the land, and later is found dead.

Season 5:

21. MIRROR, MIRROR, ON THE WALL, Part 1. Filmed March, 1989. Broadcast May 14, 1989. Jessica's old rival, Eudora, shows up with a smile and a gift, but everyone knows she is up to no good.

22. MIRROR, MIRROR, ON THE WALL, Part 2. Filmed March, 1989. Broadcast May 21, 1989. Eudora admits she stole Jessica's notes, but denies poisoning the apples she brought or murdering the detective who was following her.

Recurring cast members of *Murder, She Wrote* were Angela Lansbury, Michael Horton, Tom Bosley, William Windom, Claude Akins and Jerry Orbach. Numerous guest stars made cameo appearances.

Murder, She Wrote won a Golden Globe award for Drama for the Best TV Series in 1986 and won numerous other awards. Angela Lansbury won Golden Globe awards in 1985, 1987 and 1990 for Best Performance by an Actress in a TV Series and other awards.

Dark Mansions — 1985

Supernatural Soaper Slaps Our Shores
By Martin Hickel

Hollywood hit the Heritage House in Little River last week in the form of a 75-member cast and crew on hand for three days of location work as part of the hoped-for new fall series, "Dark Mansions."

The Aaron Spelling Productions pilot for thc ABC television network stars Joan Fontaine as yet another woman in charge of a vast financial empire (shipping, as opposed to say...breakfast cereal) this time headquartered in Seattle.

The title refers to twin mansions high on a desolate and windswept bluff near Seattle as portrayed by the famous Greystoke Mansion in Hollywood. But the grounds (here we come to it) of the mansion are none other than the meadow and bluff below the Heritage House.

Eventually, through the miracle of cinematography, these different locations will appear as "Drake Point," whose twin mansions provides the central motiff "of a family's passions and their conflicts with the running of a shipping company," according to ABC publicist Jaspar Vance.

Most of the members of this passionate family minus its matriarch, Margaret Drake (having just replaced the original comeback star of the series — Loretta Young — Ms. Fontaine does not appear in the first scenes), were busy Thursday shooting the first of their video disasters: the "mysterious death" of a daughter who tumbles off a cliff during a picnic.

Michael York, in his first TV series, is the "Europe-educated son," Paul Shenar is an adopted son, Lois Chiles, his wife, and then four grandchildren — Melissa Sue Anderson, Nicolette Sheridan, Yves Martin and Grant Alexander. Linda Purl goes over the cliff in the opening flashback, then reappears as Margaret's biographer. Spooky stuff. Dan O'Herlihy is the head of the clan but not for long.

Before the fog rolled in, shooting was moving along nicely under blue skies. But Producer-Director Jerry London's crew kept right on with the picnic sequence involving all the principals when the inevitable billowing Mendocino moisture arrived, turning what had started out like a fun-time on the lawn into something resembling real work.

Meanwhile the second unit, using stunt doubles, filmed the off-the-cliff tragedy scene nearby.

Melissa Sue Anderson, who portrayed Mary on the long-running "Little House on the Prairie," described the production team as "the most organized I've seen since then." Once again Anderson's lovely ice blue eyes are supposedly sightless, but this time her blindness is only "psychosomatic."

"I'm only blind for 13 weeks. It's in my contract," she said.

Anderson, Linda Purl and Lois Chiles were beautifully dressed in Ralph Laurent fashions that were the envy of their local stand-ins Joan Batteiger, Susan Maeder and Pat Turner.

"Yes, Aaron dresses his girls," Chiles said. "When I was on 'Dallas' we'd wear our own clothes if we wanted to look nice," she said referring to the quality of the Aaron Spellman Production.

Greg Hillman, Jeff Walsh and Jim Lamb served as stand-ins for the male leads. All the stand-ins were hired by Toni Lemos, the local production coordinator.

During set-ups, all the stars said they were enjoying the chance to be working on the coast.

"I've made films in exotic places all over the world," said York, an English actor who now makes his home in Hollywood, "but this is actually my first film work in Northern California. My wife and I have been across the country many times by plane, but now we're finally getting a chance to see it."

Although he had no idea whether he would be returning to film additional episodes for the series, York said "I very much hope so, based on what I've seen already."

—*Fort Bragg Advocate-News*, April 25, 1985

Dark Mansions aired on ABC on August 23, 1986. Available on YouTube.

Michael York and stand-in Greg Hillman (*Lemos*)   Stand-in Pat Turner and Lois Chiles (*Lemos*)

Stand-in Susan Maeder and Linda Purl (*Lemos*)   Yves Martin and stand-in Jim Lamb (*Lemos*)

Grant Alexander and stand-in Jeff Walsh (*Lemos*)   Stand-in Joan Batteiger and Melissa Sue Anderson (*Lemos*)

Destination America — 1986

Filmmakers Shoot Harbor Scenes For Pilot Series

Filmmakers this week are at work in Ashville, NC, creating a two hour pilot series for ABC called "Destination America."

Last week crews finished shooting in and around Noyo at the Harbor Trailer Park.

Produced by Stephen Cannell Productions, headquartered in Hollywood, scenes from the trailer park were used because of the Noyo Bridge background, explained Charlotte Clay, publicist for the company.

Appearing in the pilot are Bruce Greenwood, Rip Torn and Corinne Bohrer. Torn is a well-established actor with many screen credits. Greenwood played in a short run series by NBC called "The Leg Man."

Executive producer and creator of the show is Patrick Hasburgh who created "Hardcastle and McCormick," a popular television show.

According to Clay, Greenwood plays Corbet St. James, the son of a wealthy patrician family whose emotional differences with his father (played by Torn)—especially after the death of his much beloved brother in Vietnam force him to seek a blue collar life in another part of the country.

During a return home for the commemoration of a museum in the name of his brother, however, Greenwood's father is murdered. Although suspected of the murder, Greenwood is released and he begins a search to find his father's killer and at the same time himself.

Bohrer plays Greenwood's lover who befriends and is, in turn, befriended by Greenwood.

Aside from being filmed in Fort Bragg, other locations selected for filming include Los Angeles and Ashville, NC, where St. James lives in a large mansion. The mansion which will ultimately appear in the film is the same one as shown in the movie "Being There."

The pilot is tentatively scheduled to air on ABC in late spring, Clay says.

—*Fort Bragg Advocate News*, February 9, 1986

Two scenes at the Presbyterian Church in Mendocino.
Above: Robin White & Sandy Sandbothe.
Below: Father Gibson, Robin White & Clytie Mathews
(Wagner/MHR)

Filming at Noyo. Extras Jill Lemos, Doug Nunn, Ellen Callas & Tracey Burns.
Wagner/MHR)

Destination America was apparently never broadcast on television.

Mendocino Perfect For 'Strangers'
by Katherine Lee

It's a mystery how ordinary people wind up in extraordinary situations, doing things they'd never dreamed of, even committing murder.

That theme has fascinated authors and playwrights for hundreds of years and is the stuff of many a now classic movie. It's the story behind "A Perfect Stranger," a movie now being filmed on the coast.

The film is based on an original script written by Don Bohlinger and James Nathan, and rewritten by Bruce Singer. "You'll recognize the story as the film begins," says producer Peter Abrams. "The story seems like the usual murder mystery as first, but then it takes on entirely new twist."

Simply stated, "A Perfect Stranger" is about a man and a woman who plan and murder and attempt to frame someone else, but their plans go awry.

The camera rolls as Joe Don Baker and Keifer Sutherland stroll at Main & Kasten Streets. *(Mendocino Beacon/Lee)*

"The real interest is in the characters and the decisions they are forced to make by the circumstances they find themselves in," Abrams says.

"The proof of the pudding is in the cast," he continues. "The quality of the actors and the fact they are willing to do this film for far less than their normal salaries is indicative of their opinion of the script."

Actor Joe Don Baker plays the sheriff of a small West Coast town, Santa Alba. His character, "Carl Cunningham," is on the verge of retirement, due to be replaced by the deputy sheriff, played by Beau Bridges. Kiefer Sutherland is "Brian," another deputy whose career will be boosted by the sheriff's retirement.

Also in the spotlight are Wayne Rogers and Camelia Kath, as husband and wife "Jake" and "'Laura."

The film is the first project for Abrams and his partner, Robert Levy. Abrams previously produced a play, "A Talent for Murder" starring Angela Lansbury and Sir Lawrence Olivier, for "Showtime." Levy produced the movie "Rad," which was in theaters last summer, and was executive producer of "Smokey and the Bandit."

Thirty "extras" were selected by Toni Lemos, Mendocino's liason with the film industry. They include: Lucia Zacha Peterson, Jeffrey Walsh, Tracy Burns, Jim Lamb, Janet Davis, Peter Russell, Nancy Spazek, Jill Fosse, Pat and Ken Turner, John Schweicket, Agnes and Ralph Stormer, Shane and Eva Kerwin, Maynard Kaminsky, Al Mandoli, George Halter, John Vasta, Renata and Marshall Stoecker, Stuart Beck, Adam Humiston, Brian Fairlee, Roberto Felici, Susan DeVanna, Oasis Hasten, Bill Wagner, Roy Hoggard and Billy Ray Fitzhugh.

Abrams and Levy chose Mendocino after first searching the East Coast for a suitable "small town."

The story was originally set in a small East Coast town closing down at the end of a heavy tourist season. After looking at North Carolina and Florida with no luck, Abrams took the suggestion of friends and checked out Mendocino.

Despite the fact that it rained on all three preliminary trips to Mendocino from Los Angeles, the company liked what the area has to offer and so the story was changed to reflect a small West Coast town closing down at the end of a heavy tourist season.

"It's actually saved us quite a bit of money. We haven't had to change license plates and make a lot of signs," Abrams said. The movie's budget is a modest $1 million.

Scenes have been shot on Main and Kasten streets, on Main Street in front of the Ford house and the Deli, in Mendocino, at the Point Cabrillo lighthouse, in Russian Gulch, along the headlands, and north of Fort Bragg at Ten Mile River and the dunes. The company will stay 12 days.

"A Perfect Stranger" will be released in late spring or early fall, Abrams said.—*Mendocino Beacon*, October 8, 1986

Wayne Rogers, Ford House docent Dick Starr
and Beau Bridges (*Lemos*)

Jack Lemos, Joe Don Baker, Camelia Kath
and Kiefer Sutherland (*Lemos*)

Toni Lemos and Camelia Kath
(*Lemos*)

A Perfect Stranger was renamed *The Killing Time*. This minor yet effective murder thriller is available on DVD.

There is a right time for everything. A time to dance, a time to weep, a time to love, a time to hate. And a time . . . to kill.

Santa Alba, like most small towns, has a quaint and quiet charm. Strangers are welcomed with open arms, high-school sweethearts marry and have families, and everyone is on a first-name basis. But underneath the calm and orderly surface, Santa Alba is poised for a scandalous chain of events.

A newcomer playing a deadly masquerade, an insanely jealous husband, and two lovers with a murderous agenda all become players in a harrowing game of deceit, double-cross, and murder. It is a game that will pit husband against wife, friend against friend, and the masquerading stranger against them all. The time is ripe for THE KILLING TIME.—*New World Video*

Top rated actors plan coast film
Goldie Hawn, Kurt Russell in comedy

Fort Bragg will be on the big screen again, this time playing host to Goldie Hawn and Kurt Russell for the month of May.

Hawn, Russell and several other actors including Roddy McDowell, will be shooting scenes from their new movie "Contemporary Insanity" on location in the Noyo Harbor/Fort Bragg area, according to Toni Lemos, Fort Bragg-Mendocino County Chamber of Commerce film coordinator.

The location manager for Metro-Goldwyn-Meyer Productions, which is producing the film, has been scouting the local area for potential sites, said Lemos.

A Noyo Harbor dock owned by Bud and Barbara D'Arezzo of Fort Bragg may be used by MGM to secure a 100-foot yacht featured in the movie.

MGM is also searching for a house and is already considering several.

No definite contracts have been signed yet said Lemos.

Several local people are also being considered for stand-in roles.

"It's a terrific thing for the Coast," said Barbara D'Arezzo. "Good publicity for the area. And all the people they (the filming company) bring with them, they have to stay somewhere and eat somewhere, which brings business into the area."

"Contemporary Insanity" is a comedy featuring a woman (Hawn) who meets a widower (Russell) with four young children.

"It's a good comedy," said Lemos. "I read the script and it's excellent. "

Hawn and Russell will tentatively be in Fort Bragg at the beginning of May, and may stay partway through June.

No definite filming schedule has yet been set, said Lemos, adding that the rest of the characters remain to be cast.

"Everything is still subject to change," she said.—*Mendocino Beacon*, March 4, 1987

Kurt Russell and Goldie Hawn with director Garry Marshall aboard the yacht *S.S. Immaculata*. (*MGM Pictures*)

Roddy McDowall, Goldie Hawn and Edward Herrmann aboard the yacht in Noyo Harbor.

Movie makers start shooting next month

Fort Bragg will be inundated next week with the office crew, and perhaps some cast, of "Overboard," Goldie Hawn and Kurt Russell's new movie, as preparations begin for shooting, scheduled to start around May 4.

Construction crews for the film, which had formerly been named "Contemporary Insanity," are already onsite.

Scenes from the film, produced by Metro-Goldwyn-Meyer Productions, will be shot at the Noyo Bowl and Restaurant, Purity Market, and Noyo Harbor, and in Caspar and Mendocino.

Other locations have not been finalized yet.

A 100-foot yacht featured in the movie is scheduled to arrive in Noyo Harbor the first week in May, but dock space has not been found, though the film company is scouting several possibilities.

Casting for the film, which features Roddy McDowell in addition to Hawn and Russell, has not yet been completed, according to Ron Pennington, publicist for MGM.

"We just began reading scenes with Hawn and Russell last Thursday," he said.

Several local people will play stand-in roles.

Filming is expected to last 12 weeks.

—*Fort Bragg Advocate-News*, April 22, 1987

Movie crew to arrive on weekend

Preparations to begin shooting "Overboard" are approaching final countdown as cast and crew arrive this Saturday from Southern California.

Filming is scheduled to begin Monday. Some of the cast and crew will be staying at the Tradewinds Lodge in Fort Bragg, according to film publicist Patti Hawn, sister of lead actress Goldie Hawn.

Casting has been completed for the film, which stars Goldie Hawn and Kurt Russell. Hawn plays a woman who meets a widower (Russell) with four children.

The oldest child, Travis, who is 14, will be played by Brian Price. Jared Rushton and Jamie Wild play paternal twins Charlie and Greg, and Jeffrey Wiseman plays the youngest child, 7-year-old Joe.

"Overboard" also features Edward Herrmann as Grant Stayton, Hawn's husband.

Roddy McDowell takes a minor roll as a manservant aboard Stayton's yacht, is the film's executive producer.

The 100-foot yacht, which is scheduled to arrive at the end of this week from Oregon and will be docked in Noyo Harbor, is privately owned and has been leased for the film.

Filming at Noyo Flat. *(Wagner/MHR)*

Captain Flints at Noyo Harbor becomes the set for CRABS 'R' US. *(Wagner/MHR)*

Extra Jacob Archuletta and Kurt Russell. *(Wagner/MHR)*

Onsite construction crews are building a miniature golf set for the film. Crews have also built a facsimile of a local private residence used in the film for use on the set in Southern California.

Scenes from the movie, which is produced by Metro-Goldwyn Meyer Productions, will be filmed at the Noyo Bowl and Restaurant, Purity Market, an appliance store, a fertilizer plant, Point Cabrillo lighthouse, and a mobile home trailer park as well as in the Noyo Harbor area, according to Patti Hawn.

Street scenes will also be shot, and local stand-ins will be used, said Hawn. Arrangements for the stand-ins have not yet been made.

MGM is considering using the Fort Bragg Veteran's Hall for an indoor set representing a police station and a small hospital, said Hawn.

The Mendocino County Board of Supervisors has reportedly agreed to rent the hall to MGM as long as MGM's use does not interfere with previously scheduled activities.

—*Fort Bragg Advocate,* April 29, 1987

Kurt Russell and Goldie Hawn in the Fort Bragg Senior Center's parking lot. *(Wagner/MHR)*

Four scenes at Wonders of the World, the miniature golf course and pony rides set erected at Hidden Pines Campground south of Fort Bragg. *(Wagner/MHR)*

Jack's Corner

The movie making with Goldie Hawn came to Mendocino last week and some locals were pleased to pick up $50 per day working as extras. Mendosa's also picked up a little extra by supplying munchies for the movie crew. Every little bit helps our town's economy. Don't knock it.

—*Mendocino Beacon*, June 10, 1987

Filming completed for 'Overboard'

LITTLE RIVER—As the big white DC-9 took off from the Mendocino County Aiport here, a very small boy, perched on his father's shoulders, waved and called "bye, bye Goldie."

That was Saturday's farewell here to film star Goldie Hawn and the MGM movie company, which has spent the last five weeks on the coast filming "Overboard," directed by Garry Marshall.

Estimates are the company left between $3 and $4 million here, benefitting businesses and individuals. Construction crews were here for eight weeks. Much of the filming was in the Noyo area.

The company used 250 local people for background scenes. Jacob Archuletta, 9, had a small speaking part, according to Toni Lemos, local coordinator.

Hawn, Kurt Russell and their personal staff rented Marge and Bud Kamb's Mendocino Farmhouse on the Comptche-Ukiah Road for their stay.

—*Mendocino Beacon*, June 10, 1987

Extras Alex Fosse and Tyler Fosse with Goldie Hawn. *(Wagner/MHR)*

A few tickets are still available for premier 'Overboard' show

There are still a few tickets left for the world premier showing of "Overboard," a movie filmed here in Fort Bragg last summer starring Goldie Hawn andKurt Russell.

The first-ever showing has been arranged as a benefit for the Mendocino Coast Hospital Foundation's purchase of a dedicated mammography unit for the hospital.

The Foundation has only a few thousand dollars more to raise for the instrument, which is already in use at the hospital. The price of the mammography unit was $42,000.

According the Foundation director Suzanne Binette, raffle tickets for the premier showing are still being sold for $1 a chance, and are available at the Coast Chamber office on Main Street, at For the Shell of It, Coast Video, Cheshire Books, Estes Marine and Mendocino Barbershop.

"Overboard" will show Dec. 15 at the Coast Theater. Regular tickets, with all the proceeds going towards the state-of-the-art unit, cost $25.

—Fort Bragg Advocate, December 10, 1987

Overboard

EDITOR— The benefit performance of the MGM film, "Overboard," held at the Coast Theatre on Dec. 15 raised over $6,000 for the Mendocino Coast Hospital Foundation.

The funds have been applied to a new dedicated mammography unit purchased for the Hospital in October.

To date, the Foundation has raised, through fundraising vents and donation, over $43,000 towards the purchase price of $46,200.

The Foundation would like to thank everyone for their generosity which helped ensure the success of the premiere.

Paul Delagnes, President,
Mendocino Coast Hospital Foundation

—Fort Bragg Advocate-News, December 17, 1987

Lifestyles of the rich and outrageous!

Goldie Hawn is a super-rich spoiled brat. Over-bored you might say! Kurt Russell is a struggling carpenter who should know how to handle brats . . . he raised four of them! One night Goldie goes overboard on her yacht . . . winds up in Kurt's world . . . and sparks begin to fly that even the Pacific Ocean can't put out! Directed by Garry Marshall and written by Leslie Dixon, "Overboard" is a swimingly funny riches-to-rags love story . . . a wet-and-wild throwback to the classic screwball comedies of the '30s! — *CBS/FOX Video*

Everything worked in both the filming and production of *Overboard.* The stars, film crew, extras, locals and the weather all cooperated to make everything come together. Although critics were widely divided on the film's merits, the picture is worth seeing. Yes, the plot is completely predictable, but the performances and laughs make for enjoyable viewing.

Goldie Hawn, Kurt Russell, Jared Rushton, Jeffrey Wiseman, Brian Price & Jamie Wild *(MGM Pictures)*

(MGM Pictures)

**Lights... camera...
Mendocino Coast action!**
by Rebecca Bush

The movie moguls of Hollywood are at it again here on the Mendocino coast.

This week, a crew of almost 80 are in Fort Bragg, shooting the final portions of the film *Wired*, based on the book **Wired: The Life and Times of John Belushi** by Bob Woodward.

Filming started Monday at MacKerricher Park. That was chosen as the cemetery site where Belushi was buried after he died at the age of 33 of a drug and alcohol overdose in 1982.

MacKerricher was picked by *Wired* director, Larry Peerce, for its similarities to Martha's Vineyard on the coast of Massachusetts where Belushi had lived.

There were some 22 gravestones set up (made of a sort of paper mache') and carefuly painted by the scene designer. He put turquoise stains on copper lettering and dripped "seagull droppings" on top of some of them for an authentic weather-worn look.

Belushi's headstone is only a boulder cut in half with "BELUSHI" carved on it, littered with beer bottles, a pair of black sunglasses (similar to those that became Belushi's Blues Brothers trademark), and a few notes written by fans that frequent it to make a final toast to the man who brought wild abandon and outlandish impersonations to a whole generation.

The props are carefully set about. Poloroid photos are taken to insure that everything gets back to its proper place between takes of a conversation of Woodward (played by J.T. Walsh) and Belushi's wife, Judy (played by Lucinda Jenney).

Woodward had written in his book about Belushi that "he made us laugh, and now he can make us think." It's no wonder that a film is finally being made.

Publicist Vic Heutschy who has worked on such films as *One Flew Over The Cuckoo's Nest*, *Rocky* and *Star 80*, said "Woodward is 100 percent behind the project and has been very cooperative."

Belushi's family has not shown much interest in the film though, Heutschy said, after Woodward's account that included 217 on-the-record interviews. The family, including Judy who commissioned the book but later rejected it, never accepted the portrait of Belushi's life.

Belushi's final demise was predisposed in his roles as samurai, a killer bee and bemuddled newscaster in *Saturday Night Live*, which he was a part of from 1975-1979. The roles will be recreated in *Wired*.

The show cast many of the members that appeared in a National Lampoon production in New York (1973), *Lemmings*, Belushi's first major performance outside his hometown of Chicago.

He also appeared as an obnoxious toga-clad Bluto in *Animal House* (1978) and as a cart-wheeling, fedora-topped rocker in *The Blues Brothers* movie (1980) with side-kick Dan Ackroyd, played by movie-newcomer Gary Groomes, a former night-club comedian.

Michael Chiklis, a comedian and graduate of Boston University, was chosen to portray Belushi's life. It's Chiklis' first role but at the age of 24, it's a heck of a start.

According to Peerce's wife Madeline, Chiklis does a great job of impersonating Belushi and "he even sings better" though he had to gain 30 pounds to play the part.

Chiklis and Groomes will both do their own singing in the movie which will have a sound-track album issued.

Heutschy said the movie will have a lot of music and entertainment along with a subtle anti-drug message.

"The film will combine all the humor, tenderness and passion of an amazing career, one that left Belushi revered by his fans and idolized for his ability to make people laugh," Producer Ed Feldman said. "Every decade there is a performer worth remembering—Belushi was such a performer."

Footage of the film was also shot Tuesday and Wednesday at 10-Mile Beach and today the final scene will happen at the MacKerricher 'graveyard.'

With the help of over 250 locals acting as extras, the massive funeral will be recreated. Local casting was done by Toni Lemos, a resident of Mendocino who has a long record of involvement with films here on the coast. The majority of the film, with a $13.5 million budget, was shot in Los Angeles studios. The crew and cast are obviously glad to be on the beach filming in their shorts and t-shirts instead of a stuffy studio.

There will be two more days of shooting in New York for exterior footage but then the film will be ready for editing and is due out in theaters early next year.

It's taken over four years for the film to become a reality, said location manager Brian Brosnan.

Funding was near impossible here in the United States because of pressure from Hollywood to shelve any plans for a movie based on a book that had already caused much controversy because it exposed the life-styles of a lot of people, Brosnan said.

Feldman, who recently worked on the film *Witness*, raised the money in New Zealand with the help of

Extras Jeff Walsh and John Schweikert at Wired production headquarters.

Peter Ware, an Australian director he had worked with, Brosnan said.

Wired will most likely be picked up by Paramount Studios for distribution, Brosnan said.

The screenplay was written by Earl MacRauch and will stray a bit from the realistic into a surrealistic waking up from the dead, taking Belushi on a trip through his life with the help of a Puerto Rican cab driver-guardian angel of sorts played by Ray Sharkey.

"A small group of people have preconceived notions about this film but they will be quite amazed and pleasantly surprised with it. It's done with a great deal of taste and is not exploitive," said Heutschy.

Because of the swirling controversy over *Wired* and a large amount of publicity it has already created (stories about it have been featured in *People* magazine, the *San Francisco Chronicle* and a segment was aired on the television show *Entertainment Tonight*) the movie would prove to be at least moderately successful as the Mendocino Coast chalks up another appearance in the movies.—*Mendocino Beacon*, July 14, 1988

Wired was universally panned by film reviewers, who had absolutely nothing good to say about it. In addition, the scenes at MacKerricher Park were drastically cut. So it is only a Mendocino Coast film in spirit, certainly not in quality. The movie is available on DVD from Avid Home Entertainment.

Filming south of Elk *(M. Anthony/Mendocino Beacon)*

Pat Morita on location near Elk, with spectators.
(M. Anthony/Mendocino Beacon, January 26, 1989)

Extra Shane Kerwin, Film crew members Hope & Eva, Extra George Halter.

Karate Kid Daniel LaRusso risks losing it all when he places pride before principle in this dramatic film that reunites stars Ralph Macchio and Noriyki "Pat" Morita. When Daniel (Macchio) decides not to compete in an upcoming karate championship, he becomes the target of vicious Cobra Kai student Mike Barnes (Sean Kanan) who's determined to win the title back. Standing firm, Daniel's mentor and trainer Mr. Miyagi (Morita) instructs him to ignore Mike's threats—and stay away from the tournament. But when Mike's relentless abuse escalates into blackmail, Daniel finds himself forced into competition—and at serous odds with Miyagi, the one person he cherishes most. Desperately, Daniel turns to another karate instructor, Terry Silver (Thomas Ian Griffith), whose violent combat techniques are directly opposed to Miyagi's wise instruction. But when Daniel realizes that Terry and Mike are allied with Mr. Miyagi's old nemesis Kreese (Martin Kove) in an elaborate set-up for revenge—he also knows he has alienated the only person who can help him. A riveting story of independence, inner-strength and self-enlightenment, THE KARATE KID PART III is a powerful new chapter in this popular series of films.

—*RCA/Columbia Pictures Home Video*

No local newspaper articles were published about the making of *The Karate Kid III.* The film crew was in Elk for only a short time during January, 1989; most of the scenes were shot in southern California. There isn't much to be said about this film. Most critics thought that the first movie in the series was of genuine interest but by the time the producers made the third episode they had run out of fresh ideas. 'Hopeless' is one description given to this film.

Dying Young — 1990

Town bustles
with movie activities

Filming of "Dying Young" began on Monday with a staff busily occupied with the ins and outs of movie making. But according to location manager, Mike Meehan, everything "went exceptionaly well. We had a great start."

State Park rangers and Fox staff kept the groups of spectators off the set, the weather was favorable and so the filming was off to a smooth start.

By now all the large equipment trucks and trailers have been moved to town. They are parked at a location out of the heart of the village where they do not impact traffic or parking.

The stars of the movie are pretty well shielded from public contact, yet some spectators stayed at a location long enough to have been able to get a brief look of the actors.

Scenes were shot in several locations on Monday, including house scenes at the Main Street set, and a driving scene on Ukiah Street. At sunset, the location shifted from the heart of town to headlands. There, special effects created a winter scene complete with artificial snow.

Tuesday morning a few more outdoor shots ware taken before the rain moved in about 1 p.m.

A number of extras have already been called, and while some got to be on the set on Monday, a group of about 20 extras were less fortunate on Tuesday when the weather changed. Only a family of five was used for an indoor shot at the Village Laundromat, aka, the Visual Feast, but most of the others were dismissed before 3 p.m. due to shooting schedule changes.

—*Mendocino Beacon*, November 15, 1990

Southerly view of the house 'shell' erected for Dying Young on Main Street, Mendocino. *(Wagner/MHR)*

Northerly view of completed 'house,' which was demolished after filming was completed. The water tower at right was erected for the movie.

Filming on Ukiah Street. Note artificial snow on pavement. Julia Roberts on porch at right. *(Wagner/MHR)*

Three views of Julia Roberts, at the Mendocino High School bleachers. *(Christine Loss/Twentieth Century Fox)*

Movie Director Gives Mendocino Four Stars

By Christiane McLees

The movie crew has left the Coast, allowing Mendocino and Fort Bragg to return to life before the movies. But before the part of "Dying Young" shot here was in the can, Joel Schumacher, the director of "Dying Young" took some time out Wednesday of last week to speak about his experience in Mendocino and Fort Bragg during the two weeks of shooting on the Coast .

"The residents have been fabulous," said Schumacher. "Many are in the film, and they will bring a lot of character and reality to the movie."

He also said that the location has been perfect and that they have been "blessed to get it. It is an important part of the story - a life giving, warm, part of the story..."

Filming at The Visual Feast, Main and Kasten Streets. *(Wagner/MHR)*

Luck with the weather only contributed to the pleasurable experience the crew and actors enjoyed here. In Schumacher's words: "We've had good karma...This was a good way to start off the movie." He added, "Sometimes it can be a nightmare, and you wonder if you've picked the right movie."

When asked about the perceived audience of "Dying Young," Schumacher laughs and says, "I hope there is one..." But back on the subject he explains that the film is not directed at a particular audience or age group. Instead, Schumacher said, "I believe in making good movies."

Having left Mendocino on Tuesday, the film crew travels to San Francisco and Napa, where they will get more 'on location' shots. Schumacher anticipates that the film will be done in January.

A release date has not been set, but it is possible that "Dying Young" will be released in the the summer of next year.

When Schumacher was asked about the subject matter - a young woman falling in love with a man inflicted with leukemia - he said that it is not at all grim. "Death and illness is something that touches everbody's life and family...Life is tough...but when you tell stories like this, you don't tell a story about illness and death to talk about illness and death, you use it to celebrate life."

"Dying Young" is the seventh film Schumacher directed - he smilingly called it 'the lucky seven' - and he confessed a special affinity for Northern California.

—*Mendocino Beacon*, November 29, 1990

Julia Roberts, Joel Schumacher and Campbell Scott
(Twentieth Century Fox)

"It tugs at the heart and fills the soul...a four hankie triumph!"—*Mike Cidoni, ABC-TV*

Julia Roberts and Campbell Scott star in this moving love story about the power of inspiration. With little money, a poor education and no luck when it comes to love, Hilary O'Neil (Roberts) answers a want ad and finds her whole world suddenly changed. Hired as the caretaker for a seriously ill young man (Scott), she unexpectedly discovers they have much in common, even though he is wealthy and intelligent. Their growing friendship quietly develops into a deep and powerful romance that ultimately tests the boundaries of true love.

—*Twentieth Century Fox video.*

Although the 'house' was a bit unsettling to locals while it was being erected, some people missed it when it was gone. Overall it was a welcome experience to have the film company on the Coast, so it's a shame the film wasn't better than it was. It's difficult to explain what went wrong with *Dying Young.* Something to do with the title, for certain. Ultimately the blame must settle on the screenplay, because the acting is good, the photography beautiful—but essentially just another tearjerker.

Forever Young — 1992

Hollywood in Point Arena—On the scene with The Rest of Daniel
By Lisa Walters

The security was tight Monday morning as one Mendocino County Sheriff's lieutenant, two of his deputies and a security guard from the film company flagged down my car about a quarter-mile down Lighthouse Road.

They were all there, of course, to make sure no unauthorized persons or spying tabloid reporters made their way onto the set of *The Rest of Daniel,* the Warner Brothers-Icon Productions movie starring Mel Gibson that is being filmed this week at the Stornetta Ranch adjacent to the lighthouse.

Being authorized—I had been given one of the coveted *Daniel* placards for my car and had my name on the approved list—I was sent on down the road where the usually bucolic and placid scenery of the area was teeming with humanity.

And not just humanity. Trucks, trailers, vans, cranes, helicopters and the B-25 plane all added to the surreal nature of the scene.

Publicist Lauren Strogoff, whose job it was to shepherd me around, began by parking my car when I found myself unable to maneuver among the mass of vehicles on the narrow road. We were then off on a tour of the set.

Braving the typical spring weather in Point Arena (similar to a night game at Candlestick Park) we made our way down to the bluff where they were shooting a "flashback" scene involving the young Daniel and his childhood sweetheart, "Helen." As the gale-force winds blew, ("Great day for flying a kite!" commented one of the prop men) the two child actors patiently went through their paces, batting a ball back and forth and running with the kite.

Executive producer Edward S. ("Call me Ed") Feldman explained that the scene, which will run less than a minute in the movie, would take about two hours to shoot.

"We have to get everything right," he said. Feldman, who produced the film *Wired* in Fort Bragg a few years back, sang the praises of the coast while trying to explain exactly what it is an executive producer does.

"It's different on every movie and every producer is different, too," he said, as he huddled against the wind. "For me, I'm here to oversee everything in a hands-on way."

Feldman didn't say so, but it is also part of his job to okay the expense sheets the two on-site accountants present him every week. Set up in the production office in one of the rental houses, the pair was busy working on computers and issuing funds for company members'"per diems," the cash they get to pay for daily expenses.

Next to the production office was the school room where a teacher was holding classes for the two 11-year old boys who star in the movie, Elijah Wood and Robert Gorman.

Both extremely personable and polite young men, they sat for a chat after their teacher told them a reporter wanted to ask them questions about their impressions of the area.

Robert and Elijah, who currently stars in *Radio Flyer,* were excited about being included in the film company's Academy Award pool, filling out their ballots, they told me, for *Bugsy* and *JFK.*

"Of course," noted Robert, "we're too young to have seen either movie."

"But," added Elijah, "there's a $400 prize for the winner of the pool!" He added that he hoped former child star Jodie Foster would win her second Oscar.

"I'm not in the Academy so I don't get to vote yet," he confided. "You have to be nominated before they let you do that."

As the boys got called to get into costume, our next stop was the catering truck where Nicaraguan native Luis Lara has the Herculean task of providing up to 400 meals in record time to feed the company.

"Between the time the first person is served to the 400th can only take one half-hour," said production manager Mary Cay Hollander. Luis, an ebullient man who said Point Arena reminded him of his home in Nicaragua, seemed up to the challenge as he enthusiastically went about putting out a hot lunch for the cast and crew.

A hot lunch was needed Monday as the wind-chill factor seemed to drop by the hour. Gibson's partner in Icon Productions, the producer (as opposed to executive producer) of the film Bruce Davey, was shaking my hand in introduction when a gust blew his cowboy hat down the street. Luckily, he retrieved it, but it seemed a good time to go and get back to the wamth of Gualala.

Strogoff, who said it was nice that local people show so much interest when a film is shot on location, invited me to stay for lunch but I declined, even though I knew Mel himself was due at the catering truck.

There's only so much Hollywood glamour I can take in one day.

—*Independent Coast Observer,* April 3, 1992

Point Arena Lighthouse Museum curator (and former Air Cavalryman) John Sisto stands with one of the two 50-year-old Mitchell B-25 bombers which were used in filming at the Lighthouse. *(ICO/David Torres)*

Director talks about Daniel
By Lisa Walters

Holed up in his "office," a bedroom in one of the rental houses at the Point Arena Lighthouse, Steve Miner was gulping down a plate of Mexican food while frentic activity swirled all around him.

"We're set up for the establishing shot," announced one assistant, who burst through the door carrying a walkie-talkie.

"Mel's ready for the scene," another crew member informed him as Miner's personal assistant, Noa, handed him a soda and removed the remains of his half-eaten burrito.

It was just another typical day on location for the 43-year-old Miner, director of the Warner Brothers-Icon Productions movie, *The Rest of Daniel,* starring Mel Gibson that was filmed at the Stornetta Ranch next to the lighthouse last week.

The level of intensity for the director and his crew stayed at the same fever pitch for most of the six-day shoot as the company had to contend with the ever-changing Point Arena weather ("Fog, depart!" executive producer Edward S. Feldman implored one morning while looking up at the sky) as well as the normal hazards of movie-making such as equipment failures and breakdowns.

"The fog and the weather were our biggest problems. We had one really great day," said Miner, who had escaped the pressure for an hour Thursday when he sat alone with his fishing pole at the end of the bluff overlooking the ocean.

"I didn't catch anything but the serenity was worth it," he noted. "It's such a beautiful area. I've been coming up here to go steelhead fishing for many years. I love the Gualala Hotel."

His affection for the coast figured heavily in the decision to use it as a pivotal location in the film, the home of Daniel's great love, "Helen" and scene of some spectacular aerial shots involving the vintage World War II B-25 bomber.

"It's very tempting to think about living here," said the divorced father of two children, ages nine and seven. "I hate L.A."

Miner grew up in the opposite end of the country, in Westport, Connecticut—"where they shot *The Stepford Wives*"—and where his mother was the town's film librarian.

"But I didn't really ever study film in school," he explains. "I just decided that was what I wanted to do."

After a youthful sojurn in Colorado as a a "ski bum," Miner returned to his home state where he became an apprentice editor for local educational, industrial and sportsfilms, including stockcar racing for *Wide World of Sports.* As he learned his craft, he moved on to direct "a couple of movies, lowbudget" and eventually raised enough moncy to produce his first big-time success, the hit horror film, *Friday, the 13th.* Following the first *13th,* he directed the second and third sequels in the popular series. His most recent credits include *Soul Man* and the Disney film, *Wild Hearts Can't Be Broken.*

Director Steve Miner (*Warner Bros./Icon*)

Miner says that though the lengthy process of filmmaking may seem tedious at times for much of the crew, such is not the case with the director.

"A director is responsible for everything once we're at the set—shooting scenes, working with theactors and cameraoperators—the overall feel and look of the film. And then I run dailies with the producers for about an hour every night.

I also work on the script and the castng beforehand and once shooting's done I go into the editing room for 10-12 weeks. Then I meet with the sound people and composer to score the film."

In the case of *Daniel,* Miner says shooting is due to be completed by early May. The film is expected to be released sometime between Thanksgiving and Christmas.

When the movie does come out, there's a good chance it won't have the same title, which many find a little too ambiguous.

"It's really just a working title," Miner notes. "It was supposed to refer to the fact that he's frozen for 50 years and therefore, resting, and also to the fact that the movie is about the rest of his life. Choosing a new title, he says, will be a "group decision" made by a "combination" of people.

Miner says he hopes the movie will attract a "crossover audience of most ages and sexes." Though he says a director never knows how the Motion Picture Association will rate a film, "It definitely won't be an R!"

Despite the weather and equipment problems, Miner feels the experience of working on *Daniel* has been great. "While admitting that some actors can be difficult or they wouldn't be actors"— he has nothing but good things to say about stars Gibson, Isabel Glasser, Jamie Lee Curtis, George Wendt and Elijah Wood.

"As a matter of fact, they are just the opposite of difficult. This film has been a collaborative effort all the way."

As for the Coast, Miner had one more comment as he got up to go and direct the next scene: "I'll definitely be back!"

—*Independent Coast Observer,* April 10, 1992

A look down the temporary runway of metal plates laid down on the bluff shows the set of "Helen's" house, gazebo and garage. (*ICO/David Torres*)

Coastal Observations

What are your impressions of the Point Arena area? Asked by Lisa Walters on the set of "The Rest of Daniel."
Photos by David James

Edward S. Feldman, executive producer: "The area around Point Arena and Mendocino is one of the absolute wonders of nature in the world. When we needed an exotic locale to have in the movie, we came here."

Christina Hershey, company nurse: "It's beautiful. The area, before we got here, is untouched and pristine. Some place we've wanted to escape to."

Luis Lara, company caterer: "I like it except last night I was driving here and I got lost! It's beautiful. I wish I could live here. It looks like the Pacific Coast of Nicaragua where I'm from."

Scott Fieldsteel, assistant chief lighting technician: "I love it. It's the place I would choose to vacation, my favorite part of the world. I've been coming up here since 1979. I was up here three years ago for *Karate Kid III* and it's good to be back."'

Mary Cay Hollander, production coordinator ("Den Mother"): "A very quaint little town. The cooperation and excitement about us being here is really fulfilling."

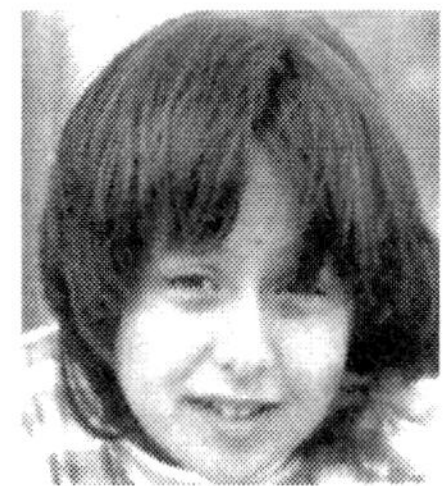

Robert Gorman, actor, age 11: "I think it's a real nice town with the ocean view and so peaceful and quiet and everybody's real nice."

Elijah Wood, actor, age 11: "It's very beautiful. The ocean's great—the thing about the ocean is the big huge rocks that remind me of pirate movies. The people are very nice. There's not much crime here compared to L.A. It's like the country."

(Independent Coast Observer, April 3, 1992)

The Rest of Daniel was re-named *Forever Young*. Although the movie received critical reviews, *Forever Young* is a beautifully-made film that tells a poignant story. It is one of the top ten motion pictures made on the Mendocino Coast.

Red Burke from Fort Bragg brought down his 1920s-vintage Essex to add an authentic touch to one of the scenes. His classic automobiles have also appeared in *Racing with the Moon* and *Same Time Next Year*.
—*ICO/David Torres*

In 1939 test pilot Daniel McCormick (Mel Gibson) has the world by the tail, **and** he's having the time of his life. He has the perfect job—flying B-25s for the newly formed Air Corps. He has a terrific best friend — loyal buddy and truly brilliant scientist, Harry Finley (George Wendt). And he has his true love at his side — his childhood sweetheart and beautiful soul-mate, Helen (Isabel Glasser). Life has given him everything he wanted.

Almost.

Daniel has only one problem: he can look danger in the face unflinchingly, but just thinking about emotions, much less declaring them, makes his throat close up without fail. He gets weak-kneed at the mere prospect of proposing marriage to Helen. And every time he does, Daniel decides that he can wait until tomorrow to pop the question.

But a tragedy suddenly strikes Helen, and Daniel's tomorrows are snatched from him in one terrible instant. Now he must confront a life alone, knowing that he never truly declared his feelings for the woman he will always love.

Daniel (Mel Gibson) gives young Nat (Elijah Wood) a flying lesson.
(Warner Bros./Icon Productions)

Grief-stricken, Daniel volunteers for a top-secret cryogenics experiment conducted by his friend Harry — an experiment that accidentally puts him into frozen slumber for more than 50 years. He awakens in 1992, lost, alone and out of step. Through a tender friendship with a fatherless young boy (Elijah Wood) and the boy's mother (Jamie Lee Curtis), Daniel finally learns that, while time waits for no man — true love waits forever.

(Warner Bros./Icon Productions)

Daniel (Mel Gibson) and Helen (Isabel Glasser).
(Warner Bros./Icon Productions)

'Pontiac Moon' filming starts Monday

Movie cameras will be rolling again in Mendocino starting Monday, Oct. 25. Disphunkshunal Films will shoot a movie, tentativley titled "Pontiac Moon" in several locations around town and on the Coast through Nov. 3.

Little detail about the plot of the film has been made public, only that the story takes place in 1969 and centers on a family that is suffering from agoraphobia and how it overcomes its affliction. But a couple of minor details can be gathered by reading through a location and filming schedule that was presented to the Board of Supervisors for approval. The season must be winter because for all the scenes the roads have to be wet down, and in one scene a little boy is playing with a snake.

The movie company has requested a number of measures including road closures and parking prohibition during shooting for which it has gained permission. The company is trying to move as quickly through the shots as possible as they are aware of the road impediments the filming represents. Between Oct. 25 and 28, the film crews can be found in one of the following locations: the Mendocino Coast Recreation Center; Lansing Street between Palette Drive and Main Street; Main Street from the corner of Heeser and Main to Main and Lansing, the old Shell Station, Brewery Gulch Drive; Albion Ridge Road between Middle Ridge Road and Highway One; Highway 20 between Highway 101 and 1; and on Highway 128 between the Mendocino County line and Highway One. From Nov. 1 through 3 filming is scheduled on Highway One between Little Lake Road and Albion Ridge Road.

The only scene where dialogue will be happening is set to take place between Oct. 29 and Nov. 3 at Little Lake Street. When shooting is done along State roads, a helicopter will be part of the company's equipment.

—*Mendocino Beacon*, October 14, 1993

Mary Steenburgen and Ted Danson stand next to the 1949 Pontiac Chief on Little Lake Street. *(Kalvass)*

Above: The "Pumpkin House," Little Lake Street, Mendocino, before movie set construction. *(Mendocino Beacon)* — Below: The house after two-week construction time showing added side wings. *(Wagner/MHR)*

Ted Danson, director Peter Medak and Ryan Todd on Lansing Street. *(Kalvass)*

Two scenes being filmed on Lansing Street. (Above: *Kalvass* — Below: *Wagner/MHR*)

A smooth start for 'Pontiac Moon'
Filming attracts spectators, employs locals

By Christiane McLees

After almost three weeks of preparations, Dysphunkshunal Films began shooting scenes for "Pontiac Moon" on Monday. With a small crowd of spectators on location, local and visitors alike, the film crew has been shooting scenes at the Mendocino Recreation Center. on Lansing Street and Highway One.

"Pontiac Moon" stars Ted Danson, Mary Steenburgen and Ryan Todd. Danson is well known for his 11 years as Sam Malone behind the bar at "Cheers." He has also starred in the movies "Cousins," "Three Men And a Baby," "Body Heat" and most recently 'Made in America," and he just finished "Getting Even With Dad," with Macauley Culkin.

Steenburgen starred in "Parenthood" opposite Steve Martin and won an Oscar for her performance in "Melvin and Howard." She was also in "Back to the Future, Part III" and can be seen in in the upcoming feature film, "What's Eating Gilbert Brape." The 11-year-old Todd has had minor roles in movies such as "Backdraft" but is making his debut in a major role in "Pontiac Moon."

The film is directed by Peter Medak, whose credits include "The Ruling Class," and "The Krays," and the upcoming "Romeo is Bleeding." Bob Schaffel and Youssef Vahabzadeh, whose most recent production includes "Diggstown," starring James Woods and Lou Gossen, Jr, are the producers, with Sharon Roesler coproducing. The script is written by Finn Taylor and Jeff Brown.

In "Pontiac Moon" Mendocino turns into Meridian Bay, a fictitious west coast town that is somewhat insular. It is in this small town where the Bellamy family is dealing with the problems caused by Washington Bellamy's (Ted Danson) wife Katherine's (Mary Steenburgen) agoraphobia, the fear of being in open or public places. Washington Bellamy teaches at the local elementary school and among the students is his son Andy, who is being shaped by his mother's affliction. Her projection of her own fears onto her son make it hard for Andy to fit into the real world and he becomes somewhat of an outsider at school. But one day, his dad has had enough of it all and takes his son on a trip to the east, in an attempt to keep the family from being sucked into his wife's affliction any further. The father's voyage with his son parallels Apollo II's 1969 journey to the moon.

The filming and preparations so far employed about 60 local people, who have been involved as carpenters, drivers, security, locations help and extras. Monday morning about 100 local children were part of the first scene shot at the Rec Center.

Maria Moon, Rec Center director, has nothing but positive remarks about the crew, who is responsible for the transformation of some of the center's outdoors. "They've been wonderful," Moon exclaims, also explaining that the crew has shown sensitivity for Mendocino people's concerns and is trying not to step on anyone's toes.

Location manger Beth Meinick attests to that perception. In an interview on Friday, Meinick said that Dysphunkshunal Films is trying everything to make the process go as smoothly as possible. In order for people and businesses to prepare for filming in their areas, she and other crew members have gone from door to door to talk about concerns and how to remedy them. Pointing at diagrams of all shooting locations she drew up which include all businesses and residences, she said she knows of all the deliveries for shops, patients to doctors offices, and civic events that could be impacted by the filming and is working on ways to accomodate everyone's needs. "If we can get a handle on what people's schedules are we'll do the best we can," Meinick said.

The film company has brought in a crew of 110 people, who according to Meinick will be fed through a caterer the company is bringing with it, but all produce will be bought locally, just as all other supplies and building materials have been purchased locally.

She said that community response has been positive, with the exception of two or three individuals who were "intractable, but had legitimate concerns." One of her main concerns is that people who had scheduled to see Mendocino Theatre Company's production of "The Dresser" which opens this weekend are thinking about postponing tbeir night out for fear they won't be able to get to the theatre. Meinick said that although there will be filming at the Pumpkin House Friday and Saturday night, people should hve no trouble getting to the show. She suggested that people approach the theatre from Williams Street, as well as park west and south af the Schoeni Theatre.

"I've been here for nine years and there have been several movies," said Pumpkin house resident Linn Bottorf, "But these are the nicest people I've worked with." Bottorf had to endure hammering and sawing from 7 a.m. to 7 p.m. every day for the past couple of weeks as the addition for the house is being completed, but did it gladly. "It's fascinating what's going on," he said. "And when the noise get too bad, I go visit friends."

Aside from trying to make the filming as pleasant and non-intrusive an experience as possible, the film company has also donated a large chunk of money to the Recreation Center. moon said that $11,600 have been donated for a new community playground, as well as several thousand dollars towards matching the grant that the center need to repair the building. In addition to the money, the center got a new coat of paint and charcoal trim, a side porch for the Infant Childcare Center, a fertilized

Mendocino Recreation Center becomes Meridian Bay School. Ted Danson walking at right.

Identified extras , left to right: Allegro D'Albert, Emily Kalvass, Katy Anderson, & Jackie Elder. *(Kalvass)*

Extras Amy Mansfield, Sarah Sharaf, Fionna Yancy-O'Ceallegh and Sarah Levene—between takes.

and now green lawn, and a white picket fence around the front of the property. "I'm thrilled because this was some of the stuff we desperately needed," Moon said.

—*Mendocino Beacon*, October 21, 1993

Danson behind the scenes

By Christiane McLees

Sitting in his trailer a few minutes before the next scene is to be shot, Ted Danson revealed a little bit of the person behind the many characters he has portrayed in movies and on televisiorn. Danson admitted tha he came to Mendocino without knowing much about the area, but in terms of his personal convictions he seems to fit right in.

About six years ago he founded the American Oceans Campaign with lawyer friend Bob Sulnick. Danson was trying to prevent off-shore oil exploration off Santa Monica area at the time and has been a supporter of the cause ever since. "The ocean is a perfect metaphor for what happens on land," Danson said. "If you look at the coastal waters you can see the health of the planet..."

A group of scientists, lawyers and advocates are working in of-fices in Washingion, D.C., Santa Monica and Seattle on the AOC which has worked on thc reauthorization of the clean water act, is lobbying for a nalional oil moratorium and was instrumental in stopping oil exploration.

To help the organization, Danson makes public appearances and gives press confereaees. "I am by no means an expert," he said. "but I get the media to listen to the experts, which is what I think is a function of celebrities."

Danson hasn'l been on the Coast long enough to explore the area and might not have the time to do so either, as filming is keeping him fully occupied.

Asked why he chose to work on "Pontiac Moon" and whether he liked the idea of working with young aclors—he jusl finished filming a movie with Macauley Culkin—Danson said that "The unbeliev-able words and beautifully written script" drew him to it. "lt's funny, moving, it's about family and it's intelligent." he said. A recently rekindled connection wilh his father may have had some influence in picking a movie where he plays a father, Danson admits.

He also admits to missing "Cheers." Working long hours on the show five days a week, he got very close to the people he worked with, whom he calls "some of the best friends I ever had."

—*Mendocino Beacon*, October 28, 1993

Danson delights residents

By Christiane McLees

The Little River Inn's dining room and bar were packed when 110 people descended upon the local establishment Tuesday night to meet actor Ted Danson and support Project Gradua-tion. Event organizers, beaming with joy, announced that about $5,800 were raised.

"We raised in one night, what usually takes us one year," said Dianne Lex, Project Graduation Chair.

People waited patiently to get their chance to talk to the actor who cheerfully served drinks, answered questions, gave autographs and posed for a barrage of pictures. There seemed to be consensus among the crowd that Danson is "a really nice guy" and that sup-porting a safe and sober graduation and meeting him had been well worth the $50 per person tickets.

Carol Greenberg, who just recently moved to the Coast from Los Angeles, was the woman who is responsible for getting Danson behind the bar. Having been a Hollywood publicist for 15 years, Greenberg used her connections to get the actor for the school fundraiser. Once it was clear that Danson was going to be able to attend, Greenberg said selling the tickets was "like popcorn at the movies." And when Little River Inn owner Susan McKinney offered to donate all food and drinks for the evening, the event was set.

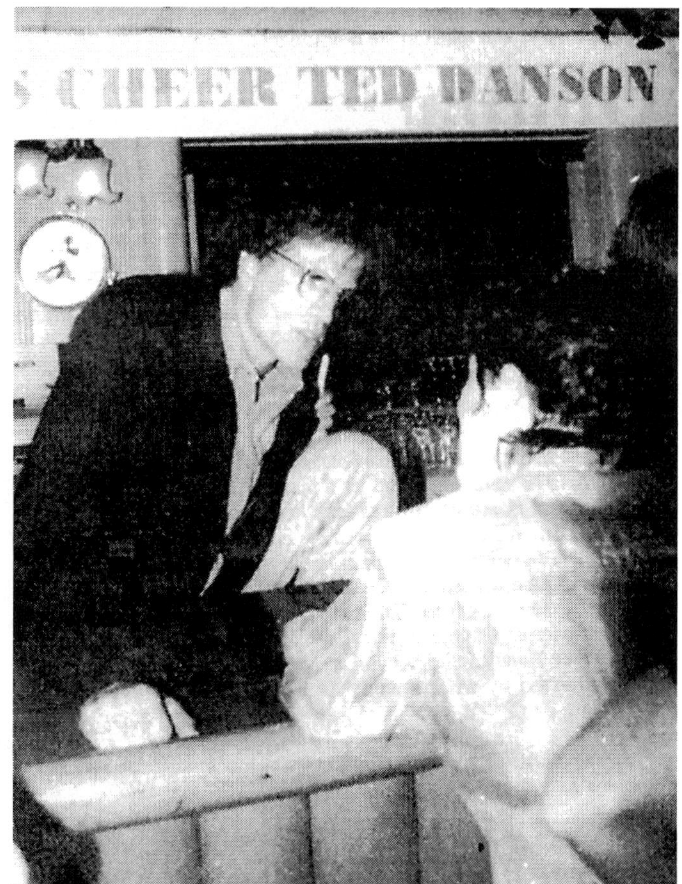

It was a cheerful event, but it wasn't the bar of "Cheers" that actor Ted Danson tended for an hour. *(McLees/Mendocino Beacon)*

About her generous donation, McKinney said, "A lot of my employees are Mendocino High School students ....I'm indebted to the community, besides, who would miss a night like tonight ... an all time magical night."

On Saturday Danson paid a visit to the Mendocino Coast En-vironmental Center to find out how he could be of assistance in causes that are dear to the local people.

The center's co-proprietor C. J. Jones praised Danson for his work on the American Ocean's Campaign but urged him to talk more about trees when he is talking about water. "After the ocean's been saved, the issue is timber," Jones said. "The logging practices are just as destructive as what is going on in the Ama-zon." Jones mentioned the interconnection of the trees with the water by talking about the disapearance of the once so plentiful salmon population due to a disappearance of healthy spawning grounds for the fish.

Danson said that he intends to push for the protection of a 30 to 50 mile inland zone as part of coastal waters in the national Ocean Sanctuary Act.

Rachel Binah, chair of the state Democratic Party's Environ-mental Caucus, urged Danson to support the Headwater's bill and help to defeat the approval of the North American Free Trade Agreement. "If the mills are being moved to Mexico," Binah said, "this will become a third world country if we ship out our resources to be developed somewhere else..."

After being presented with a poster depicting the "Bird of the Mendocino Coast" as a thank you from MCEC for his continued work for the environment, Danson took a ride around the block in an electric car.—*Mendocino Beacon*, November 4, 1993

Science teacher Washington Bellamy (Ted Danson) is fascinated by the mysteries of life. He lives with two of them — a wife (Mary Steenburgen) who hasn't left the house in seven years, and an eleven-year-old son (Ryan Todd) who dreams of rockets but has never even taken a ride in a car.

In the summer of 1969, as a whole nation awaits the Apollo XI mission to the Moon, Washington and his son undertake a fantastic journey of their own. Their goal: to match the mileage from the Earth to the Moon in Washington's 1949 Pontiac Chief, which has an odometer reading just 1,800 miles short of the distance. If Washington's calculations are correct, they will arrive at the Spires of the Moon National Park just as the astronauts land on the Moon.

Father and son travel a road rich with adventure, wonder and delight. By journey's end, they discover just what they've been looking for — the renewed love of a wife and mother, and a future that shines as bright as the Moon.

—*Paramount Pictures Video*

"Original, off-beat and very funny . . . It's a great ride!"
—Bob Healy, *Satellite News Network*

(Paramount Pictures Video)

Pontiac Moon was shown in only a few theaters, which is a shame considering how good the film is—an example of the tyranny of movie reviewers, who obviously didn't understand or care for the plot, thus depriving the movie-going public of great entertainment. Without exception, everyone who has seen this film, either the one showing in Fort Bragg or on videotape or DVD, has praised it highly. It is a favorite of this author and ranks with the Mendocino Coast's best films.

'Sea Cliff Inn' Haunting In Progress

By Christiane McLees

They like the house and almost buy it when Susan has a vision of the place she really wants. The house the young yuppie couple end up buying, and what happens to them in it, viewers will find out in "The Haunting of Sea Cliff Inn."

The TV movie stars Ally Sheedy as Susan and William Moses as her husband, Mark, who escape city life to buy a bed and breakfast inn in Mendocino. But the inn is haunted with the spirit of a dead man who is searching for his lover.

Sheedy is best known to movie audiences for her role in "The Breakfast Club." Moses played the detective on recent Perry Mason movies. The third co-star is Lucinda Weist who played a nurse in "One Flew Over the Cuckoo's Nest."

"Mendocino has all the things a haunted house movie needs to have," said director Walter Klenhard, when asked why he came here to shoot the film. "It has the crashing waves, the fog, the moods and it has isolation."

He said the film is not a horror picture but about "what happens when people come face to face with the supernatural and have to deal with it."

Filming at the end of Rundle Street. *(Wagner/MHR)*

Klenhard, who appears laid back as he sips his coffee, explains that he came to Mendocino to write the script for the film. He wanted to get an idea of what the town was all about before making it the scenery for the film.

He shows understanding of the little town that often feels inundated with tourists and filming activities.

"Mendocino isn't Mendocino until when the local people come out. During the weekend it's something different," he said.

Mendocino will be Mendocino in the movie filmed by May Day Productions. And local real estate agent, Mary Weaver, plays the same in the film.

Filming began on Monday and is expected to be wrapped up on Friday.—*Mendocino Beacon*, May 12, 1994

Kelley House Calendar

by Wally Smith

In "Haunting" I exchanged an entire page of dialogue with Ally Sheedy, the female lead in the TV movie. The filming was on the Kelley House lawn, and she approached me as I prepared to run up the Stars and Stripes.

First speaking role I ever qualified for. It must have taken May Day Productions four or five hours to set up the scene for filming— and somewhere between three and five minutes to actually film it!—*Mendocino Beacon*, May 26, 1994

> *The Haunting of Seacliff Inn* was broadcast on USA on September 22, 1994. It is available on DVD from MCA/Universal Home Video.

Rehearsing at the Kelley House, with Ally Sheedy, extra Wally Smith, and (on porch) MHR Director Pat Turner. *(Wagner/MHR)*

The Fugitive — 2001

Filming returns to Mendocino

Tim Daly, star of "The Fugitive."
(*Mendocino Beacon*, Februay 8, 2001)

Filming on Ukiah Street. At left is is Mykelti Williamson, who portrays Lt. Philip Gerard, with gun aimed at bank robber (Nick Chinlund) and hostage. Other scenes were filmed on Ukiah Street and Kasten Street.

Last week a cast and crew of 125 took over Mendocino's Lansing and Ukiah streets to film the second part of an episode of "The Fugitive," a Warner Bros. television series starring Tim Daly.

The first part, "Jenny," was filmed mostly in Seattle in January, with some shots taken last Saturday here in the Mendocino Area. Stacy Edwards from "Chicago Hope" is cast as Jenny Butler, an inn owner who Dr. Richard Kimble, played by Daly, falls in love with.

In the second part, "Strapped," a pair of bank robbers hold Kimble and Jenny hostage and force Kimble to help them hold up a bank.

The setting is a small Northern California town named Cliffside. The Mendocino Savings Bank was transformed into the Emerson Savings and Loan for the filming.

The stories are different from an earlier version of the series that starred David Janssen.

According to a Warner Bros. spokeswoman, 97 extras and one crew member were hired locally. Forty-five members of the regular "Fugitive" crew were brought down from Seattle, plus 15 actors and stunt people. She said 65 additional crew members were brought in from California.

Several local inns and Fort Bragg motels were filled with cameramen, grips, technical crew and actors. The former Seagull restaurant building in Mendocino was used as a base for buffet lunches for the nearly 250 involved in the filming, and for the extras while they waited their turn to be on screen.

According to a crew member, the food was handled by a Los Angeles catering firm that set up buffet style meals in the building. Crew members were more than polite to bystanders and Daly appeared to be unaffected and a bit modest as he mixed with cameramen, makeup and costume people.

California Highway Patrolmen handled traffic during the filming. A film permit was obtained from the County Administrator's office.

According to the spokeswoman, "Jenny" will air on Feb. 16 on CBS television, and "Strapped" will air on Friday, Feb. 23.—*Mendocino Beacon*, Febuary 8, 2001

Local residents Sharon Robinson and ruth weiss, extras in "The Fugitive."

The Majestic — 2001

Award winning cast for the "Majestic"

By Naomi Jarvie

Filming on "The Majestic" began this week in Fort Bragg using about 200 coastal resident extras in 1950s and late '40s attire. Jim Carrey costars with new actress Laurie Holden.

Strolling around town in the evening and on the weekend were several well-known character actors; Martin Landau, James Whitmore, Allen Garfield and David Ogden Stiers, best known for his portrayal of Major Charles Winchester III, the pompous, outspoken wartime surgeon in the television series "M*A*S*H."

Carrey, a top comedian, tackles a dramatic role in "The Majestic." Screenwriter Michael Sloane says, "Carrey is doing unbelievable work, blossoming into a great dramatic actor."

Fort Bragg is transformed into the fictional town of Lawson for the film. Carrey plays Peter Appleton, a writer blackballed during the '50s McCarthy investigations. He takes off in his car and has an accident near Lawson with amnesia as the result. He is mistaken for Luke Trimble, thought to be lost in World War II and son of the owner of the now defunct Majestic Theater, Harry Trimble, played by Landau. The film is set in the '50s, but has an atmosphere evoking the late '40s and reminiscent of the many soldiers lost in the war.

Asked if the movie script was taken from a book, screenwriter Sloane said, "No, it came from my fevered little brow."

This is Sloane's first major film and he is enthused about working with old friends. He said the production designer, Greg Melton, the director, costume designer, two key hair stylists and some crew members all attended the same high school. Melton's father was the high school drama teacher. Sloane said they all attended classes and worked on school productions together.

"Melton really inspired us, his students," Sloane said. He added that it was great to be working with old friends, but also that every one of them is at the top of his craft.

Tidbits about the film include that the "Skunk Train" will be filmed inside as well as outside and that it took two dozen makeup and hairstylists to ready the 300 extras for Tuesday's shooting at the depot, plus dressers, beginning at 4 a.m.

—*Fort Bragg Advocate-News*-May 3, 2001

A partial fake roof constructed on the Skunk railroad depot for scenes in "The Majestic."

Jim Carrey, star of "The Majestic."

Antique cars used in "The Majestic" parked in Mendocino.

The 'set' at Big River Beach.

Most of "The Majestic" was filmed in Ferndale, in northern California. Scenes filmed on the Mendocino Coast were at the California Western ('Skunk') Railroad Depot in Fort Bragg, Point Cabrillo Lighthouse near Caspar, and Big River Beach at Mendocino. Supposedly threats were made against Jim Carrey and the sets were closed. Not even the media were allowed to take any candid photographs.

Shark Swarm was created as part of the *Maneater* film series. Directed by James A. Contner and written by Matthew Chernov and David Rosiak, the film stars Daryl Hannah, John Schneider and Armand Assante. It was released to generally unfavorable reviews.

Corporate real estate tycoon Hamilton Lux (Armand Assante) sets his sights on developing the quaint seaside town of Full Moon Bay into a prime getaway for the wealthy, but runs into some unexpected problems. Lifelong fisherman Daniel Wilder (John Schneider) and wife Brooke (Daryl Hannah) own property exactly where Lux wants to build high-priced condos, and aren't planning to sell. Lux secretly laces the local waters with a toxin deadly to marine life, decimating the fishing industry in an attempt to starve Daniel out.

Alas, the chemical reacts differently on the area's sharks, drastically increasing their aggressive tendencies and transforming them into engines of pure destruction moving in coordinated swarms. Without fish to feed on, shark attacks on humans rapidly increase. Lux uses media contacts to paint the attacks as random incidents. Daniel, his marine biologist brother and a concerned E.P.A. agent must expose Lux's plan and rid the area of the chemically-altered sharks before the town's entire population is devoured by hungry sharks.

❖

"We went and signed up to be extras in this movie, ***Shark Swarm,*** and so far, we have had a blast! The people are really nice to be around, the stars, and the production people, and even the director, and others important to this production are all really wonderful people!

We have been in 2 days of extra shooting, and hope to be in the last day of extra shooting soon. It IS exciting! for the moment, but it will be a life time of memories as well."

— *Lisa Chiapero*, July 6, 2007

Cast members at Carine's Fish Grotto, Noyo Harbor

Shark Swarm was filmed for a Hallmark TV mini-series. The production crew mainly used Fort Bragg as they were on the water a lot out of Noyo Harbor. They also filmed on Main Street in Mendocino, at the Mendocino Hotel and Twist of Mendocino, plus other locations.

— The Mendocino County Film Office —*Debra De Graw*

Need for Speed — 2013

In July 2012, DreamWorks Studios committed to a film based on the *Need for Speed* series of video games by Electronic Arts, using a script written by brothers George and John Gatins. Director Scott Waugh and DreamWorks head Steven Spielberg cast Aaron Paul as the male lead and Imogen Poots as the female lead. In 2013 Dominic Cooper, Kid Cudi, Ramon Rodriguez, Rami Malek, Harrison Gilbertson and Michael Keaton were cast in the film.

Principal photography began in Macon, Georgia, with other filming locations at Road Atlanta in Braselton, Georgia, the 13th Street Bridge in Columbus, Georgia; and Phenix City, Alabama, and Campus Martius in Detroit, Michigan.

California production locations include sections of Highway 1 north of Point Arena, the Point Arena Lighthouse, and Highway 253 between Boonville, and Ukiah; also Highway 128, between Navarro and the Navarro Bridge, linking Highway 128 North to Highway 1 south to Point Arena.

For the film's chase sequences, the filmmakers decided against the use of computer-generated imagery, instead employing practical effects, which required the cast to receive extensive driving lessons. For the final race sequences and the car crashes the production unit used propped supercars.

In 2013 *Need for Speed* generated over $50k in Transient Occupancy Tax alone, as Dream Works brought in close to 200 crew members to stay in Mendocino County. The grand total spent in Mendocino County by DreamWorks Studios was close to $3 million.

Crabs! — 2015

Filming *Crabs!* in Fort Bragg
By Kelci Parks

Movie makers have descended on Fort Bragg's streets and beaches to film a horror/comedy film called **Crabs!** The crew will be shooting in and around Fort Bragg until mid-March.

The film is a love letter to classic practical effects horror films like **Gremlins** or **The Lost Boys**, but with a contemporary tongue-in-cheek sensibility, said producer Noah Lang. It follows a group of locals caught in a battle for survival against a growing horde of mutated horseshoe crabs.

Director Pierce Berolzheimer and his family have been spending time in the Fort Bragg/Mendocino area for many years and the film was specifically written to take place here.

"It not only serves as a beautiful and pristine backdrop, which makes the horror elements of the film that much more stark when the action begins, but it is also crucial to the design of the story, Lang said.

The cast and crew have been well-received by the community. Everyone in Fort Bragg seems to know us at this point and realizes that, first, we aren't making a huge Hollywood film and can't afford much, and second, we are trustworthy people and professionals who take this craft seriously. Many people and places in town have gone above and beyond for us and we truly appreciate that level of support. That is the only way small, independent films can keep surviving.

Local casting calls were dispersed throughout the community via flyers and social networking asking for applicants. About 60 background actors were used for key sequences and five local actors were cast in speaking roles. Internships were offered and filled through local outreach. They have been involved in everything from the art department and office production support to the camera department and grip and electric.

Suzi Long, of Mendocino, described her time on set as both comical and memorable. "I have a starring role," she joked, "I am eaten by a giant crab in the window of a restaurant. They had to do the shoot three times and they had a propellant machine that spit [fake] blood, mashed bananas and wads of latex on the inside of the window after I was pulled awayby the giant crab."

Long said after a few takes the supply of mashed bananas had been spent and crew members started frantically looking for apple sauce or another substance that could be mixed with the fake blood.

"Next to me was a big tray of vegetarian egg rolls, so Long said, "Hey, how about egg roll insides?"

The idea was a hit, and she and several crew members then unwrapped about 10 egg rolls and dumped the carrots and cabbage into the cannon."

"I will never eat another vegetarian egg roll as long as I live," she said, implying their transformation into cinematic guts had slightly altered her view of the popular Asian cuisine.

When they are not filming, cast and crew say they enjoyed local beaches, bars, hiking trails and downtown shopping. They also raved about the local food, but wished restaurants were open later.

Most of the filming is relatively nonintrusive, however a press release by the city advised residents of street closures. —*Fort Bragg Advocate-News*-March 6, 2015

Chico State Graduates Win Emmy Award For Documentary

By Barbara Arrigoni

The story of an 1850 shipwreck on the Mendocino Coast, fragments of Chinese pottery and an archaeologist's search form the basis of a documentary film that won an Emmy Award for two former Chico State University students. Graduates Matt Ritenour and Arik Bord won an Emmy for the film, The Impact of the Frolic, at the Northern California Region Emmy Award ceremony held Saturday at the a San Francisco Jazz Center. It won in the category of historical/cultural programs.

"It felt like such an honor to be nominated," said Ritenour. "I felt we had no doubt; there was no chance we were going to win. It felt like a win just to be nominated."

Ritenour and Bord got involved in making the film at the Advanced Laboratory for Visual Anthropology at Chico State. Ritenour directed, Bord was the director of photography and Chico State staffer Daniel Bruns edited the film. They worked on it for a year.

The pair originally began the project with the Valene L. Smith Museum of Anthropology and then worked on it during the summer to bring it to broadcast length and quality.

The story began with a group of Northern California Indians who were making beads. Archaeologist Thomas Layton stumbled on the tribe and beads, which later led to a long-ago shipwreck. The film follows Layton's archeological research on the sailing vessel Frolic and was based on the archeologist's two books: **The Voyage of the Frolic** and **Gifts from the Celestial Kingdom**.

"Those were a great help," Ritenour said. "We had stories to go from. *The Frolic* is important because it shows the connection and communication and trade between countries at a time when California was first being settled." *The Frolic* was originally used to carry opium, but then became involved in shipping commodities between China and the United States.

In 1850, *The Frolic* shipwrecked on the Mendocino Coast. Later, the Mitom Pomo Indians found beer bottles and broken bowls filled with ginger and other things that had washed onshore. The Pomos took the items and adapted those to making the tools and technology they understood, making beads from the pottery and arrow tips from the glass, Ritenour said.

"When Layton found the arrow tips out of the beer glass, he found a forgotten ship and history," Ritenour said. "It was right at the beginning of California being founded. It was the start of those relationships. Europeans and settlers hadn't been that far yet. The ship is really a catalyst for history and the expansion of settlement of California."

Ritenour also voiced appreciation to the Academy of Television Arts and Sciences. "I'd like to thank them for recognizing such an important topic and honoring it, for drawing attention to the project that I think is important for cultural and historical preservation."

—*Chico Enterprise-Record*-July 8, 2015

The *Impact of the Frolic* is available on DVD from: www.csuchico.edu/anth or can be streamed over the Internet at: http://vids.kvie.org/video/2365321356/.